TEACHER'S GUIDE

A HISTORY OF THE UNITED STATES

LAND
PEOPLE
NATION

SECOND EDITION

Anna Uhl Chamot
Kathleen Anderson Steeves

Longman

Land, People, Nation: A History of the United States
Teacher's Guide, Second Edition

Pearson Education, 10 Bank Street, White Plains, NY 10606

Editorial director: Ed Lamprich
Senior development editor: Virginia Bernard
Development editor: Elise Pritchard
Senior production editor: Kathleen Silloway
Production editor: Lynn Contrucci
Marketing manager: Alexandra Smith
Production manager: Ray Keating
Senior manufacturing buyer: Edith Pullman
Cover design: Patricia Wosczyk
Cover photos: *Beginnings to 1877:* Tom Till Photography, Inc. (top);
  The Guide Sacajawea with (Lewis, Clark) by American artist N C Wyeth.
  The Granger Collection, New York (bottom L); Joseph Sohm; Visions of
  America / CORBIS (bottom R). *Since 1865:* Bob Pool, Tom Stack and
  Associates, Inc. (top); Ken Kavanagh, Photo Researchers, Inc. (bottom L);
  Ulrike Welsch, Photo Researchers, Inc. (bottom R)
Text design: Warren Fischbach
Text composition: Rainbow Graphics
Text font: Minion 11/13
Maps: Map Resources, adaptations by Wendy Wolf
Photo credit: Page 75: National Aeronautics and Space Administration
Text credit: Page 125: The excerpt from the speech "I Have a Dream" by
  Martin Luther King, Jr., reprinted by arrangement with the Estate of
  Martin Luther King, Jr., c/- Writers House as agent for the proprietor,
  New York, NY. Copyright 1963 Dr. Martin Luther King, Jr., copyright
  renewed by Coretta Scott King.

ISBN: 0-13-042571-0

Printed in the United States of America
1 2 3 4 5 6 7 8 9 10—TCS—09 08 07 06 05 04

Contents

Program Overview

Land, People, Nation: A History of the United States is a two-book series for upper elementary and secondary students who need to develop academic language skills for learning history and geography. These books are designed for English language learners at the intermediate level of English proficiency and can also be used by native English speakers who need support in listening to and reading, speaking, and writing about history and geography.

The instructional approach in Land, People, Nation is based on the theory that active learners are better learners. That is, students who actively think about what they are learning and understand how they are learning will be more effective in acquiring and recalling new information and skills.

The major objectives of Land, People, Nation are to:

1. Provide a standards-based overview of major events and personalities in U.S. history from earliest times to the beginning of the twenty-first century
2. Develop an understanding of the features of world geographical regions
3. Apply historical thinking skills to narrative and visual content
4. Develop proficiency in academic English through content-based instruction in U.S. history and geography
5. Use learning strategies that help students become more efficient and autonomous learners, and that they can transfer to other language and content learning tasks

THE INSTRUCTIONAL APPROACH

The instructional methodology used in Land, People, Nation is the Cognitive Academic Language Learning Approach (CALLA). This instructional approach integrates three important components: content-based materials, academic language development activities, and learning strategy instruction.

- A content-based second-language curriculum involves the incorporation of subject matter appropriate to the student's age and grade level with the teaching of second-language skills. Scientifically based research supports the development of second-language academic proficiency through content-based instruction.
- The language development component of CALLA focuses on academic language skills. This is typically the type of language that occurs in classrooms when teaching and learning in the content areas are taking place. This academic language emphasizes literacy skills, for students need to be able to read to acquire information and to write to express what they are learning. Academic proficiency requires not only literacy skills, but also a specialized vocabulary and the ability to comprehend and produce the types of grammatical structures and discourse features found in each content area.
- The learning strategy instruction component of CALLA is based on a sociocognitive model of learning that emphasizes the information processing capability of the learner and the role of social interaction in learning. Learning strategies are techniques that students can use on their own to help them learn new information and master new skills. Learning strategies can be applied to both language and content learning. Research indicates that students can be taught learning strategies that help them become more effective learners. A description of the learning strategies and their use in these books is on p. vi.

U.S. HISTORY AND GEOGRAPHY CONTENT

The content of Land, People, Nation has been developed with the recognition that history and geography standards, developed in the mid-1990s, are used widely as the basis for the development of school curricula and assessments. Additionally, the historical thinking standards are significant in understanding and using history. They are addressed intentionally as they interact with the learning strategies. The chart at the back of each student book illustrates the interaction of history/geography standards, historical thinking standards, and learning strategies for every unit.

For all students of history, concepts are more easily grasped when they are presented in varying ways. This book makes extensive use of images, graphs, maps, and primary documents to provide opportunities for learners to approach any topic in multiple ways and to encourage students to ask questions about the content.

ACADEMIC LANGUAGE DEVELOPMENT ACTIVITIES

In addition to developing a conceptual understanding of the major events and people in U.S. history, Land, People, Nation also presents an instructional approach for developing contextualized academic language skills through practice with a variety of language activities, including:

- Reading comprehension, in which students practice reading for different purposes, inferring meaning from context, identifying main ideas and supporting details, recalling factual information, making interpretations, determining whether a certain item of information is included in a reading selection, and gaining information from illustrations, paintings, photographs, diagrams, graphs, charts, maps, and time lines

- **Listening comprehension**, in which students practice listening to a teacher's explanation or account of events and biographies of historical figures, taking notes on the main ideas and supporting details, and then summarizing the important points
- **Developing written reports**, in which students develop research skills and use the writing process to write about different types of historical information, from planning the organization of a report to determining the language needed for the report and then developing, revising, and sharing successive drafts
- **Academic speaking**, in which students practice using academic oral language to engage in discussions and make presentations and reports on history topics

LEARNING STRATEGIES

Learning strategies can be applied to all types of learning tasks, including reading, listening, speaking, writing, vocabulary development, understanding and remembering information, and problem solving. Effective learners use a variety of strategies to assist them in gaining command over new concepts and skills. Less effective learners can be taught to use learning strategies that help them become more successful learners. Considerable research supports the identification and teaching of learning strategies in the classroom, and the view that transfer of strategies to new tasks is facilitated when students are provided with opportunities to use strategies on their own.

Teachers can play an active and valuable role by helping students learn and apply learning strategies for different learning activities. In *Land, People, Nation* specific learning strategies are embedded in each lesson. In addition, both students and teachers are provided with names of strategies and directions on how they can be applied to different language and content tasks. These books present repeated examples of particular learning strategies. At first, each strategy is named and explained. Then students are given reminders to use the strategy. Finally, students are asked to identify the strategy or strategies they plan to use for a specific learning task. In this way, the explicit initial instruction in learning strategies is gradually faded so that students will begin to apply the learning strategies independently and generalize them to new learning tasks.

Learning strategies presented and taught explicitly throughout these books are shown in the chart on p. vi.

In addition to explicit learning strategy explanations and directions for use in the student books, the Teacher's Guide indicates where strategies are taught implicitly in the context of a learning task by providing the name of the strategy in parentheses. Teachers may wish to call students' attention to these additional opportunities to use learning strategies.

ORGANIZATION OF LESSONS

Lessons are organized on CALLA principles. Each lesson begins with a **Preparation** phase that includes vocabulary development and the elicitation of students' prior knowledge about the topic of the lesson. Next is the **Presentation** phase that provides new information through reading, listening, and/or visuals. In the **Practice** phase, students check their comprehension of the material presented and engage in activities to consolidate their learning. During **Self-Evaluation** activities, students are asked to assess their own content learning and use of learning strategies. Finally, the **Expansion** phase provides opportunities for students to apply what they have learned. Most Expansion activities appear in the Teacher's Guide under Historical Thinking and Application Activities.

HOW ESL TEACHERS CAN USE *LAND, PEOPLE, NATION*

The aim of *Land, People, Nation* is to teach students the major concepts and accompanying academic language that they need to study U.S. history and geography at the secondary school level.

Land, People, Nation can be used in content-based ESL and sheltered content classes to extend and supplement the regular texts used for students at the intermediate level of English proficiency. The exercises in these books are designed to develop students' academic language skills and to encourage the use of learning strategies. Grammar exercises are not included because the focus is on using language for functional purposes rather than the study of language forms and structures.

Many of the activities in these books involve students working in pairs or small groups so that they have maximum opportunity to use language actively to understand concepts, read for information, solve problems, and discover principles. Mixed-ability grouping is recommended so that more proficient students can provide assistance and serve as models for less proficient ones. The Answer Key is provided on pp. 147–163.

HOW CLASSROOM TEACHERS CAN USE *LAND, PEOPLE, NATION*

Classroom teachers at the upper elementary and secondary school levels who have English language learners in their

LEARNING STRATEGIES PRESENTED IN *LAND, PEOPLE, NATION*

STRATEGY	DESCRIPTION
Tell/Use What You Know	• Think about and use prior knowledge to assist in completing a task. • Recall and build on what has already been learned about the topic.
Predicting	• Make logical guesses about what will happen. • Anticipate information to come. • Use text headings to predict content. • Predict choices and consequences.
Making Inferences	• Use context to make logical guesses about meanings of new words or phrases. • Read or listen between the lines to understand implied meaning.
Selective Attention	• Listen or read (scan) for specific information. • Focus on key words, phrases, or ideas. • Find main ideas and details.
Planning	• Set goals. • Plan how to accomplish the task. • Plan the sequence.
Using Resources	• Use reference materials and the Internet. • Question experts. • Use a model.
Summarizing	• Create a mental, oral, or written summary of information.
Classifying	• Relate or classify words or ideas according to attributes.
Graphic Organizers	• Use or create a visual representation (such as Venn diagrams, time lines, and charts) of important relationships between ideas.
Taking Notes	• Write down important words and ideas.
Cooperating	• Work with others to complete tasks, build confidence, and give and receive feedback.
Using Imagery	• Use or create an image to understand and/or represent information.
Evaluating	• Judge how well you have understood and applied what has been taught. • Judge the effectiveness of the learning strategies used.

classes can use *Land, People, Nation* to help these students learn the major concepts and language they need to study U.S. history and geography.

Classroom teachers do not need to be language specialists to use these books because the language development component is embedded in the material presented. By following the suggested procedures for teaching each lesson, teachers will be providing students with opportunities to use their developing English skills to understand teacher presentations, read for information and main ideas, engage in discussion of subject matter topics, and write simple research reports.

The learning strategies strand is particularly important for English language learners because they may need additional techniques for acquiring subject-matter knowledge through a second language. By teaching students to use learning strategies, teachers can develop their students' ability to become more independent and effective learners.

Many activities call for pair or small-group work. This can be especially beneficial to English language learners if native English-speaking students are included in the pairs or groups. Native English-speaking peers can act as tutors and as language models. Less able students are often chosen as tutors for English language–learning peers because they can also profit from a review of the concepts presented— they learn the concepts by teaching them to others.

COOPERATION BETWEEN ESL AND CLASSROOM TEACHERS

English language learners can make the transition from ESL programs to the general curriculum most successfully when ESL and classroom teachers work closely together in planning and evaluating the progress of their students. ESL teachers need information about the language demands of the general education classroom, and classroom teachers need to know the degree of language proficiency and subject matter knowledge of English language learners entering their classes.

In order to facilitate communication between ESL and classroom teachers, the Teacher's Guide provides two reproducible checklists that chart the language, content area, and learning strategy objectives covered in *Land, People,* *Nation.* The checklists are on pp. 164–167. The teacher is encouraged to reproduce and complete a checklist for each student, evaluating the student's proficiency in the various academic language skills and understanding of the history and geography concepts presented. Use of Expansion activities may result in teachers adding content objectives in the additional spaces provided. These checklists can be shared with the student's other teacher(s) and filed in the student's record files for the coming year.

Teaching Suggestions

Land, People, Nation features a variety of learning activities that are basic to student success in the academic program. A list of these featured types of activities appears below. General guidelines and procedures for teaching each type of learning activity are provided on pp. ix–xiv. Following these general guidelines are detailed teaching suggestions for the lessons in the two student books. Where appropriate, these detailed lesson plans refer the teacher to the teaching procedures described in the general guidelines.

Students will need a notebook or binder for recording answers, writing journal entries, and writing reports. For each volume of *Land, People, Nation* we suggest that the binder or notebook be divided into five parts, one for each unit.

TYPES OF LEARNING ACTIVITIES

- **Unit Opener:** Each unit begins with a list of the unit objectives and a set of questions to elicit students' prior knowledge about the unit's topics. After discussing the questions and viewing the accompanying maps or illustrations, students write their ideas in their journals. The unit opener also includes a time line of the major events presented in the unit.
- **Vocabulary:** The vocabulary exercises are designed to provide practice with new words and their meanings before students encounter them in the lessons.
- **Learning Strategies:** Learning strategies are accompanied by an icon. When a learning strategy is introduced, it is named and defined, and the usefulness of the strategy is explained. Strategy instruction is scaffolded. After the introduction of a strategy, subsequent instances appear as reminders only. Eventually students are asked to identify a strategy by its definition, and finally they are asked to choose an appropriate strategy for a learning task. The goal is to help students learn to use the learning strategies independently. In addition, the general guidelines for teaching specific learning activities (pp. ix–xiv) indicate in parentheses points in each type of activity at which the teacher can reinforce appropriate learning strategies.
- **Reading Selections and Comprehension Exercises:** Each unit contains a variety of lessons which emphasize reading comprehension. The reading selections are only slightly rewritten to accommodate English language learners; for the most part, they present authentic textbook language that students encounter in the general academic curriculum. The reading comprehension exercises that precede and follow the selections assess students' understanding of the main ideas in the reading passage.
- **Listening Comprehension:** In the listening comprehension exercises, students listen to the teacher's presentation of new information about a historical figure or topic, take notes on important ideas and supporting details, and write summaries of the information presented. Listening texts are provided in the Teacher's Guide and are written as mini-lectures to simulate teacher presentations in history classes.
- **Taking Notes (Outlining):** Students are provided with opportunities for taking notes and making a basic outline of material that is listened to or read. The outline format used is a T-list, in which students write main ideas in the left column and the corresponding details and examples in the right column. Scaffolding is provided through partial notes in the beginning units so that students listen for and fill in missing information. Later, the scaffolding cues are reduced so that students learn to take accurate notes without prompts.
- **Academic Discussions:** In order to participate effectively in the classroom, English language learners must learn how to take part in class discussions on academic topics. These books provide many opportunities for students to engage in this type of academically oriented discussion in which the focus is on the identification of an issue, the solution of a problem, and the higher level cognitive skills required to analyze, synthesize, and evaluate. Open-ended discussion topics are presented in the books under the heading, "What do you think?"
- **Oral Presentations:** Opportunities are provided for students to explain what they know or have found out about a topic through carefully planned and practiced oral reports. These are developed first as written reports, and as each student presents his or her report, the other students take notes on the information.
- **Writing:** Writing skills are developed through lessons in which students learn how to plan their written reports, confer with peers about how well their ideas are communicated in written form, and evaluate several drafts of a report. This ensures that the final report illustrates both thinking skills and an organized and coherent form. This process approach to writing reports focuses on the communication of intended meaning. Spelling, punctuation, and grammatical accuracy are checked after the basic report has been conceptualized and several drafts have been written. Additional opportunities for writing include taking notes (see

above), writing summaries, answering questions, and writing reflections in journals.

- **Using Reference Materials:** Research skills are acquired as students use a variety of reference materials, including almanacs, encyclopedias, the Internet, and textbooks, to locate information and develop oral and written reports. Useful websites are provided in the Teacher's Guide and student books to help students use the Internet to access history information.
- **Map and Graph Skills:** The ability to read maps and graphs is important for understanding both social sciences and mathematics. In each unit, exercises are provided in which students must read and interpret maps or graphs, develop time lines, identify geographical locations, or compare statistical information. These study skills are an important component of general learning strategies.
- **Visual Learning:** In addition to reading maps and graphs, students are also provided with opportunities to learn from illustrations of artifacts, reproductions of paintings, photographs, and cartoons. They are asked to analyze and draw conclusions from a variety of images.
- **History Mysteries:** The History Mystery boxes in each unit contain a challenging quote or comment and a question that asks students to make a prediction or inference based on what they have learned in the unit.
- **Historical Thinking and Application:** Discussion questions, suggestions for further research, and application projects designed to help students analyze, compare, and apply what they have been learning are provided at the end of each lesson in the Teacher's Guide.

GENERAL GUIDELINES FOR TEACHING SPECIFIC LEARNING ACTIVITIES

This section outlines suggested teaching procedures for each type of basic lesson activity contained in these books. In addition to explicit learning strategy instruction in the student books, learning strategies are also embedded in each type of activity. Embedded strategies are indicated in parentheses throughout the teaching suggestions so that the teacher can use the different types of activities to review or remind students of the learning strategies previously presented explicitly.

How to Preview Each Book

Help students get a general and comprehensive preview of the book by taking a Book Walk. Have students first look at the cover and tell you what they think the book is about (*using imagery, making inferences*). Then have them turn to the table of contents and silently read the contents of each unit. Ask them questions to assess the knowledge they already have of the topics listed (*tell what you know*).

Sample questions posed in *Land, People, Nation: A History of the United States—Beginnings to 1877* are

- Who do you think were the earliest Americans?
- Do you know the names of any explorers in America?
- What is a colony?
- How did the United States become an independent nation?
- What two parts of the United States fought each other in the Civil War?

Students can also be asked similar questions about their native countries or other places they have lived. This provides them with an opportunity to begin integrating information about U.S. history with their existing knowledge of the history of other countries (*tell what you know*). Point out the list of maps following the book's Contents.

Next, turn to the map of North and South America (p. x). Have students identify places where they have been (*tell what you know*). Then have students look at the map of the United States (pp. viii–ix). Have them identify where they live and other places in the United States where they have traveled. Explore their knowledge of the United States by asking questions about the number of states, when the country was started, who the first settlers were, etc. (*tell what you know*).

Have students look at the unit openers throughout the book. Discuss the illustrations and have students tell you what they think each unit is about (*using imagery, predicting*). Finally, have students turn to the Glossary on pp. 140–144. Discuss how the Glossary is like a dictionary and how it is different. Ask the students how they think the Glossary will be useful to them as they use the book.

By going through the book in this fashion, students will learn to use advance organization to provide them with a general but comprehensive preview of the material to be learned.

How to Use the Unit Openers

Unit openers introduce the topics to be studied with maps or illustrations, general objectives, questions to discuss and react to in students' journals, and a time line of major events presented in the unit. Discuss the maps and illustrations and have students tell what they already know about what they represent. Go over the unit objectives and check what students may already know about the topics (*tell what you know*). Use the "Tell what you know" questions and the unit time line as springboards for a discussion of the topic and what new information students expect to find out (*predicting*). After the discussion, have students write their ideas, reflections, and predictions in their notebooks. Finally, use the unit time line as a way to link ideas from the previous unit to important events that students will be learning about in the current unit.

How to Teach Vocabulary Lessons

The vocabulary lessons present key words that may be new to students and provide different kinds of exercises to help students learn their meanings. Students need to use new words actively in various contexts before they acquire these words as part of their own vocabularies. They need to encounter new words in a meaningful context and through all four language modalities—listening, reading, speaking, and writing. Several learning strategies are introduced to help students learn and remember new vocabulary words.

First, have students look at the vocabulary words to see which words they already know and which they will need to study (*selective attention*). Encourage students to look for cognates, or words that are similar to words in their native language (*tell what you know*), and to make guesses about probable word meanings (*making inferences*).

In some vocabulary lessons, students can classify the new words according to functions or semantic categories (*classifying*). Have students look at the new words and imagine seeing the person, thing, scene, or action that the word represents (*using imagery*). Students are also asked to use the new words in sentences that they generate from their own experiences.

Students are encouraged to work together (*cooperation*) to figure out the meanings of new words, look up definitions in dictionaries or in the Glossary (*using resources*), and quiz each other to keep track of their individual progress in vocabulary learning (*evaluating*).

How to Teach Learning Strategies

Learning strategy icons and explanations are clues for both students and teacher that one or more strategies should be used to assist in the accompanying activity. Strategy instruction is scaffolded as follows:

- The strategy is **introduced**, named, defined, and a rationale for its use is presented.
- The strategy is named, a brief definition and/or rationale is given, and students are **reminded** to use it.
- Students are asked to **identify** the strategy or strategies they will use for an upcoming task, or they are asked to identify the strategy they used in a just-completed activity.
- Students are asked to **select** a strategy or combination of strategies to use for an upcoming learning task.

1. **Introducing a New Learning Strategy:** When a new strategy is introduced, model the strategy for students. Modeling is most effective when the teacher "thinks aloud" as he or she works through the activity that

students will do later. Following is an example of teacher modeling for page 44 of *Beginnings to 1877*:

When I see that a reading has headings, I read the headings first to get an idea of what the reading is about. For instance, on page 44, I see that the title of the reading is "Spanish Colonies," so I know in general what the reading is about. But then I read the four subheadings to get more specific information. I can figure out where to look for the answers to each of the questions on page 44. When I scan for specific information, I am using a learning strategy called selective attention. It's a good strategy to use when I have to find specific facts.

"Do any of you use selective attention? Tell me what you do."

After modeling the strategy, identify the name of the strategy and explain why it is useful and how students can use it. You may paraphrase the explanation in the strategy box. Then ask students if they already use this strategy and if so, to give examples of how and when they have used it.

2. **Strategy Reminders:** Use the strategy reminders to ask students what they remember about the strategy and its use. Encourage students to use the strategy with the activity that follows the strategy description. After they have completed the activity, discuss how well they believe they used the strategy, whether it helped them complete the task, and with what other tasks they could use the strategy—including activities and assignments in other classes.

Your reminders to use strategies should become gradually less direct and prescriptive. Fading of explicit strategy reminders provides scaffolding that encourages students to make the transition from using strategies at the teacher's request to using strategies independently.

3. **Having Students Identify a Strategy:** After several reminders about using a particular strategy the text provides a brief description of a strategy and students are asked to say or write its name. In this way, the name and usefulness of a particular strategy is reinforced and students begin to think of strategies as tools that they can use independently.

4. **Having Students Choose a Learning Strategy:** The final step in the scaffolded strategy instruction is to encourage students to select strategies that they have found personally effective for a particular type of task. Ask students what strategies they will choose (or have chosen) for an activity and then explain why they have chosen that strategy or strategies. There are no right or wrong answers as long as students can justify their chosen strategy. In this

way, students begin to build a personal repertoire of learning strategies that they can use independently and effectively for a variety of learning tasks.

How to Teach Reading Lessons

Reading to learn is a skill that is used across the curriculum. These books provide extensive practice in reading for information, reading for the main idea, skimming, scanning, making inferences, and drawing conclusions. "Before You Read" activities precede reading selections, and various types of comprehension checks appear after the reading. The emphasis is on reading for meaning, and therefore the reading selections should be read silently. (See "How to Teach Speaking Activities" and "How to Teach Writing Lessons" for oral reading suggestions.) Explain to students that the reading selections are very similar to the kind of reading they will encounter in regular textbooks, and that there may be unfamiliar vocabulary. However, they should try to get as much meaning as possible from what they read, and using learning strategies is an effective way to help them understand what they read. In addition to teaching the learning strategies when the icons indicate a strategy teaching moment, you may wish to include additional strategy instruction as suggested below:

- Have students look over the headings of a reading selection, study the pre-reading or comprehension check questions, or rapidly skim the reading selection as a way of previewing the information to be read (*planning*).
- Have students practice scanning a selection for specific information, or learn to attend to the words and phrases that signal main ideas (*selective attention*).
- Encourage students to guess at the meanings of new words from the context clues surrounding them. The clues may be in the surrounding text, in linguistic markers such as "This means that . . ." or "such as . . .", or in the maps and illustrations accompanying a reading selection (*making inferences*). Teachers can help students practice the strategy of making inferences to guess at meanings of new words in the following ways:
  –Have students read the selection silently once for general overall comprehension.
  –Have students read a second time and copy in their notebooks any vocabulary words that are completely unfamiliar (*selective attention*).
  –Have students sit in small groups to help each other figure out the meanings of the words that each has copied (*cooperating*).
  –If students need further help, they can consult a dictionary or the Glossary (*using resources*).

Students can also predict the information that will be found under certain section headings, or in a given selection. At times, have students read only the first part of a selection, then predict the information that will follow in the next part.

By asking students to actively recall what they already know about the topic, you will help them activate their prior knowledge (*tell what you know*). By consciously relating their own previous experiences and knowledge to the new information they acquire through reading, students will build a deeper understanding of U.S. history. Teachers can help students practice the strategy *tell what you know* in the following ways:

- Before reading, discuss the reading topic with books closed. Ask students to tell everything they already know about the topic.
- While reading, have students differentiate between information that they already know and new information by taking notes on new information.
- After reading, ask students to relate what they have just read to their own life experiences.

Various strategies can assist students in remembering the information they read. Students can be asked to take notes of the important facts as they read (*taking notes*). (See the next section, "How to Teach Listening Comprehension Lessons" for suggestions on teaching note-taking skills.) Students can also develop brief oral or written summaries of the reading selections (*summarizing*) either individually or in pairs or groups (*cooperating*).

After completing the comprehension exercises, students should check their own work by looking back over the reading selection to find out which questions were answered correctly, and to correct those that were not (*evaluating*). Finally, students should be encouraged to ask the teacher or their peers for clarification when they do not understand and cannot figure out the meaning of any part of a reading selection (*using resources*).

How to Teach Listening Comprehension Lessons

The purpose of the listening comprehension lessons is to provide students with opportunities to understand information from material presented orally. The listening comprehension lessons are designed to simulate the types of teacher lectures and explanations that occur frequently in the general education history classroom. For instance, teachers often provide background information about a topic, explain the sequence of events, describe key concepts, and explain the relationship between cause and effect. This type of teacher presentation requires effective listening comprehension skills on the part of students. The lessons on listening in these books provide practice with this type of academic listening. The listening comprehension texts appear in the Teacher's Guide only and are to be read aloud by the teacher to simulate a mini-lecture by a general education history teacher.

For listening comprehension lessons, students are asked to take notes on the main ideas and details or examples of the material read by the teacher. To do this, they must use two learning strategies, *selective attention* and *taking notes*.

Ask students to listen carefully for the language markers that provide clues for the type of information to follow (*selective attention*). For instance, markers such as "Today, we're going to talk about . . ." indicate the main topic of the presentation. Markers such as "The most important thing to remember about . . ." indicate that a main idea is about to be presented. When students hear markers such as "For instance . . ." or "An example of . . . ," they know that they can expect an example or a detail. And when students hear a marker such as "Finally, . . ." or "In conclusion," they know that the summary is about to be presented.

The second strategy used in the listening comprehension lessons is *taking notes*. This is a complex strategy that requires both practice and overt instruction by the teacher to make it useful to students. The note-taking system recommended in these books is called the T-list. Students should copy the T-list from the student book into their notebooks. In a T-list system, a large *T* is drawn on the note-taking paper. Main ideas are written in the left column, and the supporting details and examples are written in the right column. This system of note taking is simple and provides students with a way of separating main ideas from details. Scaffolding is provided to help students gain familiarity with note taking. Parts of the T-list are already filled out in the earlier listening comprehension lessons, and the cues are progressively diminished in subsequent lessons. For example, all the main ideas may be provided in the left column at first, and fill-in-the-blank phrases for the details may be provided in the right column. Students must listen for the details in order to complete the notes in the right column. Gradually, this scaffolding is reduced, and eventually students independently take notes on the entire listening presentation.

Students are taught to write notes in abbreviated form, recording only essential words and figures. To introduce each listening comprehension lesson, the teacher writes a sample paragraph from the listening text on the board. Students are encouraged to look for the key words and phrases that communicate the meaning. Following students' prompting, the teacher erases the nonessential words, abbreviates where possible, substitutes numbers for number words, and in general transforms the text to look like a sample of note taking. Students follow this example when they take notes themselves, rather than attempting to write entire sentences verbatim, which many inexperienced note takers tend to do. (Sample paragraphs

for this introductory exercise are provided in the Lesson Plan for each listening comprehension lesson.)

After students complete their individual T-lists, have them work in pairs or small groups and compare the information they have noted, pooling information so that together they can reconstruct as much of the listening comprehension selection as possible (*cooperation*).

Finally, have students use their T-list notes to construct a short summary of important points in their own words (*summarizing*). This summary can be mental, oral, or written.

How to Teach Speaking Activities

The speaking skills practiced in *Land, People, Nation* involve group discussions on history topics, problem-solving activities, classification activities, presentations of oral reports, and evaluations of each other's oral presentations. In most cases, these discussion activities are part of vocabulary, reading, listening, or writing lessons. When students prepare written reports and then present them orally, they practice using academic language in a meaningful context. Discussion activities involve either pair or small group work in which students lead the activity and the teacher acts as facilitator. In addition, "What do you think?" activities throughout the units present open-ended critical thinking questions and discussion topics in which students express and support their opinions about issues raised in the lessons. By engaging in these academic speaking activities, students have an opportunity to integrate new information acquired in the unit into their own conceptual framework.

Learning strategies that can be used in the speaking and discussion activities vary depending on the specific task, but all discussion activities call for the social learning strategy *cooperating*. By working in pairs and small groups, students learn to pool information and assist each other in the learning task.

For the lessons in which students prepare and present oral reports, students first plan the structural organization of the presentation or report (*planning*). If they find that they lack some of the required language to express their intended meaning, they can consult a reference book such as a dictionary or encyclopedia or the Internet and/or ask a teacher or classmate for the word or expression needed (*using resources*). Only after this initial planning stage are students ready to begin preparing an oral or written report by taking notes on the information to be presented (*taking notes*).

Students who have had experience in making oral presentations in their previous schools will also be able to use prior knowledge and experience in organizing their talks and presenting them with appropriate voice level and pace. Oral presentations should be practiced at home, if possible with a tape recorder, before class presentations.

After students give oral presentations, they privately answer questions judging the pace, delivery, comprehensibility, and organization of their own report (*evaluating*). A checklist of self-evaluation questions appears on p. 37 of *Land, People, Nation: Beginnings to 1877*. These questions can be used subsequently for all oral reports.

How to Teach Writing Lessons

The writing activities included in *Land, People, Nation* emphasize writing key ideas and brief summaries of information gained from reading or listening (*taking notes* and *summarizing*), writing reflections in notebooks, and writing reports. The main objective is for students to communicate their understanding of the topic being studied. In some cases this understanding will be expressed in inaccurate or incomplete English; teachers should respond to the intended meaning their students are trying to communicate, at the same time making note of frequent errors that can provide the basis of corrective lessons.

Library and Internet research is called for in many of the writing lessons. Teachers can help make these lessons useful for English language learners by investigating the school's library catalogue on the subjects to be researched, and requesting temporary reserve status for appropriate books. In addition, important websites for studying U.S. history are provided at the back of the student books. Some English language learners may not have had access to a library previously, so they can profit from library sessions which provide them with information about how to find a book and how to make correct references to source material. Similarly, teachers should provide guidance to students as needed for accessing the Internet and identifying trustworthy Websites that can provide accurate and objective historical information.

The unit openers provide several questions to elicit students' prior knowledge about some of the events or personalities in the unit. After discussing these questions, students are asked to write their reflections in their notebooks. Additional opportunities for recording their ideas in their notebooks are provided throughout the books. The notebook writing activities are intended to encourage individual and thoughtful responses to the content studied (*evaluating*). Teachers can respond to the notebooks with comments and questions, but should refrain from indicating "right" or "wrong" answers.

As a first step in developing a written report, have students plan the organization and expository discourse structure required for the report (*planning*). A sample report appears on p. 33 of *Land, People, Nation: Beginnings to 1877* in which students' attention is called to the underlying organizational framework. This consists of an introduction, a body, and a conclusion; linguistic markers are used to signal the three different sections and to distinguish main ideas, details, and sequence of events. This organizational framework is intended to serve as a model for all the reports, both written and oral, that appear in the books.

After *planning* the report, students may need to use reference materials or consult the teacher, classmates, or family members in order to identify the ideas and language needed for the report (*using resources*). As they identify what will be included in the report, students should write down the important information needed for the report (*taking notes*).

A process approach to writing is encouraged for developing written reports. This means that students are expected to engage in prewriting activities such as those described above, make multiple drafts of their reports, seek input from their peers (*cooperating*), and evaluate their successive drafts critically so that the final draft is representative of their best and most thoughtful effort (*evaluating*).

Some lessons call for students to read their final written reports to a group of classmates who will take notes on the information. This is the sole occasion in these books in which a student is expected to do oral reading. (See the section above on "How to Teach Speaking Activities" for suggestions on presenting oral reports.)

How to Teach Map and Graph Skills

Land, People, Nation is extensively illustrated with maps and different types of graphs that portray information about the history and geography topics studied. Maps for individual lessons show the location of historical events or geographical regions. Thus students have many opportunities for acquiring information graphically as well as verbally.

In order to help students develop effective map and graph skills, have them focus on that part of the map or graph that provides the specific information needed (*selective attention*). Ask students to make a mental picture of a map to aid in developing accurate geographical knowledge (*using imagery*). Students can recall previous map and graph knowledge to assist them in comprehending the graphic material presented in these books (*use/tell what you know*). In order to assist learning and retention, students are occasionally asked to express graphic information in written form (*taking notes*).

Reproducible maps for classroom activities are on pp. 168–176 at the back of this book.

How to Teach Visual Learning Skills

In addition to maps and graphs, *Land, People, Nation* provides illustrations of artifacts and original documents, paintings, photos, posters, and cartoons. Teachers can use these illustrations to develop students' visual learning skills by having them describe what they see, compare and contrast, infer meanings, and speculate on the people, ideas, objects, and context portrayed. These visual learning activities are often accompanied by opportunities for students to record insights gained in their notebooks.

How to Teach the History Mysteries

Each unit contains a History Mystery. This is usually a quote or comment that addresses a topic discussed in the unit under study. However, it is not easily answered without thinking about the subject in more depth. In some cases, the History Mystery will ask students to use prior knowledge (*use/tell what you know*) or predict how the quote or illustration might foreshadow something to come in the future. It might also answer a question about what they are studying from a different perspective, encouraging them to practice using historical thinking. The purpose of the History Mystery is to provide students with a challenging idea that will encourage them to identify what they know already about a topic, and then use that information to solve the "mystery."

The History Mysteries also provide students with an opportunity to model strategies used by historians in their work: identify known information (*tell what you know*), guess at answers to an historical problem (*making inferences*), and add more information (*using resources*) to finally solve the mystery. Teachers can use the mysteries as expansion activities. The mysteries might be posted in the classroom where students add evidence as they research the topic and discuss the unit under study, recording the clues in their notebooks. Teacher questions that will assist students in solving the mysteries are provided in the Teacher's Guide lesson plans. Students may also begin to develop their own "mysteries" or questions that they wish to explore further.

How to Teach Historical Thinking and Application Activities

Most Expansion activities appear only in the Teacher's Guide and generally appear under the heading Historical Thinking and Application Activities. The objectives of the suggested discussion questions in Historical Thinking are to develop students' ability to focus on cause-effect relationships, to make inferences and predict outcomes, to relate their own previous knowledge and experience to the material being studied, to express their own values, and to apply what is being learned to their own lives (*selective attention, making inferences, tell what you know, evaluating*).

These questions can be used as brainstorming activities in which students contribute their ideas and speculations, the teacher writes all contributions on the board, and finally the group organizes the information and writes a brief summary of the discussion (*summarizing*). The teacher may want to also develop the habit of checking facts in the encyclopedia, on the Internet, or in other reference materials (*evaluating*).

A major purpose of these discussion questions is to extend students' ability to express concepts in English. At first, students may not be able to express all their ideas in English. Teachers should encourage the expression of ideas even in less than adequate English, and focus on intended meanings during these discussions. If the teacher is bilingual or has a bilingual aide, students can be allowed to respond to these higher order questions in their native language first, then find out what language is needed to express the same ideas in English.

Various types of home assignments and additional class activities are included in these Expansion activities. The objectives of these are to provide additional academic language experiences and to develop knowledge about and appreciation for students' native culture(s) or other cultures of their choice, and to further examine visual material or documents. In these activities students may conduct interviews with each other or with family members, work in groups to develop a project, or practice research skills and the use of reference materials to develop brief reports (*using resources, cooperating, taking notes, summarizing*). In some activities, students may be asked to interview family members or friends to discover information about people, events, and geographical features of their native countries or home states. These may be conducted in their native language(s), but reports to the class should be in English.

LAND
PEOPLE
NATION

BEGINNINGS TO 1877

Lesson Plans

Land, People, Nation: Beginnings to 1877

Simple directions for each exercise are included in the student books. These directions are intended for teachers as well as students. Teachers are encouraged to go over the directions carefully with students to be sure that they understand what they are to do.

The presentation of most lessons should take about 20 to 30 minutes. Additional time for expansion and review activities should be planned depending on the needs and interests of students. Longer lessons involving the development and presentation of reports can be spaced over several days.

The detailed Lesson Plans (pages 1–74) provide the following information for each lesson:

- History Objectives (and Geography Objectives, if applicable)
- Language Objectives
- Historical Thinking Objectives
- Learning Strategy Objectives
- Procedures for teaching the lesson following CALLA phases (Preparation, Presentation, Practice, Self-Evaluation, and Expansion) (most Expansion activities are included in Historical Thinking and Application Activities)
- Text for listening comprehension exercises
- Historical Thinking and Application Activities: Expansion activities that include suggested higher order questions for developing thinking skills, class activities, projects, and assignments.

The Answer Key for *Land, People, Nation: Beginnings to 1877* is provided on pp. 147–154. The Checklist of Language, Content, and Learning Strategies Objectives is provided on pp. 164–165. This checklist can be reproduced as a progress report for each student and used to facilitate communication between the ESL and classroom teacher. Maps for photocopying are on pp. 168–175.

The Earliest Americans

....

History Objective: Identify prior knowledge about early migrations to America.

Geography Objective: Use images of geographic regions.

Language Objectives: Develop oral language; record prior knowledge in notebook.

Historical Thinking Objective: Interpret data from a time line and images to increase knowledge of history.

PROCEDURES

1. See "How to Preview Each Book" and "How to Use the Unit Openers," p. ix.
2. Have students look carefully at the photographs on these pages that show artifacts from many of the indigenous peoples of North America. The background image is a Pueblo village in the southwestern United States. Ask students what they can tell about the first Americans by the pictures. What kinds of houses did they live in? How did they dress?

HISTORICAL THINKING AND APPLICATION ACTIVITIES

1. Connect to students' lives by discussing questions such as: *How do people know about the first people to come to your country (state)? Who were the first people in your country (state)? Did they come from someplace else? Where?*
2. Have students interview their parents or other family members to find out as much information as possible about the earliest history of the family's original country (state) of origin. Students may find additional information on the Internet by looking for the history of their country or state. Then ask students to share this information in class, either orally or in writing.

The First to Come to the Americas

History Objectives: Increase knowledge of academic vocabulary; draw upon data from various sources to gain knowledge about migration; identify patterns of early migration to the Americas; increase and assess knowledge about the origins of the first Americans.

Geography Objectives: Use maps to explain movement of people on the Earth's surface; use geographic information to develop concepts related to Asian migrations to America; use maps to organize geographic information.

Language Objectives: Develop vocabulary related to early migrations; read for comprehension; develop vocabulary by using context clues to understand new words; evaluate reading comprehension; recognize familiar information phrased differently; correct false statements.

Historical Thinking Objectives: Build historical comprehension; identify methods for investigating history before it was recorded; use data from maps and narrative; reconstruct meaning from narrative and visual data.

Learning Strategy Objectives: Explicit: Understand the usefulness of the learning strategy *predicting* and practice this strategy with section heads; evaluate how well the learning strategy *predicting* assisted in reading comprehension; understand usefulness of the learning strategy *making inferences* and practice using it to identify new words in the reading text. **Implicit:** Practice the learning strategy *evaluate learning*.

PROCEDURES

Preparation

1. **Before You Read: Vocabulary.** See "How to Teach Vocabulary Lessons" on p. x.

2. Discuss grouping of words in three categories: *People, Things People Do, Other Words.* Explain that it is easier to remember new words when they are grouped according to their meanings or characteristics. Have students write the definitions in their notebooks. Ask them to write the words they already know or can guess next to the correct definitions.

3. Review dictionary skills and alphabetical order. Then have students look up the remaining words in the Glossary and determine the correct definitions. Have students work with partners to compare their answers and decide cooperatively on correct ones.

4. <u>Vocabulary Game</u>. Have students work in pairs and take turns reading definitions to each other. The student listening to the definition should have the book closed and recall the vocabulary word from the definition read. Then have student pairs make up original sentences using the vocabulary words.

5. See "How to Teach Learning Strategies" on p. x.

6. **Before You Read: Predicting.** Model the strategy *predicting* by thinking aloud as you look at the section headings of the text on p. 6. Say what kind of information you expect to find under each heading. Tell students that thinking ahead about what a text might be about is a useful learning strategy named *predicting*. Have students give examples of times when they have used this learning strategy.

7. Tell students that they can understand what they read much better if they first get a general idea of what a reading selection will be about by following these four steps to *predicting*:
   a. Read and understand the title.
   b. Read the headings of each section.
   c. Look carefully at maps and illustrations and read the captions.
   d. Tell yourself what you think the text will be about.

8. Have students read the directions and copy the correct headings in their notebooks. Discuss the title "The First to Come to the Americas" and have students volunteer ideas on what the reading selection is about. Write *The First to Come to the Americas is probably about . . .* at the top of the board, then write the ideas contributed by students.

9. Have students complete their own sentence telling what the story is probably about. They may write a new sentence or choose one of the sentence completions on the board.

Presentation

1. Preview and discuss the map, illustrations, and captions on pp. 5–7.

2. Have students close their eyes and make a mental picture of the route the early Asian hunters followed.

3. See "How to Teach Reading Lessons," p. xi.

4. <u>History Mystery</u> (p. 7). Introduce students to the "History Mystery." Tell students that there is a History Mystery in every unit. They are not expected to know the answer, but it is a question that requires them to think further about a topic or to apply the knowledge they now have in a deeper way. Because the mysteries deal directly with "being historians," they may not be "solved" immediately. (See "How to Teach the History Mysteries," p. xiv.) Give students some clues to get them started in problem solving. In the case of this unit's mystery, the teacher could begin with questions to students: *How can you find out about events that happened last week? What happens if there is no written record or no one to talk to?* If they answer the mystery, then the teacher may go further by providing objects as examples of non-written records or by referring to the opening photos in the unit. Ask students to discuss what they could learn about a people by their art and objects. When students have "solved" the mystery, they will have acquired some of the tools of the historian, and the teacher can apply those skills to later history discussions.

Practice

1. **Understanding What You Read: Using Context.** Introduce the learning strategy *making inferences*. See "How to Teach Learning Strategies" on p. x.

2. Tell students to quickly read over p. 6 to find the words listed on p. 8. When they find each word, they should then read the sentence (and if necessary the paragraph) in which it appears to make a logical guess of its meaning.

3. Students should write each new word and a phrase that gives the meaning of each word in their notebooks. Students may not be able to write grammatically correct definitions yet, but in this exercise the purpose is to demonstrate whether or not they have been able to infer the meaning of each word.

4. Have students work in pairs or small groups to go over and discuss the definitions they have written. Encourage them to cooperate to improve each other's and their own definitions so that they are as accurate as possible.

Self-Evaluation

1. **Understanding What You Read: Comprehension Check.** Explain to students that there are three possible responses to each statement. *True, False,* or *Not Given,* meaning that the information was not given in the reading selection on pp. 6–7. They must pay attention to the facts presented in the reading selection and relate them to the statements in the comprehension check.

2. Have students work individually, reading and marking the comprehension statements with *T, F,* or *NG.* They should mark the ones they are sure of first, and then take time to go back to the more difficult items.

3. Have students check their answers by rereading pp. 6–7 and locating the sentences in the reading selection that provide information for their answers. Ask them to write the sentences in their notebooks beside the answers. (Items marked *NG* will not have corresponding sentences.)

4. Have students correct all false statements so that they are true. Then have them read the new statements to the class.

HISTORICAL THINKING AND APPLICATION ACTIVITIES

1. Discuss the following questions in class and have students write their reflections in their notebooks.

   - Do you think farmers would migrate, or would they settle in one place? Why?
   - What is the difference between climate and weather?

2. Connect to students' lives by discussing the following questions: *Have there been any migrations of large groups of people in modern times? From where? To where? Why? About how many people? How could you find out?*

3. Use a globe to have students show their own countries (or states) of origin and the routes taken to (or within) the United States. Have students write a short paragraph telling about their family's trip to the United States or their family's move from one part of the United States to another.

4. Discuss these questions with students: *Are there any mammoths today? What could have happened to them? How do scientists know about mammoths? How do historians know about Ice Age hunters and their travels?*

5. Have students investigate the following questions individually, in pairs, or in groups. They may write the results of their investigations in their notebooks and then share them with the class. Questions: *Are there any land bridges today that connect two continents or two other geographical areas?* (Look at a world map.) *Are there still caribou and bison? Where?*

6. Have students go through the reading selection on pp. 6–7 again to identify any other words that are new to them. Have them list these words and then use context clues to develop definitions. Their definitions can then be discussed as a small group activity in class.

7. Ask students if they, like historians of early Americans, used any clues that are not written. If so, what did they use? What did they learn from these clues?

8. Conduct a brainstorming activity with students by asking the following question: *What would happen here if the average yearly temperature were 20° colder?* Write all student contributions on an overhead transparency. Discuss and correct as needed. For extra language practice, ask students to write their ideas in their notebooks.

9. As an assignment, ask students to develop (orally or in writing) additional comprehension statements with possible *T, F, NG* responses, based on pp. 6–7. Then have students sit in small groups to ask each other the questions they have developed.

REGIONS OF THE WORLD PAGES 10–11

The Polar Regions

> **Geography Objectives:** Identify characteristics of Polar Regions; use maps and bar graphs to compare and contrast two Polar Regions.
>
> **Language Objectives:** Develop oral language and reading comprehension.
>
> **Historical Thinking Objectives:** Practice using maps to gain information about world regions; compare and contrast regions.

PROCEDURES

Presentation

1. See "How to Teach Map and Graph Skills" on p. xiii.
2. Preview maps and section headings. Identify the Polar Regions on a globe. Then have students close their eyes and form a mental picture of where the two Polar Regions are on the globe.

Practice

1. Explain the lesson layout: reading, maps, questions, graphs, more questions.
2. Explain how graphs are to be read (temperature on vertical line and letters indicating months on horizontal line). Practice oral reading of temperatures, such as "twenty-four degrees below zero." Have students ask each other questions such as, *What was the temperature in June at the South Pole?*
3. **Map Skills: Comparing Regions on a Map.** After students have read p. 10 silently, have them answer the Map Skills questions on p. 11.

Self-Evaluation

1. **Understanding Bar Graphs: Temperatures in the Polar Regions.** Have students work in pairs or small groups to study the graphs and answer the questions.
2. Have students share answers with the whole class.

HISTORICAL THINKING AND APPLICATION ACTIVITIES

1. Connect to students' lives by discussing the following question: *What changes in your daily life would you have to make if you lived in the Polar Region?* Have students think about homes, transportation, clothing, and recreation. (Note: If you are teaching in or near the Arctic, you can reverse this question and have students discuss aspects of their lifestyle that would change if they were to move to a warmer region.)
2. As an assignment, have students look up Polar Regions, Arctic, and Antarctic in reference books such as junior encyclopedias or geography texts, or have them use the Internet to find three additional facts about Polar Regions that they can share orally with the class.

The Inuit, page 12

> **History Objective:** Learn about characteristics of the Inuit culture.
>
> **Geography Objective:** Examine how native peoples interact with their region.
>
> **Language Objective:** Develop academic listening comprehension.
>
> **Historical Thinking Objective:** Identify central ideas of historical narrative by listening and taking notes.
>
> **Learning Strategy Objectives:** Understand the importance of *taking notes* during academic presentations and practice this learning strategy with a listening text.

LISTENING AND TAKING NOTES

PROCEDURES

Preparation

1. See "How to Teach Listening Comprehension Lessons" on p. xi.
2. Tell students they should pay attention to the organization of the listening passage about the Inuit. First, they will hear the topic of the passage, then they will hear three main ideas with some details or examples, and finally they will hear a conclusion that tells what the passage was about.
3. See "How to Teach Learning Strategies" on p. x.
4. Ask students to describe when they take notes in class, why they take notes, and how they take notes. Explain that *taking notes* is a learning strategy because it helps us understand and remember new information.
5. Explain to students that they will use a special way to take notes for all of the listening texts in this book. First, they must choose which words to write down. Show them how to do this as follows: Write this paragraph from the listening text on an overhead transparency and ask students to tell you which words can be erased without losing the meaning:

Now you are going to hear how the Inuit found food to eat in the Arctic region. Early Inuit fished and hunted for food. They fished and hunted sea animals such as seals and whales. They also hunted large land animals such as caribou and polar bears. Sometimes they cooked their meat, and sometimes they ate it raw.

As students indicate which words are less important, erase them. Write abbreviations to replace any words that can be abbreviated. Ask students to reconstruct the passage from the words remaining on the board.

Presentation and Practice

1. Have students copy the T-list on p. 12 in their notebooks.
2. Read the listening text. In their notebooks, have students write the information missing from the blanks on the T-list previously copied.
3. Discuss with students how they used the learning strategy *taking notes* and whether it helped them remember the information.
4. Have students sit in small groups to compare and complete their notes.

Self-Evaluation

Have students individually write short summaries of the important points about the Inuit, using their completed T-lists as a guide.

Listening Text for "The Inuit"

Today you are going to hear about a group of Native American people who live in the cold Polar Region around the North Pole. Today these people are called Inuit (IN yoo it) ("real people"). The most important things to remember about these people are how they came to North America thousands of years ago and how they learned to eat and keep warm in the cold Polar Region.

First, you are going to hear how the Inuit came to America. They were the last group of hunters to come across the land bridge from Asia and they came across a frozen ocean, probably on sleds. They did not move south like other hunters before them. Maybe they liked the cold region, or maybe they were not welcome when they tried to move south. Today, the Inuit still live in the North American Polar Regions of Alaska and Canada.

Now you are going to hear how the Inuit found food to eat in the Arctic Region. Early Inuit fished and hunted for food. They fished and hunted sea animals such as seals and whales. They also hunted large land animals such as caribou and polar bears. Sometimes they cooked their meat, and sometimes they ate it raw.

Finally, you are going to hear how the early Inuit learned to keep warm in a Polar Region where no other people were able to live. The Inuit kept warm in two ways. They learned how to make warm clothes and how to build special houses. Inuit used the fur of animals and feathers from birds to make warm clothes. They made fur parkas or jackets to keep their bodies and heads warm. They made pants and boots out of the animal skin. Early Inuit made different types of houses because there were no trees to build wood houses. Some Inuit made tents from animal skins. Some Inuit made houses from whalebone and dirt and grass. When the Inuit went hunting, they also built houses of blocks of snow. These houses are called *igloos.* The Inuit stayed warm in their houses and in their fur clothes.

In conclusion, today you have learned how the Inuit came to America and how they found food to eat and built places to live in the cold Arctic Region. They live today in Alaska and Canada, and they still live in many of the same ways they did a long time ago.

HISTORICAL THINKING AND APPLICATION ACTIVITIES

1. Ask students to discuss their ideas on the following questions: *Why didn't the Inuit become farmers? How do igloos made of blocks of snow keep people warm? Why did the Inuit stay in the cold Polar Regions instead of migrating south like other groups of early Americans?* If students are not sure of the answers, have them research the information on the Internet or in an encyclopedia.
2. Using their completed T-lists, have students prepare their own oral versions of the listening text, adding markers such as *first* and *second*, and sentence connectives such as *and* and *but*. In small groups, students can take turns reading their individual versions and asking for input from the group on ways to improve their oral presentation. Finally, students can make tape recordings of their individual presentations. These tapes will be the start of a series of dated individual tapes that students will make for each listening comprehension lesson in the book, and will be a record of their oral language development for this type of activity.
3. Ask students to look at the photographs of the Inuit. Then ask the following questions: *What information can you add to what you know about the Inuit from*

looking at the pictures? What do you already know about the Inuit from the listening text that they can confirm from the pictures?

MAP SKILLS Reading Maps for Information, page 13

History Objective: Examine migration and settlement of indigenous people.

Geography Objectives: Find information on a map; identify the names and locations of major North and South American indigenous cultures.

Language Objectives: Develop reading comprehension and oral language; practice recognizing the main idea.

Historical Thinking Objective: Use maps to gain knowledge about historical movements.

Learning Strategy Objectives: Understand the importance of the learning strategy *selective attention* and use it to find the main idea.

PROCEDURES

Preparation

Discuss the map on p. 13 and the areas where specific Native American groups settled. Have students indicate map area directions such as *northern, southern, southeastern* and *southwestern*. After students have studied the map, have them close their eyes and make a mental image of the map. Ask them to visualize the northeastern part of the United States. Ask, *What Native American tribe lived there?* Repeat for other map areas.

Presentation and Practice

1. Have students read p. 13 silently, using information from the map to complete the sentences, then writing the complete sentences in their notebooks.

2. **Before You Read: Finding the Main Idea.** Introduce the learning strategy *selective attention*. See "How to Teach Learning Strategies" on p. x. Model this learning strategy by reading aloud a paragraph and asking yourself, *What is the most important sentence in this paragraph?* Read each sentence in the paragraph and think aloud about why it is or is not the most important idea in the paragraph. Explain to students that *selective attention* is an important learning strategy when you need to focus on a specific part of a text (reading or listening).

3. Have students read the two-paragraph text on p. 14 silently, using the learning strategy *selective attention* to identify the main idea of each paragraph. They may use the map on p. 13 for help.

Self-Evaluation

Tell what you learned. Ask students to write five facts they learned about indigenous American cultures in their notebooks.

HISTORICAL THINKING AND APPLICATION ACTIVITIES

1. Ask students to discuss the following questions: *Why are maps useful? What is your definition of culture? What are some similarities and differences between your native culture and culture(s) in the United States? What else do you already know about the Mayas, Aztecs, or Incas?*

2. Provide students with textbooks, library books, and encyclopedias, or have students use the Internet to find more information. Brainstorm what kinds of additional information about Maya, Inca, and Aztec cultures they would like to have (such as, pictures of artifacts, cities, statues, etc.). Show them how to use the index, and review alphabetic order. Then have each student practice looking up information and writing down two or three additional facts about the Mayas, Aztecs, and Incas that they can share with others in a small group activity.

Moctezuma Meets Cortés, page 15

History Objectives: Gain information about the Aztec civilization and its encounter with Spain; increase knowledge of history concepts.

Language Objectives: Develop academic reading comprehension; recognize cause and effect; write complete sentences.

Historical Thinking Objectives: Explain causes in analyzing historical events; explain change over time.

Learning Strategy Objectives: Recognize *cooperation* as a learning strategy and practice the strategy to answer comprehension questions.

PROCEDURES

Preparation

1. Review what students have learned about Aztecs on pp. 13–14, including additional information gathered through research.

Presentation and Practice

1. Have students read the passage on p. 15 silently once for comprehension. Then have them read it a second time to make a list of words that are completely unfamiliar (students cannot even *make inferences*).
2. In small groups, have the students discuss the words each has in a list, helping each other make logical guesses about probable meanings. Go from group to group to clarify word meanings where necessary.
3. Check comprehension by asking questions such as: *What was the main idea? (What was the story about?) What did Cortés (the Spanish) want? What did Moctezuma do? Why? What did the Aztec people do? Why? Then what did the Spanish do? What happened a year later? Who owned Mexico then?*

Self-Evaluation

1. **Understanding What You Read: Comprehension Check.** Introduce the learning strategy *cooperation*. See "How to Teach Learning Strategies" on p. x. Ask students why they think you often ask them to work together in pairs or groups. Discuss their answers—hopefully some students will say that they learn from each other when working together! Reinforce (or introduce, if necessary) this idea and explain to students that *cooperation* (working together) is a learning strategy that can help them solve problems and find answers more easily than working alone.
2. Have them practice the strategy *cooperation* to answer the *why* questions at the bottom of the page. Explain that they must give reasons (some of which must be inferred or guessed at, from the text), and that they must write complete sentences. The answers should be written on scratch paper.
3. Have students sit in small groups to discuss individual answers and decide as a group on the best answers. Then ask students to record the best answers on the appropriate lines in their notebooks.

HISTORICAL THINKING AND APPLICATION ACTIVITIES

1. Connect to students' prior knowledge by discussing the questions that follow. *Many times in history, a strong army from one country has attacked another country. Can you give examples that you know about from history (of your own country or another)? What reasons can you see for such invasions? Is the army that invades always wrong? Why or why not?*
2. Repeat the brainstorming activity and use of indexes for finding information explained for p. 14, but concentrating this time only on Aztec civilization.

The Iroquois and the Anasazi, page 16

History Objective: Find out about the culture and way of life of the Iroquois and Anasazi.

Geography Objective: Use maps to gain information.

Language Objective: Develop academic listening comprehension.

Historical Thinking Objectives: Identify the central ideas of historical narrative; compare cultures of two indigenous people; use maps.

Learning Strategy Objective: Identify and use the learning strategy *taking notes* with information presented orally.

LISTENING AND TAKING NOTES

PROCEDURES

Preparation

1. See "How to Teach Listening Comprehension Lessons," p. xi.
2. On a classroom map locate: New York State, Arizona, New Mexico, Colorado, and Utah. Point out to students the Four Corners area, where Arizona, New Mexico, Colorado, and Utah come together. Attach labels of Native American tribes (Iroquois and Anasazi) to geographical areas. Ask students to tell what they already know about these Native American peoples.
3. Ask students what learning strategy they will use as they listen to information about two important Native American peoples (*taking notes*). Have them explain why this strategy is useful (it helps them understand and remember information).
4. Review note-taking techniques by writing the following sentences on the board and using the erase-a-word technique explained in the lesson plan for p. 12.

The council was made up of leaders from all of the tribes and they met together to settle arguments between the tribes. So an important thing to remember about the Iroquois is that they learned to live in peace.

Presentation and Practice

1. Read the listening text and have students write the missing information in the blanks on the T-list previously copied in their notebooks.

2. Then have them work in pairs or small groups to compare their T-lists and pool the information they acquired from listening.

Self-Evaluation

Have students individually write short summaries about the Iroquois and the Anasazi, using their completed T-lists as a guide.

Listening Text for "The Iroquois and the Anasazi"

There were many interesting North American indigenous people, and some of them still exist. Today you are going to hear about two Native American peoples: the Iroquois (IR o kwoi) and the Anasazi (AN a SA zi). The most important thing to remember about these two different groups of people is how they learned to make their lives better.

First, we are going to talk about the Iroquois. They were a group of several tribes, and they lived in the area that today is New York State. Since this was a land of forests and lakes, the Iroquois got their food from hunting and fishing, and they also farmed. For many years the different Iroquois tribes had wars with each other. Before the first Europeans explorers came to their land, a number of the tribes were convinced by two leaders, Hiawatha and Deganwidah, to stop fighting each other. They formed a council and called it "The League of Great Peace." The council was made up of leaders from all of the tribes and they met together to settle arguments between the tribes. So an important thing to remember about the Iroquois is that they learned to live in peace.

Now you're going to hear about some Native Americans who lived in a very different part of North America. The Anasazi settled in the Southwest, in the area that is today called the Four Corners. Four states—Arizona, New Mexico, Colorado, and Utah—come together at this place. This is a dry desert region. The Anasazi lived by farming on a mesa that they climbed to each day from their houses in the cliffs. They grew corn and beans and also hunted. Their houses were like apartments today, built into the sides of the cliffs high above the desert. These houses provided very good protection from the enemies of the Anasazi and from the weather. The Anasazi women also made beautiful pots of snake-shaped coils of clay that they decorated with paints made from plants. Around the year 1300, there was a drought, or a very long time without rain. The Anasazi were unable to grow enough food to live on the mesa, so they left their protected houses and moved to the valley, near the Rio Grande River. The amazing cliff houses of the Anasazi can be seen today in the states of Colorado and New Mexico. The Pueblo and Zuni people today are descendents of the Anasazi.

In conclusion, today you have learned about two Native American cultures in North America: the Iroquois and the Anasazi. The most important thing to remember about these people is that they learned to make their lives better. The Iroquois learned to live in peace with each other, and the Anasazi learned to build communities in a desert region.

HISTORICAL THINKING AND APPLICATION ACTIVITIES

1. Discuss these questions with students: *The Iroquois lived in a forest region and the Anasazi lived in a desert region. How did the region where each Native American culture lived influence their lives?* Make a list that includes as many different aspects of life as students can think of (e.g., food, clothing, and houses).

2. Bring in library books on different Native American tribes. Let students browse through the books and select one tribe to investigate further. Allow students to take one book home to find out three important facts about the tribe selected. Students may also find additional information on the Internet about the tribe they have selected. Have each student then share the facts discovered in a small group discussion.

FOODS NATIVE TO THE AMERICAS — PAGE 17

History Objective: Identify foods we eat that were first discovered/developed by Native Americans.

Language Objectives: Develop oral language; practice alphabetization skills.

Historical Thinking Objective: Categorize items and compare over time.

Learning Strategy Objectives: Introduce and practice the learning strategy *classifying*; practice the learning strategy *cooperation*.

PROCEDURES

Preparation and Presentation

1. <u>Which foods do you eat?</u> Discuss names of foods and clarify meanings. Ask students familiar with some of the foods illustrated to describe their appearance, taste, and use.
2. Ask students to name foods they eat that early Native Americans would not have known.

Practice

1. <u>Classifying.</u> Introduce the learning strategy *classifying*. See "How to Teach Learning Strategies" on p. x. Discuss the concept of classifying, and have students suggest ways in which they could classify themselves (e.g., by gender, by ages, by colors of clothes, by height, etc.). Read with students the reasons for using this strategy and examples of how it can be used in the Learning Strategy section on p. 17.
2. Review alphabetical order by having students line up according to their names, then write an alphabetical list of names.
3. Have students list foods in alphabetical order in their notebooks.
4. Working in small groups, have students read and follow the directions for the Classifying activity. Ask students what learning strategy they are using when they work with others (*cooperation*).

HISTORICAL THINKING AND APPLICATION ACTIVITIES

1. Discuss with students questions such as: *Which of the foods illustrated can be prepared in the greatest number of ways? No meats are mentioned on the list. What reasons could there be? What food do you think is found in the most places in the world? Why?*
2. Connect to students' lives by comparing Native American foods to foods enjoyed in their native countries or by their families. Ask students to bring to class a list of five foods that are typical of their native countries. In class, have students interview each other to develop a master list of all the different foods on individual lists, with no food mentioned more than once. In small groups, have students make a chart to classify these foods in different ways, such as how they are eaten (raw or cooked), the time of day when they are usually eaten (breakfast, lunch, dinner), occasions when they are eaten (special celebrations, every day, on certain days). Students should ask each other for clarification when necessary. Finally, ask students in each group to alphabetize the list and then share it with the class.

Explorers and Explorations

History Objective: Identify prior knowledge about European explorers and explorations in North America.

Geography Objective: Identify the geographic relationships between Europe and different locations in North America.

Language Objectives: Develop oral language; record prior knowledge in notebook.

Historical Thinking Objective: Use a time line to gain knowledge of events and people related to exploration in North America.

PROCEDURES

1. See "How to Use the Unit Openers," p. ix. The image is an old engraving of a Spanish ship similar to those used by European explorers in the fifteenth and sixteenth centuries, the era of Columbus.
2. Have students look at the map and identify the countries they recognize.
3. Discuss the map on pp. 18–19, identifying the coast of America, the Atlantic Ocean, Africa, and Europe. Point out the different countries and areas that European explorers came from. Discuss the map of Europe and help students identify Scandinavia (Denmark, Norway, Sweden), Spain, England, France, and the Netherlands.
4. Provide students with copies of the map on pp. 18–19 (see Teacher's Guide, p. 170). Have students choose five different colors, and then color the five regions of Europe, each with a different color. Ask them to make a key by coloring the boxes labeled for each country or region with the corresponding colors.
5. Have students work in pairs to ask each other what colors they have chosen to represent each country or region and to check that they have colored the boxes correctly. (Note: In this unit, students will color areas of North America the same colors as the European countries by which they were claimed.)

HISTORICAL THINKING AND APPLICATION ACTIVITIES

1. Connect to students' prior knowledge by discussing questions such as: *Did any European explorers explore in your country (or state)? Who were they? Where did they explore? Did any non-European explorers explore in your country (or state)? Who were they? Where did they explore? Did people from your country (or state) explore in other places? Who? Where?*
2. Have students interview their parents or other family members to find out information about early explorers of their countries or from their countries of origin. Students born in the United States should use the country or countries of origin of their parents, grandparents, or great-grandparents (as far back as necessary). Students can share this information in class, either orally or in writing.
3. Show students how to use an atlas to measure the distances from various points in Europe to different parts of North America. Have students use the Internet to discover how many hours a flight takes from different European countries to different points in North America (e.g., Spain to Mexico, London to New York, Paris to Montreal). Refer back to this information when students study the different voyages in the fifteenth to seventeenth centuries and the length of the time each trip took then.

History Objective: Extend academic vocabulary about European exploration.

Language Objective: Develop academic vocabulary related to exploration.

Historical Thinking Objective: Use words in historical context.

Learning Strategy Objective: Practice using the previously introduced learning strategy *classifying* to assist in vocabulary learning.

PROCEDURES

Preparation

1. See "How to Teach Vocabulary Lessons," p. x.

2. **Before You Listen: Vocabulary.** Have students work in small groups to discuss the vocabulary words and their definitions.

3. In small groups, have students quiz each other on the definitions of the fourteen vocabulary words. Then, have students close their books. Provide each group with a list of the definitions. Ask students to cooperatively provide a word for each definition. In this way, groups, instead of individuals, compete against each other.

4. See "How to Teach Learning Strategies" on p. x.

5. Remind students of how to group words by their meanings and how this learning strategy makes it easier to remember the words.

Practice

1. Have students work in pairs to group the new vocabulary words into the three categories given.

2. Then have each student imagine a context in which each new word could occur, and describe the imaginary context to his or her partner.

HISTORICAL THINKING AND APPLICATION ACTIVITIES

1. Connect to students' interests by discussing the following questions: *Which continent do you live in now? Choose a different continent and name one of its countries. Did people establish colonies in this country? Who were they? What happened? What oceans or seas does this country have coasts on? Who explored in this country? Are there many sailors in this country? Are there many merchants? Why or why not?*

2. Working in pairs, assign each group of students two of the vocabulary words and ask them to create pictures that illustrate each word. Have each pair share their pictures with the class, explaining their pictures. Hang illustrations in the room as students study the unit.

Why People Explore, page 21

History Objective: Identify the main reasons why Europeans explored in the fifteenth to seventeenth centuries.

Language Objective: Develop academic listening comprehension.

Historical Thinking Objectives: Appreciate historical perspectives; identify central questions of historical narrative.

Learning Strategy Objective: Practice using the learning strategy *taking notes* with information presented orally.

LISTENING AND TAKING NOTES

PROCEDURES

Presentation

1. See "How to Teach Listening Comprehension Lessons," p. xi.

2. On a world map, identify Europe, the Middle East, and Asia (India, China, Japan). Show students the distances by land from Europe to these different areas of Asia.

3. See "How to Teach Learning Strategies" on p. x.

4. Ask students what learning strategy they will use as they listen to information about the reasons for European explorations in the fifteenth to seventeenth centuries (*taking notes*).

5. Review note-taking techniques by writing the following sentences on the board and using the erase-a-word technique explained in the lesson plan for p. 12.

Let's think about some of the reasons why people explored in the fifteenth, sixteenth, and seventeenth centuries. In those days, there were three main reasons why people explored. These reasons were trade, riches, and religion.

Practice and Self-Evaluation

1. Have students copy the T-list on p. 21 in their notebooks.

2. After students have listened to the passage below and completed the information on the T-list in their notebooks, have them work in pairs to compare their T-lists and pool the information they acquired from listening.

3. Have students individually write short summaries about the reasons for European exploration in the fifteenth to seventeenth centuries.

Listening Text for "Why People Explore"

Today, we're going to talk about the reasons why people explore. Exploration is always dangerous, yet there have always been explorers in the history of our world. Explorers have gone to regions of the world that they did not know, they have discovered things new to them, and they have met people different from themselves. Even today, there are explorers who travel to dangerous places like frozen Antarctica—or even into space. There are many reasons why people go to unknown and dangerous places to explore.

Let's think about some of the reasons why people explored in the fifteenth, sixteenth, and seventeenth centuries. In those days, there were three main reasons why people explored. These reasons were trade, riches, and religion.

The first important reason why people at that time explored was for trade. They wanted to sell their products to other countries and also to buy useful products from countries far away. Europeans wanted Asian spices such as pepper, ginger, and cinnamon because these spices made spoiled food taste better. Remember—there were no refrigerators in those days to keep food fresh! The spice trade was by land. Look at a map of Asia and Europe. It was a long way by land and very dangerous because of deserts, mountains, and bandits.

So, in the fifteenth century, Europeans wanted spices from Asia, but there was a problem. The spices were very expensive because they had to be brought by land from a long way away. How to solve this problem? Well, some Europeans thought that it might be cheaper and less dangerous to bring spices (and other valuable Asian products like silk) by sea instead of by land. But nobody had gone from Europe to Asia by sea.

Some European kings and queens and rich merchants decided to pay for explorations by sea to find a new trading route to Asia. Fortunately, new inventions made this exploration easier, though it was still very dangerous. For example, the astrolabe was an invention that helped sailors navigate by the stars. New compasses and maps helped sailors find their way. Also, there were improvements in ships, and this meant that some sailors were willing to take a chance on sailing into unknown and dangerous seas. Between 1450 and 1700, many brave explorers sailed from Europe around Africa to Asia. And some also sailed to what we now call America.

A second reason why Europeans wanted to explore was to find riches such as gold and silver. This was an important reason for kings and queens of Europe, who needed money to fight wars, build, and buy luxuries. They bought ships and hired captains and crews to find the gold and silver they had heard about in stories from the Americas. These adventurous explorers also hoped to get rich themselves. Some explorers, such as Cortés and Pizarro, did find gold. These Spanish explorers made Spain the richest and most powerful country in Europe for a long time.

Other explorers found things to trade, such as sugar cane, cocoa, tobacco, and furs. Europeans also began another kind of trade at this time, bringing Africans as slaves to the Americas. This trade made kings and queens and other powerful people richer. But millions of slaves suffered and died.

A third reason for exploration in those days was because of religion. Some people went to new places because they wanted to be free to practice their religion—in Europe they were not allowed to practice their religion. Other explorers wanted to share their religion with new people in America. They wanted to convert Native Americans and African slaves to Christianity because they believed that Christianity was the only true religion. So some explorers had religious reasons for explorations.

In conclusion, in the fifteenth, sixteenth, and seventeenth centuries, there were three main reasons why Europeans explored new lands. They explored for trade, for riches, or for religion. And some explorers explored for a combination of these reasons.

HISTORICAL THINKING AND APPLICATION ACTIVITIES

1. Expand students' understanding of reasons for exploration by asking some of the following questions: *What reason for exploration do you think was the most important for the kings and queens? Why? What reason for exploration was the most important for common people? Why? Would you have wanted to go exploring in the fifteenth century? Why? Why not?*
2. Discuss with students whether there are any explorers today (e.g., astronauts, medical explorers, scientific expeditions). Ask students to speculate about the reasons why today's explorers explore.

Christopher Columbus, pages 22–25

History Objectives: Identify prior knowledge about Christopher Columbus; extend knowledge of Columbus' voyages and interaction with indigenous people; examine use of new technology used by explorers; review information about Columbus using new vocabulary.

Language Objectives: Use oral language skills to identify and discuss what is already known about Columbus; read biography of Columbus for overall comprehension; develop academic vocabulary by using context to understand new words.

Historical Thinking Objectives: Read historical narratives; interpret data on maps; reconstruct meaning of historical passage by using new vocabulary.

Learning Strategy Objectives: Understand the usefulness of the learning strategy *tell what you know,* and practice this strategy by working with a group of classmates to write down collective prior knowledge about Columbus; understand why the learning strategy *making inferences* can help in understanding new words; practice this learning strategy by using context to make logical guesses at the meanings of new words in the reading text.

PROCEDURES

Preparation

1. See "How to Teach Learning Strategies" on p. x.
2. **Before You Read: Tell What You Know.** Introduce the learning strategy *tell what you know* by modeling how you apply your own prior knowledge to a new topic. For example, write on an overhead transparency the words *Famous Explorers.* Describe famous explorers that you know about and jot down on the transparency their names and what they did. Finish by making a comment such as, *I'm surprised that I already know a lot about famous explorers. I can use what I know to learn more about these explorers. This is a great learning strategy. It is called* tell what you know. *When I think about what I already know, it helps me to focus on new information about the same topic.* Ask students to describe how they already use this strategy and encourage them to continue using it for academic learning in school.

3. Have students work in groups of three or four to discuss their prior knowledge about Columbus. Hispanic students may have more prior knowledge about Columbus than students from other national origin groups. Have students summarize their collective prior knowledge in complete sentences in their notebooks. Then have students share their sentences. Record all sentences on an overhead transparency.

4. **Before You Read: Using Maps for Comprehension.** Discuss the map on p. 22, and the first route that Columbus took to the New World and back to Spain. Have students close their eyes and make a mental picture of the relationship (distances and directions) between Europe and the Americas.

Presentation

1. Read the following title aloud to students: *Why is Christopher Columbus Important?* Ask students to tell why they think Columbus was important. Write their ideas on a transparency.
2. Tell students to read silently the biography of Columbus on pp. 23–24 to see if their ideas on the historical importance of Columbus agree with the ideas presented in the reading. Remind them to use the learning strategy *tell what you know* as they read.
3. After students have read the text, ask for volunteers to identify the reasons given in it for the importance of Columbus in history. Compare those to the reasons given by the students before reading. If any of the students' reasons are different from those in the text, ask them to explain and justify their reasons.
4. Technology Helped Early Explorers. Have students work in pairs to read the captions below the pictures on p. 24. Ask them the following questions: *Why would explorers think these inventions were so important? What would be different for the explorers if they did not have these instruments or new technologies (ways of doing things)?*

Practice

1. See "How to Teach Learning Strategies" on p. x.
2. Remind students to use the learning strategy *making inferences* to use the context to guess at the meanings of new words. For example, show a transparency of a text from a high school U.S. history textbook in which you have selected two or three words that you will pretend not to know. Read the text aloud and when you get to the "new" words, underline them and say, *That's a new word for me. I'm going to read*

the rest of the sentence, then read the sentences that come before and after to help me figure out what this word means. Hmm, I think this new word means _____. Ask students if they ever do the same thing when encountering new words. Tell them that this is a good learning strategy that can help with both reading and listening. Have them identify the name of the strategy (*making inferences*).

3. **Understanding What You Read: Using Context.** Have students sit in groups of two or three to find the vocabulary words in the reading selection on pp. 23–24. After they have located the words in the reading, have them look at the sentences on p. 25 and decide which vocabulary word best fits in the blank in each sentence. Ask them to write the sentences with the correct words in their notebooks. Encourage students to keep going back to the text to help them make the correct inference about each vocabulary word.

4. Have students list additional new words (if any) from the text on pp. 23–24 and practice the new strategy with these words.

Self-Evaluation

1. **Tell what you learned.** Have students refer to the "Before You Read: Tell What You Know" activity on p. 22. Review with them the prior knowledge they had about Columbus before reading the text on pp. 23–24. Discuss new information they learned from the reading, including any misconceptions they may have had in their prior knowledge about Columbus.

2. Have students write in their notebooks five new or corrected facts about Columbus that they learned through reading pp. 23–24.

HISTORICAL THINKING AND APPLICATION ACTIVITIES

1. Have students apply what they learned in the reading on Columbus by discussing questions such as: *Columbus thought that he had reached the Indies when he landed in America; what lands and bodies of water would he have had to cross to really reach the Indies?* (Look at a globe.) *What was happening in other countries around 1492? The year 1492 was an important year in Spain; what else happened in Spain that year besides Columbus's voyage to America?* (Hispanic students may know that this year marked the conquest of Granada, in which the last Moslems in Spain were defeated, and also the expulsion of Jews from Spain. Both of these events helped to consolidate the political power of the Catholic monarchs, Isabella and Ferdinand.)

2. As an assignment, have individual students select a country or geographical area for research. Provide library books, textbooks, and an encyclopedia for students to consult. Ask students to find out what important events took place in the area they selected during the fifteenth century (1400 to 1499). Have them write down three or four interesting facts and share them in class the next day.

3. Point out that the astrolabe, sextant, and movable sails were so important to sailors that they did not want to go onto the ocean without them. Ask, *What technologies do you think are so important today that you could not do without them? Why?*

4. Discuss the following questions with students: *What is the reason that you think Columbus is so important in history? Do you agree with the reasons given in the class? Why or why not?*

5. Ask students to look at things from a different perspective. Suggest that they are fishing in the ocean off the coast of Hispanola. They see a strange ship in the distance, then see it come nearer and men come to the shore. Ask, *What do you think they might be thinking? We do not have information about how the Taino reacted to seeing Columbus. Why do we not know this, even though we know a lot about Columbus? What does this information tell you about the stories we know in history?* (Since we only know when something has been written down or drawn or recorded, it often limits our perspective.)

REGIONS OF THE WORLD PAGES 26–27

The Wet Tropical Regions

Geography Objectives: Define and compare regions using their human and physical characteristics.

Language Objectives: Read for comprehension; demonstrate comprehension by writing answers to questions.

Historical Thinking Objective: Use visual and mathematical data in graphs.

Learning Strategy Objectives: Implicit: Practice the learning strategy *using imagery* to use maps and bar graphs to interpret information; practice the learning strategy *making inferences* with any new words encountered in the reading.

PROCEDURES

Presentation

1. See "How to Teach Map and Graph Skills," p. xiii.
2. Go over the section headings with students and ask them what kind of information they expect to find in the reading selection.

Practice

1. Explain to students that there will probably be some new words in the reading selection, but that they can make guesses about their meanings. Then have students read the selection silently.
2. Discuss the map on p. 26 with students, and have them identify Wet Tropical Regions in Europe, Asia, and North and South America.
3. **Map Skills: Finding Wet Tropical Regions.** Have students use the maps on pp. viii–x, 18–19, and 26 to answer the questions. Point out that the two states closest to the Tropic of Cancer are Wet Tropical Regions.
4. **Making Bar Graphs: The Climate of San Juan, Puerto Rico.** Remind students how information is displayed on bar graphs, and have them practice reading aloud the temperatures and rainfall measurements for different months in San Juan, Puerto Rico. Have students copy the two bar graphs in their notebooks. Help students chart the average temperature and the average rainfall for March and April on the two bar graphs. Students can complete the bar graphs independently, with a partner, or with continued teacher support.
5. Have students work in pairs or small groups to answer the questions on the bottom of p. 27.

HISTORICAL THINKING AND APPLICATION ACTIVITIES

1. Find out which students have lived in a Wet Tropical Region. Ask them where they lived. Have them describe whether and how the climate made their way of life different from the way they live in their present geographical region.
2. Have students look up Wet Tropical Regions in a geography textbook, in an atlas, in a junior encyclopedia, and on the Internet. Have them find two or three more facts about Wet Tropical Regions that they can share orally with the class. Remind students to tell the class where they found the new information.

Estevan, pages 28–29

History Objectives: Learn about Spanish interaction with native peoples, early expeditions, Estevan, and the search for gold; discuss role of slavery in Spanish exploration and conquest; learn about Spanish place names in the United States; apply learning to other situations.

Geography Objective: Analyze geographic information about the organization of people and places on the earth.

Language Objectives: Develop academic vocabulary; read for factual comprehension; engage in higher level thinking discussion; read and write answers to questions about the reading selection; develop oral language through discussion and research.

Historical Thinking Objectives: Draw upon data on historical maps; ask historical questions; use reference skills; interpret data of events over time; draw upon data on maps to answer historical questions.

Learning Strategy Objectives: Explicit: Understand why the learning strategy *using imagery* can heighten comprehension of a narrative text by imagining the sequence of events in the text; practice this learning strategy by "making a mental movie" while reading the narrative about Estevan. **Implicit:** Practice the learning strategy *making inferences* to think about names of states with Spanish origins; use the learning strategy *using resources* (reference materials, the Internet, and human resources) to investigate geographical place names.

PROCEDURES

Preparation

1. **Before You Read: Vocabulary.** See "How to Teach Vocabulary Lessons" on p. x.
2. Have students copy the vocabulary words in their notebooks. Ask them to first match vocabulary words with definitions on their own, using the Glossary or a dictionary, if necessary. Then have students work in pairs, reading to each other the words and their definitions, and deciding together on correct

definitions for each word. Still working in pairs, have students make up original sentences using the vocabulary words and write them in their notebooks.

Presentation

1. See "How to Teach Learning Strategies" on p. x.
2. Ask students if, when they read, they have ever imagined what is happening in the story they are reading. Encourage students to volunteer descriptions of scenes they have imagined while reading. Explain that imagining what is happening in a story or historical narrative is a learning strategy called *using imagery*. It is useful for understanding a reading or listening text because it engages you in the story and alerts you to a comprehension problem when your "mental movie" does not make sense.
3. See "How to Teach Reading Lessons," p. xi.
4. Write the title *Estevan* and the four headings in the reading selection on the board. With books closed, ask students to tell what they think the story is about. Under each heading, write down student contributions as they are made. Hispanic students may have a great deal of prior information about Spanish rule in Mexico and Spanish expeditions, and should be encouraged to share this information with the rest of the class. (Note: *Estevan* is spelled *Esteban* in modern Spanish, but appears as *Estevan* and *Estevanico* in historical documents written before spelling standardization.)

Practice and Self-Evaluation

1. Have students read the story of Estevan silently. Remind them to use the learning strategy *using imagery* as they read. After they have read the selection, ask students to describe their "mental movie" of this narrative. Ask them to explain whether and how this strategy helped them understand the text.
2. **Understanding What You Read: Using Maps for Comprehension.** Have students take out their copies of the map on pp. 18–19. Distribute copies of the map on pp. viii–ix (Teacher's Guide, p. 168). Ask students to identify the areas in North America claimed by Spain as a result of Estevan's expedition. Then have them color these areas the same color as they colored Spain.
3. **Understanding What You Read: Comprehension Check.** Directions for the Comprehension Check are the same as those for the Comprehension Check on p. 9 (Teacher's Guide, p. 5).
4. **What do you think?** Divide students into pairs or small groups. Ask them to read *What do you think?*

and respond to the questions. Each pair/group should find the answers to the questions, and one student in each pair/group should write them on a separate sheet of paper. Then discuss the answers as a whole class activity.

Presentation

1. See "How to Teach Map and Graph Skills," p. xiii.
2. Before reading the text at the top of p. 30, have students look at the map of the United States on pp. viii–ix and identify state names that they think might be Spanish.
3. **Map Skills: Some Spanish Claims in North America.** Have students read the information at the top of p. 30 to confirm or correct the inferences they just made. Distribute copies of the map (see Teacher's Guide, p. 171). Ask students to color in the seven states on their copy of the map. Have them use the map on pp. viii–ix to help them.

Practice

1. Tell students that questions 1–10 can be answered in words or short phrases (short answers are acceptable when the question asks for basic factual information). Have them write the answers in their notebooks.
2. After students have answered questions individually, have them work in pairs to check their answers.
3. Have students take out their copies of the maps on pp. viii–x and pp. 18–19 and look at them again. They should color the seven states the same color as they colored Spain.
4. Have students look at the photographs and try to identify the states without looking at the captions. Ask, *What geographic feature in the state made you think of Texas, Montana, or Colorado?* Ask students to tell which of the states they would like to live in, and why.

Expansion

1. <u>Investigating Names.</u> Divide students into pairs or small groups. Ask each pair/small group to write down the names of the areas where they used to live (country, state or province, city, or town).
2. Then have students investigate the origin of the names, either by asking family members or by checking in encyclopedias or online at the local historical society or Chamber of Commerce. Students should report on this activity to the class.
3. As a follow-up, have students go through the same process for the state and city in which they currently live and go to school.

HISTORICAL THINKING AND APPLICATION ACTIVITIES

1. Have students work in groups of three or four to discuss the following question: *How would your life be different if you were a slave?* After the group discussion, have students write a short essay expressing their personal view.

2. Ask students to tell the story of Estevan at home, and then ask their parents if this story reminds them of any story in the history of their native country. Have them share such stories with the rest of the class, indicating similarities and differences with the story of Estevan.

DEVELOPING REPORTS   PAGES 32–38

European Explorers in North America

History Objectives: Learn about European explorers in North America (Cabeza de Vaca, Ponce de León, de Soto, Champlain, Hudson, Cabot, Cartier); practice using information on fact sheets to develop a report.

Language Objectives: Read for comprehension; develop oral language; write short reports; make an oral presentation; listen for comprehension; take notes on presentations of classmates.

Historical Thinking Objectives: Use maps to identify areas explored by Spain, England, and France; use data presented in time lines.

Learning Strategy Objectives: Explicit: Practice previously introduced learning strategy *tell what you know* to identify prior knowledge about European explorers; practice previously introduced learning strategy *selective attention* to listen for specific information in classmates' reports; understand how using or creating a *graphic organizer* can help in understanding information and can serve as a study guide; practice using *graphic organizers* to create a chart from information presented orally. **Implicit:** Use the learning strategy *evaluate learning* by evaluating own oral report.

PROCEDURES

Preparation

1. **Before You Begin: Tell What You Know.** Ask students if they know the names of any European explorers in North America (Columbus, Cortés, Fray Marcos—Estevan was not European). Remind students that they may have studied some of these explorers in school in their native country and/or in the United States in an earlier grade or earlier in this unit.

2. See "How to Teach Learning Strategies" on p. x. Remind students that using the strategy *tell what you know* means recalling what you have already learned about a topic (even if you learned it in another language) and using that prior knowledge base to build on new information about the same topic.

3. Have students work in pairs to brainstorm their prior knowledge about European explorers in North America and write in their notebooks as many names as they can recall. Then have each pair report to the class. Compile a class list of all the names mentioned. Encourage students to tell any information they have about the explorers they mention.

4. <u>History Mystery</u> (p. 33). The History Mystery can be introduced before students move to the report writing (or at the teacher's discretion, after the reports). Students are asked to think about what would make the Spanish explorers believe that there were cities made of gold, even though no one had ever found any gold. Students can be given clues to think about how the geography of this land, new to the Spaniards, would look. What do they know about how the Southwest looks? (You may refer back to a statement on p. 29.) An encyclopedia or picture book about the southwestern United States would have pictures that illustrate how the setting sun makes the pueblos look golden. One response is that people new to a land saw something that looked like something they believed did exist and they, perhaps, expanded the story when they told it to others. (A similar situation to early sailors seeing sea monsters.)

Presentation

1. See "How to Teach Writing Lessons," p. xiii.
2. Go over the five steps given at the bottom of p. 32 so students understand the procedures they will be following to develop their reports.
3. **Step 1: Reading a Report (p. 33).** Have students read the model report on Cabeza de Vaca silently. Then have them identify the following markers:
   - Words that tell what the report is about
   - Words that indicate a main idea

- Words that indicate an example or detail
- Words that introduce the concluding paragraph

4. **Step 2: Studying a Fact Sheet (p. 34).** Divide the class into six groups. Each student in a group will be responsible for studying the fact sheet on one of the six explorers (pp. 34–36). Remind students to use the maps to help them understand the routes of these European explorers. (Note: These maps are approximations of explorers' routes because limited data are available.)

5. Ask more advanced students to use reference materials such as encyclopedias, history texts, and the Internet to find out additional information about their explorer.

Practice and Self-Evaluation

1. **Step 3: Writing a Report (p. 37).** After students have studied their explorer, have them write individual reports in their notebooks, using the model on p. 37. They should write in pencil or on the computer so that revisions can be made later.

2. **Step 4: Presenting Your Report (p. 37).** Have students go over their reports carefully and rewrite or make corrections as appropriate.

3. As a home assignment, have students practice reading their reports aloud five times or more. It is helpful to use a tape recorder so that each student can play back his/her report and evaluate it according to the three questions given on p. 37.

4. Provide time for students to practice their reports while showing the route of their explorer on the map. This can be done in small groups, in which case all members of the group should be reporting on the same explorer.

Presentation and Practice

1. **Step 5: Listening and Taking Notes (p. 38).** Ask students to copy the chart on p. 38 in their notebooks. Have them sit in their original groups and take turns presenting their reports to each other. While one student is presenting, the others should be taking notes on the information in their charts. Remind students to use the learning strategy *selective attention* as they listen for specific information in order to complete their charts.

2. Have students reread the information about Cabeza de Vaca on p. 33. Then have them complete the chart with information about this explorer.

Self-Evaluation

1. After each presentation, group members may ask the presenter questions for clarification to be sure that they understand the information presented.

2. After completing their charts, have students sit in pairs or small groups to compare their charts, pool information, and help each other correct inaccurate information or fill in missing information.

3. See "How to Teach Learning Strategies" on p. x. Ask students how they might use the chart they have just completed about European explorers in North America. Write their answers on an overhead transparency and discuss. Then tell students that the charts they have made are one kind of *graphic organizer*, that this learning strategy is helpful for remembering important information, and that it can be used later to review the main ideas of a topic they have studied.

4. **Understanding What You Read: Using Maps for Comprehension.** Have students turn to their copies of the maps on pp. viii–x and pp. 18–19 and color the areas explored by these four explorers the same colors as the countries for which they claimed the areas (England, France, the Netherlands, Spain).

5. **Tell what you learned.** Have students write summaries about the six explorers in their notebooks.

HISTORICAL THINKING AND APPLICATION ACTIVITIES

1. As a whole class or in small groups, have students discuss these questions: *We know that European explorers in North America (and in other areas) suffered many hardships, so why do you think that they continued to explore new lands? What adjectives would you use to describe these early explorers? (What qualities did they probably have?)*

2. As a class activity, provide students with U.S. history books, library books on European explorers in North America, and a junior encyclopedia. Have them find out and write down three facts each (name, area explored, dates) about another European explorer, then share this information in small groups.

3. Have students discuss the following questions in small groups and write their group's answers: *How might North America be different today if no land had been claimed for Spain? For England? For France? For the Netherlands?*

4. As an assignment, have students find out from the library, from their families, and/or from the Internet if there were ever any explorers from England,

France, the Netherlands, or Spain in their countries or near their countries. Have them share the information discovered with the class.

The Northern Forest Regions

Geography Objectives: Learn about the physical and human characteristics of Northern Forest Regions; use maps to locate cities; practice reading bar graphs.

Language Objectives: Read for comprehension; develop vocabulary; write answers to questions about Northern Forest Regions.

Historical Thinking Objectives: Use maps to locate important points; use graphs to build content knowledge.

Learning Strategy Objective: Practice the previously introduced learning strategy *making inferences* to use context to understand the meanings of new vocabulary words.

PROCEDURES

Presentation

1. See "How to Teach Map and Graph Skills," p. xiii.
2. Go over the section headings with students and ask them what kind of information they can expect to find in the reading selection.
3. Explain to students that there will probably be some new words in the reading selection, but that they can make guesses about their meanings. Then have students read the selection silently.

Practice

1. **Understanding What You Read: Using Context.** See "How to Teach Learning Strategies" on p. x. Have students look at the eight words and phrases given at the bottom of p. 39. Then have them skim the reading selection to find these words. Ask them to read the words before and after the word *evergreen* and then guess its meaning. Have them do the same on their own for the other new words and phrases. Ask students to write the words and definitions in their notebooks.

2. **Understanding Bar Graphs: Temperatures in the Northern Forest Regions.** Discuss the map on p. 40 with students, and have them identify Northern Forest Regions in Europe, Asia, and North America.

Have them identify two cities in the Northern Forest Regions (Yellowknife, Northwest Territories, Canada; and Anchorage, Alaska, United States).
3. Remind students how information is displayed on bar graphs, and have them practice reading aloud the temperatures for different months for the two cities.
4. Have students work in pairs or small groups to answer the questions on p. 40.

HISTORICAL THINKING AND APPLICATION ACTIVITIES

1. Have students work in small groups to discuss these questions: *Why do you think some animals in Northern Forest Regions migrate or hibernate in the winter? What do people do in regions that have very cold winters?* Each group should write their answers to the questions and then share their ideas with the whole class.
2. Have students look up Northern Forest Regions in a junior encyclopedia, geography textbook, atlas, and/or the Internet. Students may work individually, in pairs, or in groups. Have them find additional information about these regions (at least three new facts) and record them in their notebooks. Have students share these additional facts with the class and write down the additional facts provided by other students.

Think About What You Have Learned: Explorers, page 41

History Objective: Compare characteristics of modern explorers to characteristics of sixteenth- and seventeenth-century explorers.

Language Objectives: Read resource material for comprehension; write a short report on a modern explorer.

Historical Thinking Objectives: Obtain historical data; compare different stories of historical figures and eras.

Learning Strategy Objective: Implicit: Practice the learning strategy *using resources* to find information about modern explorers and exploration.

PROCEDURES

Preparation

1. Review with students the explorers studied in this unit. List the names and accomplishments on the board or on a transparency as students suggest them. When the list is complete, ask students what qualities

all of these explorers had (courage, determination to reach goals, technical knowledge, leadership).

2. Have students work in small groups to discuss these and other qualities they believe explorers need. Have them write down these qualities and then share them with the class.

Presentation

1. Brainstorm with students the names and accomplishments of modern explorers in different areas (e.g., mountain climbers, polar explorers, undersea explorers, space explorers, medical explorers: Neil Armstrong, Sir Edmund Hillary, Jacques Cousteau, Jonas Salk, Sally Ride, Chuck Yeager). If students are unable to come up with information about modern explorers independently, provide them with information about names, field of accomplishment, and one accomplishment. Have students investigate additional accomplishments.

2. Have students make a chart to record this information.

3. Review with students the procedures for finding information in reference materials and on the Internet, taking notes, and recording sources.

Practice

1. See "How to Teach Writing Lessons" on p. xiii.

2. Have students select the modern explorer they will investigate.

3. Students can work individually or in pairs or groups. Provide them with reference materials or take them to the school library or media center to conduct their research. (Current CD encyclopedias or text encyclopedias are a good place to start.)

4. Have students write down the name of their modern explorer and the sources they used to find additional information.

5. If possible, have students draft their reports on a computer.

Self-Evaluation

1. Have students read their reports to a classmate, and give and receive feedback.

2. Have students revise their reports, then edit them carefully. (See "How to Teach Writing Lessons" on p. xiii.)

3. Have students share their completed reports with the whole class.

HISTORICAL THINKING AND APPLICATION ACTIVITIES

1. The lesson is an expansion activity and requires that students ask the questions that lead them to compare lives of early explorers with those of modern explorers. After students have presented their reports, ask them to list the qualities they believe these modern explorers have. Ask, *How do they compare to the list you made when you were thinking about the early explorers?*

2. Ask students to think about and share areas that they think would be important to explore in the future.

From Colonies to Nation

History Objective: Identify prior knowledge about European colonies in the New World.

Geography Objectives: Develop an understanding that many states in the United States and provinces in Canada were originally colonies of different European countries; use geography to answer questions.

Language Objectives: Develop academic oral language; record prior knowledge in notebook.

Historical Thinking Objectives: Interpret data on time lines; draw upon data in historical maps.

Learning Strategy Objectives: Implicit: Identify prior knowledge (*tell what you know*) about the first European colonies in North America; practice the learning strategy *using imagery* to study a map.

PROCEDURES

1. See "How to Use the Unit Openers," p. ix. The photograph shows the main street of Plimoth Plantation, a "living museum" of Pilgrim life in Plymouth, Massachusetts. The map shows the United States and part of Canada today.
2. Discuss the map and identify what is north, south, east, and west of the territorial United States. Have students find the state where they live, and identify other states where they have lived or traveled.
3. Discuss with students the origin of the name of the state and city or town where they live. Is it American Indian, Spanish, French, English, Dutch? (Later in the unit they will relate this information to new information presented about European colonies and place names in North America.)
4. Have students examine the map closely to see if they can guess from the names of states which European countries might have had colonies in each area.

Explain that as they learn about European colonies in North America, they will be able to check their guesses and see if they were right.

5. Give each student a copy of the map on pp. 42–43 (see Teacher's Guide, p. 172). Have students complete the color key for the map, using the same color for each European country as they did on the map on pp. 18–19.

HISTORICAL THINKING AND APPLICATION ACTIVITIES

1. Ask, *Why do you think European countries established colonies in other parts of the world?* Have students give as many reasons as they can think of.
2. Identify the countries of origin for students in your class or have students choose a country in Africa, Asia, or Latin America. Include other nations that can be researched on Encarta (online) or in an encyclopedia. Have students answer the following questions: *Did any European countries establish colonies in this country? Who were they? When did they establish colonies? Did people from these countries establish colonies in other places? Where? When?* Have students write the information they discover in their notebooks.
3. Have students relate colonial settlement to your area. Have them find answers to the following questions: *When was your city or town established? Was it established in colonial times? Who established it?*
4. Have students interview their parents or family members, or look in a reference book to find out information about European or other colonies in their countries. Then ask students to share this information in class, either orally or in writing.
5. Have students group the time line items by theme or topic (e.g., colonies established before the Revolution). Have them draw pictures to illustrate the categories. When you have completed the unit, ask students to check their drawings to see how their understandings have changed or been affirmed.

Spanish Colonies, pages 44–45

> **History Objective:** Analyze the motives that led the Spanish to settle in North America and the Caribbean.
>
> **Language Objectives:** Read for comprehension by previewing selection, recalling main ideas and details, recognizing same information phrased differently, and scanning for specific information.
>
> **Historical Thinking Objective:** Use maps to obtain information about history.
>
> **Learning Strategy Objective:** Practice previously introduced learning strategy *selective attention* to find specific information in the reading text.

PROCEDURES

Preparation

1. See "How to Teach Learning Strategies" on p. x. Ask students to describe how they have used the strategy *selective attention* in previous lessons (e.g., p. 14, p. 38). Ask them if they use this strategy in other classes and have them provide examples.

2. **Before You Read: Using Headings.** Preview and discuss the headings in the reading selection. Ask students to copy them in their notebooks. Then have students write the number of the question beside the heading which they would look under to find the answer. Have students work with a partner to check their answers.

Presentation and Practice

1. See "How to Teach Reading Lessons" on p. xi.
2. Have students read "Spanish Colonies" silently.
3. Discuss with students how they used the learning strategy *selective attention* before and while reading.

Self-Evaluation

1. **Understanding What You Read: Comprehension Check.** The directions for the activity on p. 45 are the same as those for p. 9 (Teacher's Guide, p. 5).

2. Have students sit in small groups to check their answers. Have students read aloud the Comprehension Check questions to each other; indicate whether each is *True, False,* or *Not Given;* and then for true and false statements, read the supporting sentences that they have underlined in the reading selection. For items marked false, have students rewrite each item to make it true. Then have students look for information on the *not given* items in reference books or on the Internet; have students rewrite these items to make them true.

3. **Understanding What You Read: Scanning.** Remind students that when they scan, they must use *selective attention* to look for specific types of information. Have them practice scanning by going through the reading selection on p. 44 to identify the four states where Spain established colonies and missions. This can be a timed exercise, giving students one minute to find the information and one minute to write the names of the four states.

4. Have students use their copy of the map on pp. 42–43 and color the four states identified the same color as the color they have chosen to represent Spain.

HISTORICAL THINKING AND APPLICATION ACTIVITIES

1. You can often tell where countries had colonies by knowing what languages are spoken there. Ask, *What other countries do you know about where people speak Spanish outside of Spain? What other languages are spoken in those countries? What other countries speak French besides France?*

2. Spanish priests taught Native Americans about the Christian religion. They were *missionaries,* or people who teach their own religion to people in other countries. Have students find out whether there were/are missionaries in their native countries or in a country of their choice by using resource materials and asking their families. They can report orally or in writing to the class. Reports should include information about who the missionaries were, what religion they taught (or are teaching), and how successful they were/have been in having people adopt that religion.

The First English Colonies, pages 46–47

> **History Objectives:** Expand content vocabulary related to English colonies in North America; find out the reasons for the establishment of English colonies and learn about the first three English colonies: Roanoke Island, Jamestown, and Plymouth.
>
> **Language Objectives:** Develop academic vocabulary; read for comprehension.
>
> **Historical Thinking Objectives:** Read or listen to historical narratives; appreciate historical perceptions.
>
> **Geography Objective:** Use maps to learn about historical ideas.
>
> **Learning Strategy Objective: Implicit:** Practice previously introduced learning strategies such as *tell what you know, making inferences,* and *selective attention* to assist in reading comprehension.

PROCEDURES

Preparation

1. See "How to Teach Vocabulary Lessons" on p. x.

2. **Before You Read: Vocabulary.** Have students work in pairs to study the words in the vocabulary box. Students in each pair should first use the learning strategy *selective attention* to copy in their notebooks the words that are new.

3. Have students look up their new words in the Glossary and read the definitions. Then have them write the definition in their own words next to each new word in their notebooks.

4. Finally, have students define orally the words that were not identified as new words.

Presentation

1. See "How to Teach Reading Lessons," p. xi.
2. Preview and discuss the headings and illustrations for "The First English Colonies," pp. 46–47.
3. Have students read pp. 46–47. Or have students do paired reading in which they take turns reading a paragraph aloud and discussing it with their partner.
4. Have students summarize the main ideas in the reading orally.

HISTORICAL THINKING AND APPLICATION ACTIVITIES

1. Discuss the meaning of "government by majority rule." Ask students to list some group decisions they have made by majority rule in their families, among their friends, or in their classes (e.g., deciding what movie to see, choosing class officials). Ask, *What group decisions were not made by majority rule? Is majority rule a good way to make a group decision? Why or why not?*

2. Use the following questions to promote discussion: *Why do you think many of the Jamestown and Plymouth colonists died during the first winter in America? Do you know about any other people like the Pilgrims, who went to a new country so that they could have religious freedom? Why do you think that no women signed the Mayflower Compact?*

3. Develop a classroom compact that will assure that the class can work together to learn history well. Discuss with students: *What items will need to be in your compact? What are the most important things for each person to do? What roles will everyone have? Will different people have different roles?* Have students write the compact, sign it, and post it in your classroom.

LIFE IN DIFFERENT COLONIES, 1600–1700 — PAGES 48–52

Daily Life, pages 48–50

> **History Objectives:** Explain how and why family and community life differed in various regions and colonies in North America in the seventeenth century; analyze information on Jamestown and Plymouth colonies and Spanish settlements to find important ideas, guess at cause and effect relationships.
>
> **Language Objectives:** Develop oral academic language; write observations in notebooks; develop academic reading comprehension; scan for specific information; compare and contrast information from different sources by taking notes and discussing charts.
>
> **Historical Thinking Objectives:** Demonstrate historical understanding or formulate questions about European colonies in North America using photographs and documents; make comparisons and contrasts; take notes on reading by completing a study chart; use map skills to record information.

PROCEDURES

Presentation and Practice

1. **Discussing and Interpreting Photographs.** Initiate this lesson as a brainstorming activity. Ask students to examine the photographs and describe each. Write their descriptions on the board.

2. Divide the class into groups and assign several photographs and several questions to each group. Each group should work together to develop a paragraph that responds to the questions. Provide students with history and library books, Encarta, and/or a junior encyclopedia containing information about the Plymouth colony, so that they can check their facts and find additional information.

3. After each group has prepared a report on the photographs assigned, have them select a representative to present the report to the whole class. This representative should practice presenting the report at least five times to the small group. Group members should provide feedback and suggestions for improvement.

4. Finally, have each group representative present his or her report to the whole class.

Self-Evaluation

1. **Tell what you learned.** Have students write their conclusions about life in different colonies in their notebooks.

2. Have students take turns sharing their conclusions with classmates.

Presentation and Practice

1. **Understanding What You Read: Scanning and Taking Notes.** Remind students that *scanning* means going through a reading selection quickly in order to find specific kinds of information. The learning strategy used for scanning is *selective attention*.

2. Go over the seven kinds of information requested for the chart on p. 50. Have students contribute information for each of the seven topics listed from their reading of pp. 46–47 (or from their own prior knowledge).

3. Remind students that note-taking is done by writing down key words and phrases, but never the whole sentence or paragraph. Discuss with students the important linguistic markers that signal different parts of a text. For instance, in the selection about the first English colonies, students should pay attention to information about how the colonists acquired the land they settled on (by gift, sale, annexation, war).

4. Have students use *selective attention* to scan pp. 46–47 and the notes from pp. 48–49 to find the information requested for the chart. Have them copy the chart on p. 50 in their notebooks and make brief notes on the chart as they find each piece of information.

Self-Evaluation

1. **Understanding What You Read: Comparing and Contrasting.** Have students work in pairs or small groups to discuss the information they have written on their charts. Each pair or group should identify two facts which show that the colonies had similarities (comparing), and two facts which show that they had differences (contrasting). Then have each pair or group share their comparisons and contrasts as a short oral summary with the whole class.

2. **Understanding What You Read: Using Maps for Comprehension.** Have students find the answers to the questions at the bottom of p. 50 by looking at a classroom map or the map on pp. 42–43. Then have them color Virginia and Massachusetts the same color as they have chosen to represent England on their copies of the map on pp. 42–43.

HISTORICAL THINKING AND APPLICATION ACTIVITIES

1. Discuss this question with the class: *How was life in the North American colonies different from your life today?* Ask students to use the pictures and reports to describe contrasts. Ask, *How was life in the colonies different from life in your native country or in another country you know?*

2. Have students search for pictures of the colonies or of life in colonial times. (Use library resources, an online encyclopedia, or the Library of Congress website with key words such as colonial life, Plymouth colony, colonial workers, etc.) Create a class Colonial Collage with topics such as children, work by men, work by women, housing, play, family, and religion. Display the collage in the classroom and

have students list in their notebooks words they would use to describe life in colonial times.

3. Ask students what was happening in the early 1600s in other parts of the world. Provide them with history books on different areas of the world that cover the seventeenth century, and a junior encyclopedia or Encarta. Students may also bring information from home, either from books or through interviewing their parents. Have students choose a country or area of the world to work on in small groups. Ask each group to use the resources students collected to develop a time line of important events during the seventeenth century in the country or area they have selected. The time lines can be illustrated with maps and drawings. Each group can then share its time line and explain it to the rest of the class. Finally, the time lines should be displayed together so that students gain an understanding of what was happening in their own and other countries at the time of the establishment of the first English colonies in America.

Massasoit, page 51

> **History Objectives:** Discuss interaction of the colonists with Native Americans and the struggle for control of North America; learn about the important role of Native American leaders in relations with colonists.
>
> **Language Objective:** Develop listening comprehension.
>
> **Historical Thinking Objectives:** Listen to historical narratives; identify central questions in historical narratives.
>
> **Learning Strategy Objective:** Practice previously introduced learning strategy *taking notes* with information presented orally.

LISTENING AND TAKING NOTES

PROCEDURES

Preparation

1. See "How to Teach Listening Comprehension Lessons" on p. xi.
2. Remind students about the organization of the listening mini-lectures: statement of topic, main ideas with supporting details, conclusion.
3. Write this paragraph on the board and ask students to tell you which words can be erased without losing the meaning.

. . . Before their crops could grow, the Pilgrims were very hungry. Massasoit traded food to them. A year later, when the Pilgrims had a feast of thanks to celebrate their first good harvest, they invited Massasoit and members of the Wampanoag tribe to join them. The Native Americans came and also brought food for the feast. The Pilgrims and the Wampanoag learned they could be friends.

Follow the procedures described for p. 12 (Teacher's Guide, pp. 6–7), erasing less important words and having students reconstruct the passage from words remaining on the board.
4. Have students copy the T-list on p. 51 in their notebooks.

Presentation and Practice

1. Read the following text. Have students write the missing information in the blanks in the T-lists they copied in their notebooks.
2. Have students sit in small groups to compare and complete their notes.
3. Ask students individually to write in their own words short summaries of the important points about Massasoit, using their completed T-lists as guides.

> ## Listening Text for "Massasoit"
>
> Today, you are going to hear about an important Native American. He was called Massasoit (MAS u SOIT), which means great leader, and he was important because he was friendly to the Pilgrims who settled in Plymouth and because he believed in peace.
>
> First, you will hear who Massasoit was and what he did. Massasoit was the chief of the Wampanoag (WOM pu NO ag) tribe. He ruled an area that is today part of Massachusetts and Rhode Island. When the English Pilgrims came to Plymouth, Massachusetts, in 1620, they built their homes on land that belonged to the Wampanoag. However, the Wampanoag did not fight the Pilgrims. Instead, Chief Massasoit signed a peace treaty with the colonists in 1621, and the Wampanoag and the Pilgrims lived peacefully side by side for over twenty years.
>
> Now you will hear how the Pilgrims learned to live in this new place. The Wampanoag helped the Pilgrims to plant crops and to fish. The Pilgrims did not know how to do these things before they came to this new land. Before their crops could grow, the

Pilgrims were very hungry. Massasoit traded food to them. A year later, when the Pilgrims had a feast of thanks to celebrate their first good harvest, they invited Massasoit and members of the Wampanoag tribe to join them. The Native Americans came and also brought food for the feast. The Pilgrims and the Wampanoag learned they could be friends.

Next you will hear how the Pilgrims and Massasoit helped each other. When Massasoit was very sick, one of the Pilgrims helped him get well. When another tribe planned to attack Plymouth colony, Massasoit warned the Pilgrims.

Finally, let's see what happened after Massasoit died. Although Massasoit believed in peace, there was war after he died. His son Metacomet, who was called "King Philip" by the English, decided to attack the English colonists because he did not want them to take any more Wampanoag lands. The war lasted for two years, and many Wampanoag and English colonists were killed. Massasoit's ideas about peace were forgotten.

In conclusion, Massasoit was important in American history because he signed a peace treaty with the Pilgrims and was a good friend to them for the rest of his life. He was a man who believed that peace was more important than war.

HISTORICAL THINKING AND APPLICATION ACTIVITIES

1. Have students discuss the following questions: *Do you think it was possible for people as different as the Pilgrims and Massasoit's people to be real friends? Why or why not? What were some of the differences between these two groups of people that would make friendship difficult? What were some of the similarities between these two groups of people that would help friendship?*

2. Have students identify groups within the school or in their own communities that have difficulties working together. Have students write down the reasons why working together might be difficult (e.g., differences in age, language, culture, values, gender, neighborhood, etc.). In class, have students sit in small groups and share their information.

3. Discuss with students the special foods that are served for holidays such as Thanksgiving. List on the board or on a transparency the names of the holidays and the foods served. Ask students to share a family recipe for one of these special foods (or have students and parents bring a special dish to share with the class).

Anne Hutchinson and the Puritans, page 52

History Objective: Learn about the life of Anne Hutchinson and why she was important.

Language Objectives: Read for comprehension; develop academic language; use reference materials to find additional information; write a brief report.

Historical Thinking Objectives: Use chronology in the structure of an historical narrative; obtain data from various sources.

Learning Strategy Objectives: Implicit: Use the learning strategy *selective attention* to find additional information; practice the learning strategy *taking notes* to jot down information.

PROCEDURES

Presentation

1. See "How to Teach Writing Lessons," p. xiii.

2. Have students read the paragraph about Anne Hutchinson silently, then ask individual students to retell the information. Clarify any difficult vocabulary words.

3. **Writing a Report.** Tell students that they must pay attention to the important events in Anne Hutchinson's life, and then have them silently read the eleven listed facts. Discuss this new information and have students work cooperatively to figure out the meanings of any unfamiliar words.

4. Provide students with U.S. history textbooks, library books, and a junior encyclopedia or Internet encyclopedia so they can look up additional information about Anne Hutchinson. Ask each student to select three additional facts about her life and write them in their notebooks.

Practice

1. Have students work in pairs or small groups to decide where each additional fact fits into the chronological fact list on p. 52.

2. Have students write a report on the life of Anne Hutchinson on a separate sheet of paper. When students have finished writing, have them share what they wrote with a classmate, asking for help and advice as needed. Finally, have students write their corrected biography of Anne Hutchinson in their

notebooks. Remind them that they should have an *introduction*, which gives the purpose of the paper and its main ideas; a *body*, which again gives the main ideas, but also presents details and examples that illuminate the main idea; and finally, a *conclusion*, which reiterates the main points and tells why Anne Hutchinson was important.

HISTORICAL THINKING AND APPLICATION ACTIVITIES

1. Ask students to discuss the following questions: *What jobs did men and women do in the North American colonies? Find out about other women in the colonies. Was it unusual for a woman to do what Anne Hutchinson did? Why?*
2. Have students make a list of jobs that are traditionally done by men, and another list of jobs done by women. Have students think about why women might have hunted or plowed fields in colonial times. Ask, *Are there any jobs that men did in the colonies that were not traditional for men?*

REGIONS OF THE WORLD PAGES 53–54

The Mid-Latitude Forest Regions

Geography Objective: Analyze the physical characteristics of geographical areas.

Language Objectives: Read for comprehension; answer comprehension and inferential questions (compare and contrast; infer cause and effect; make generalizations).

Historical Thinking Objectives: Use maps to locate geographical areas; use graphs to expand information.

Learning Strategy Objective: Implicit: Use previously introduced learning strategies such as *selective attention, making inferences,* and *using imagery* to assist comprehension of an informational text.

PROCEDURES

Presentation and Practice

1. See "How to Teach Map and Graph Skills," p. xiii.
2. Ask students to tell what they know about *latitudes.* Use a globe or world map to point out latitude lines. Then have students look at the map on p. 53 and identify three latitude lines.
3. Have students skim the text at the top of p. 53 for the gist. Then ask them to retell the important information.
4. **Understanding What You Read: Using Maps for Comprehension.** Have students work in pairs or small groups to read and answer the questions at the bottom of p. 53.
5. **Understanding Bar Graphs: Temperatures in the Mid-Latitude Forest Regions.** Remind students how information is displayed on bar graphs, and have them practice reading aloud the temperatures for different months for the two cities.
6. Have students work in pairs or small groups to answer the questions on p. 54.
7. **What do you think?** Have students sit in small groups to work on the activity. Have each group discuss why the two graphs don't show the same amount of difference in temperature. Then have each group present their explanation to the class, and follow the explanations with a general discussion.

HISTORICAL THINKING AND APPLICATION ACTIVITIES

1. Have students give three reasons why almost half of the world's people live in Mid-Latitude Forest Regions. Ask, *Should more people live in different geographical regions? Why or why not?*
2. Have students find out as much as they can about the climate and geographical features of their native countries (or another country) through library research and through conversations with family members. Ask them to identify the geographical region of their native country and its main features, climate, and resources. Have students share this information in class, either orally or in writing.

The French and Dutch in North America,
pages 55–56

> **History and Geography Objectives:** Learn how, where, and why the French and Dutch explorers came to North America and founded colonies.
>
> **Language Objectives:** Read for comprehension, recognizing main ideas and details; complete sentences to demonstrate comprehension.
>
> **Historical Thinking Objective:** Practice using maps to learn about history.
>
> **Learning Strategy Objective:** Practice previously introduced learning strategy *predicting* to anticipate information in a reading text.

PROCEDURES

Preparation

1. See "How to Teach Learning Strategies" on p. x.
2. **Before You Read: Predicting.** Have students preview and discuss the headings and illustrations on p. 55. Ask them to use the headings and illustrations to *predict* what the reading will be about.
3. Write students' predictions on the board or on an overhead transparency.
4. Ask students to explain why the learning strategy *predicting* is useful for understanding a text. Remind students that when a prediction is not right, good readers (and listeners) correct their predictions and read (or listen) on.

Presentation

1. See "How to Teach Reading Lessons," p. xi.
2. Have students read silently the section about French explorers and colonies. Ask them to retell the main ideas with their books closed. (Students can also retell this information in their native language, if the teacher, aide, or peer tutor can understand. Native language retelling of information read or listened to provides a more accurate comprehension check than does retelling in English, which is subject to limitations imposed by limited English proficiency.)
3. Repeat the same procedures with the section about Dutch explorers and colonies.

Practice and Self-Evaluation

1. **Understanding What You Read: Comprehension Check.** Have students complete the sentences individually. Then ask them to sit in pairs or small groups to compare the sentence completions they have written, and to decide on the most complete answers.
2. **Understanding What You Read: Using Maps for Comprehension.** Have students take out their copies of the map from pp. 42–43. Ask them to color the areas claimed by the French. Then they can use a combination of colors (perhaps alternating stripes) to color the areas that were originally claimed by the Dutch but later claimed by the English.
3. Have students look carefully at the map showing the different European colonies in North America. Announce that they will have five minutes to study the names of today's states that were originally claimed or colonized by one or more of these European countries. After the five minutes have elapsed, have students put away the map and ask students to write the names of the four European nations (Spain, England, France, the Netherlands) as headings for four columns. Then have students write as many states as they can remember under the appropriate European nation(s).
4. Have students check their lists using the map, then evaluate how well they remembered the names of the states (all; half; not many). Discuss with students what learning strategy or strategies helped them remember the states colonized by each European nation. (Possible strategies: *classifying, using imagery, selective attention.*)

HISTORICAL THINKING AND APPLICATION ACTIVITIES

1. Use these questions to promote discussion: *What language is spoken today in Quebec? What language is spoken in New York? Why? What reasons can you give for the friendship between French trappers and Native Americans? Do you think the price that Peter Minuit paid for Manhattan Island was fair at that time in history? Why or why not?* (Hint: Look at an atlas and find the island of Manhattan in New York.)
2. Have students find out through the library and interviews with family members if their native country ever had French or Dutch explorers and colonizers. If so, have them write down three good things that these colonial powers brought to their countries, and three bad things that resulted from explorations and colonies of France and the Netherlands. This information can then be shared with the class.

History and Geography Objectives: Identify the thirteen English colonies and learn about their characteristics; use maps to compare features of the thirteen colonies.

Language Objectives: Read for comprehension; develop academic language; write study questions, and answer classmates' questions.

Historical Thinking Objectives: Draw upon data in historical maps to build knowledge about colonial locations; comprehend a variety of historical sources.

Learning Strategy Objective: Implicit: Practice previously introduced learning strategy *tell what you know* to name the English colonies studied earlier.

PROCEDURES

Preparation

1. See "How to Teach Learning Strategies" on p. x. Remind students that recalling known information related to a new topic helps them increase their understanding of the topic.
2. Preview and discuss the headings.

Presentation and Practice

1. See "How to Teach Reading Lessons," p. xi. Have students read p. 57 silently, individually, or in pairs.
2. See "How to Teach Map and Graph Skills," p. xiii.
3. **Understanding What You Read: Using Maps for Comprehension.** Have students read the directions for item 1 on p. 58 silently, and write the names of the thirteen colonies in their notebooks by scanning p. 57. Then have them write the name of the country that claimed the thirteen colonies.
4. Have students use the map on pp. viii–ix to locate the important colonial cities and towns listed in item 2. Ask them to match the names of the colonial cities and towns to the correct numbers on the map on p. 57. Have students write the answers in their notebooks.
5. After students have written individual answers about similarities between the eight cities and towns (they are all located on rivers or the Atlantic coast), discuss their answers. Ask students to volunteer reasons why

the colonists built their cities and towns on the ocean or a river, and write their ideas on the board.

Self-Evaluation

1. **Understanding What You Read: Writing Study Questions.** Explain to students that writing study questions is a good way to learn and review material that they read. They can use study questions to check their own recall of information, or to work with a classmate to review the material. Have them write ten study questions on the information about the thirteen colonies presented on p. 57.
2. Have students sit in groups of three to do the **Study Quiz.** First, they should write their names on a sheet of paper. Then they should take turns asking each other the study questions they have written. Each student's answers are to be evaluated by the other two students in the group; if both agree that the answer is correct, then a point is awarded to the student.

HISTORICAL THINKING AND APPLICATION ACTIVITIES

1. Ask students these questions to promote discussion: *The southern plantation owners needed many workers. Instead of buying African slaves, were there other ways they could they have gotten enough workers for the plantations?*
2. Provide students with history books covering colonial periods in Africa, Asia, and Latin America. Have them choose an area, then work in small groups to find out answers to the following questions: *Which nation(s) set up colonies in this area? How did the colonists earn their livings? Could the colonists make any decisions or pass any laws? Who were the workers on the farms and plantations? Were there slaves in this area of the world? Who were those slaves? How did they become slaves? Could they ever be free?*
3. Have students compare the weather and terrain in the northern, mid-Atlantic, and southern colonies today (website: www.ncdc.noaa.gov/oa/climate/research/cag3/NA.html). This site allows you to select a time and location to get average weather. The general site, www.noaa.gov, provides other options as well. Have students answer the following questions: *What differences are there? If you had a choice where to live in North America, which area would you choose? Why? What could you do to make a living in that area?*

The French and Indian War

> **History Objective:** Identify the reasons for and results of the French and Indian War (Seven Years' War).
>
> **Language Objectives:** Read for comprehension by comparing and contrasting information; write answers to questions on the reading text.
>
> **Historical Thinking Objectives:** Use maps to identify areas in North America claimed by European countries before and after the French and Indian War; use images to build historical knowledge.
>
> **Learning Strategy Objective: Implicit:** Practice the learning strategy *using imagery* to locate historical events on a map.

PROCEDURES

Preparation

1. See "How to Teach Map and Graph Skills," p. xiii.

2. **Before You Read: Using Maps for Comprehension.** Discuss the map on p. 59 with students and ask them to identify the areas claimed by different European countries. Have them refer to their color code on pp. 42–43.

3. Have students write the answers to the five questions on p. 59 individually. Have students go over their answers and correct any errors they find. Then have them sit in pairs to discuss and compare answers, making additional corrections as necessary.

Presentation

1. Have students read the information about the French and Indian War silently. (See "How to Teach Reading Lessons," p. xi.)

2. Discuss the illustration and caption of George Washington in the French and Indian War, and ask students what else they know about George Washington. Ask students to look carefully at the picture and answer such questions as: *What do you think is happening in the picture? Which person do you think is George Washington? Why do you think so? What can you tell about the location of the battle? Can you tell who is winning the battle? Why do you think the painter painted this picture?* Write students' answers on the board or on an overhead transparency.

Self-Evaluation

1. Have students read a brief biography of George Washington or look in the encyclopedia (book or CD) to check their facts.

2. **Understanding What You Read: Using Maps for Comprehension.** Have students look at the map on p. 60. Then ask students to answer the questions individually. Have students sit in pairs to discuss and compare answers, making corrections as needed.

HISTORICAL THINKING AND APPLICATION ACTIVITIES

1. Have students discuss these questions: *How might life in the United States today be different if the French had won the French and Indian War?* Provide a blank U.S. map and have students draw a new map to answer this question.

2. Have students find out (from their families, books at home, the library, or other students from their native countries) if any wars between colonial powers were fought in their native countries (or in any country in Africa, Asia, or Latin America). Have them take notes on as much information as they can find and share it with the class orally. Ask them to try to find out the reasons for the conflict, the countries involved, which country won, and what effect this had on the history of their native country (or other country studied).

| THE ROAD TO INDEPENDENCE | PAGES 61–70 |

Benjamin Franklin, pages 61–62

> **History Objectives:** Learn about the life of Benjamin Franklin and his ideas that led the way in the revolutionary movement.
>
> **Language Objectives:** Read for comprehension; develop academic language.
>
> **Historical Thinking Objectives:** Read historical narratives, stories of historical figures and eras; create time lines.

PROCEDURES

Preparation

1. See "How to Teach Learning Strategies" on p. x.

2. **Before You Read: Using Headings.** Remind students that one of the learning strategies they have used is *predicting* before reading. Ask students to describe how they have used this strategy. Ask them if and how it helps them comprehend a reading text. Make sure that students understand that getting the right answer is not the goal when using this strategy; rather, this strategy helps them begin thinking about the topic of the reading.

3. Call on individual students to read aloud each of the four questions on p. 61. Then call for volunteers to look at the headings of each section and *predict* which section will answer the question.

4. Have students write in their notebooks the questions and the headings where they *predict* they will find the answers.

Presentation and Practice

1. See "How to Teach Reading Lessons," p. xi.

2. Have students do paired reading for the selection, "Benjamin Franklin," on pp. 61–62. Each pair of students will take turns to (1) read one heading, (2) *predict* the information to follow, (3) read the section aloud, and (4) correct the prediction and summarize the main idea.

Self-Evaluation

1. **After You Read: Making a Time Line.** See "How to Teach Learning Strategies," p. x.

2. Remind students how to use *graphic organizers* to understand new information.

3. Have students work in pairs to make a time line of Benjamin Franklin's life.

HISTORICAL THINKING AND APPLICATION ACTIVITIES

1. Have students look at the quotes from *Poor Richard's Almanac* on p. 61. Benjamin Franklin put these ideas in his almanac to tell people about life and what he thought was important for people to know about life. Have students discuss these questions: *What do you think he was trying to say about life in each of the quotes? How would you say each quote in your own words? What advice might you like to give to your classmates or friends?*

2. Franklin was one of the most important people in the early history of the United States, yet he only went to school for two years. Ask students, *How was this possible? Would it be possible today? Why or why not?*

3. Provide students with library books, American history textbooks and a CD or print encyclopedia. Have them work in groups to find more information about Franklin. Each group should discover at least three more interesting facts about Franklin and share them with the class.

The Colonists Begin to Protest, pages 64–66

PROCEDURES

Preparation

1. See "How to Teach Vocabulary Lessons," p. x.

2. **Before You Read: Vocabulary.** Have students work in small groups to go over the vocabulary words at the top of p. 63. They should discuss what words they know or can guess the meaning of, what words are cognates with their first language (if any), and how to group the words into categories. The words are listed

alphabetically, but can be rearranged to make them easier to learn. Possible groupings include: things having to do with war/fighting, things having to do with government, things having to do with trade, other words.

3. After the discussion in small groups, students can work on the exercise individually, using a dictionary or the Glossary, if necessary.

4. Have students work in pairs to check their work, compare answers, and discuss any discrepancies.

5. Ask students to work individually on the second part of the Vocabulary exercise on p. 63. Give students sufficient time so they can think of original sentences to contextualize each of the five words and so they can self-monitor as they attempt to write each sentence correctly.

6. Have students share their sentences in small groups or with the whole class.

Presentation

1. See "How to Teach Reading Lessons," p. xi.

2. Preview and discuss the headings for the reading selection, "The Colonists Begin to Protest," on pp. 64–65.

3. Divide the class into five groups. Tell each group that they will be responsible for reading and summarizing the information under one of the headings that give the reasons why the colonists began to dislike British rule (paragraphs 2–6). Have each group read the introductory and concluding paragraphs. Students in each group should first read their assigned section silently, and then ask questions for clarification of vocabulary or concepts to other group members. (The teacher circulates from group to group in order to answer questions that group members cannot answer.)

4. Have each group develop an oral summary of their section to share with the rest of the class. Each group should select a reporter to present their summary to the rest of the class.

5. After sharing oral summaries, have students read silently the entire selection on their own.

Self-Evaluation

1. **Understanding What You Read: Comprehension Check.** Directions for the Comprehension Check on p. 66 are the same as those for p. 9 (see Teacher's Guide, p. 5).

2. See "How to Teach Learning Strategies" on p. x. Ask students what learning strategy they use when they scan to look for specific types of information (*selective attention*). Have students read the directions

at the bottom of p. 66 and then scan pp. 64–65 to check their own answers to the Comprehension Check.

HISTORICAL THINKING AND APPLICATION ACTIVITIES

1. Discuss these questions with students: *Which of the vocabulary words have similar words in your first language (or other language you know)? Do they mean exactly the same thing? Can you think of antonyms for any of the vocabulary words?*

2. Have students develop definitions for the following concepts: colony, independent, representation, tax. Put each word on the board or on an overhead. Ask students what they think of when they hear these words (brainstorming). Write all answers. Group responses by category (e.g., relate to people, have to do with government). Ask students in pairs to use the categories to write their own definition of each word. Then they can share them with classmates.

3. Ask students to discuss the following questions: *What do you think the indigenous people probably did when the colonists tried to settle the land west of the Appalachians? Were the colonists right in what they did?* Have students find out from their parents or other family members about unfair things that colonial powers did in their countries, and what was done about it. Have them share this information in class, either orally or in writing.

4. Ask students, *Does taxation without representation still happen? Where?*

5. Tell students that the British made the colonists pay different kinds of taxes because they needed money to pay for the army that protected the colonists. Have them discuss these questions: *Can you think of another way that the British could have paid for the army? Why do you think that freedom was important to the colonists?*

The War for Independence Begins, pages 67–68

History Objectives: Identify and organize the events leading up to the American Revolution; learn about the First Continental Congress and how the War for Independence started at Lexington and Concord.

Language Objectives: Read for comprehension; understand meaning through context; infer main ideas; review usage of *would*; appreciate how poetry can express ideas that inspired historical events; develop vocabulary.

Historical Thinking Objectives: Use visual data to determine historic meaning; identify central questions of historical narrative; explain causes to analyze historical actions.

Learning Strategy Objectives: Explicit: Practice using the previously introduced learning strategy *making inferences* to use context to understand new vocabulary. **Implicit:** Practice the previously introduced learning strategy *graphic organizers* to identify causes and effects of British and colonial actions leading to the American Revolution; practice using the learning strategy *predicting* by reading and discussing headings.

PROCEDURES

Preparation

1. See "How to Teach Learning Strategies" on p. x.
2. Ask students to study the diagram on p. 67 and describe the information in it. Ask them what learning strategy they used to understand the diagram (*graphic organizers*) and whether it helped them see causes and effects of the actions taken by the British and the colonists.
3. Preview and discuss the headings on pp. 67–68: "The First Continental Congress," "The British Respond," and "Lexington and Concord." Have students make predictions about the information presented under each heading, and write their predictions on the board. After reading, they will confirm or correct their predictions.

Presentation

1. See "How to Teach Reading Lessons," p. xi.
2. Review with students the meanings of *would*, as expressed in sentences such as: *I would like to be an excellent student. The boy said that he would not obey his parents* (intention). *I would give you the book if I had finished it* (past conditional). Have them find similar sentences on pp. 67–68 and decide if they express intention or condition (cause and effect).

Practice and Self-Evaluation

1. Have students sit in small groups to identify and circle new words they have encountered in the reading text.
2. Have students work cooperatively to guess at the meanings of the words circled by looking at the words before and after the new words (*making inferences*).

3. **Understanding What You Read: History in Poetry.** Explain to students that this activity will help them look in more depth at the perspectives of those who experienced the events of an historical era. Sometimes lines from poems become as famous as the speeches of presidents. Students should work in pairs to write in their own words what the lines mean. You may wish to share with students the image of the bridge (found at: www.pbs.org/wnet/ihas/icon/concord.html) to provide more context. You may also discuss the use of figurative language (e.g., "the shot" was not really *heard,* but the ideas were heard and influenced other oppressed groups to rebel). The poem was written after the American and French Revolutions and addresses the ideas of the powerless rising against the powerful.

4. **Understanding What You Read: Using Context.** Have students use the context to guess what the words on p. 68 mean. Students should work in pairs or small groups to develop definitions for these words and write them in their notebooks.

HISTORICAL THINKING AND APPLICATION ACTIVITIES

1. Have students (whole class or small groups) discuss these questions: *What might have happened if Parliament and the king of England had decided to give the colonists more freedom to govern themselves? Do you think there would still have been a War for Independence? Why or why not?*
2. Have students do a quick-write from the following prompt: *What would you do if you were a colonist? Would you join the revolution? Why? Why not?* After reviewing students' quick-writes, assign them to pairs or groups of three in which both views (in favor of and against joining the revolution) are represented. Have students explain and defend their points of view within their groups.
3. Ask students, *What does independence mean to you?* Have them share their ideas with the class and listen to the ideas of others. Then have students write in their notebooks their individual answers to the question.
4. Find "Concord Hymn" (at the National Park Service site: www.nps.gov/mima/hymn.htm) and post it in the class. You will also find out some information about the author, Ralph Waldo Emerson, and the circumstances surrounding the writing of this poem.

The Colonies Declare
Independence, pages 69–70

> **History Objectives:** Explore the major ideas in the Declaration of Independence; memorize famous historical material.
>
> **Language Objectives:** Read for comprehension; write answers to questions; write a summary; memorize the first part of the Declaration of Independence.
>
> **Historical Thinking Objective:** Identify central questions of historical data.
>
> **Learning Strategies Objectives:** Practice previously introduced learning strategy *predicting* to anticipate new information in text; understand how the learning strategy *summarizing* can be used to check one's understanding of a text and practice using this strategy; identify the strategy to use to anticipate new information (*predicting*).

PROCEDURES

Preparation

1. See "How to Teach Learning Strategies" on p. x. Discuss with students how they have already used the strategy *predicting* and how it has worked for them (answers will vary).

2. **Before You Read: Using Headings.** Preview and discuss the headings on p. 69. Have students look up meanings of unfamiliar words in the Glossary or a dictionary.

3. Have students write brief answers to the two questions independently, then have them compare answers with a classmate.

Presentation

1. See "How to Teach Reading Lessons," p. xi.

2. Have students read p. 69 silently. Then ask them to revise their answers to the two questions according to the information read.

3. See "How to Teach Learning Strategies" on p. x. Discuss with students what they already know about writing summaries. Explain that *summarizing* is a learning strategy and is particularly useful in checking how well you have understood something read or listened to. Summaries can be written, oral, or mental.

Practice

1. **Understanding What You Read: Making a Summary.** Explain to students that the four questions on p. 70 should be used as a guide for writing the summary of the text on p. 69.

2. Have students write summaries individually, then meet in pairs or small groups to compare their summaries, working together to correct individual summaries as needed.

Presentation and Practice

1. **Understanding What You Read: Citizens' Rights.** Read the first excerpt from the Declaration of Independence aloud to students.

2. Have students work in small groups to discuss the words and meanings listed next to the excerpt, asking each other (and the teacher) for clarification as necessary.

3. Have students work in pairs reading the excerpt to each other, taking special care with pronunciation, intonation, and pauses. Have students help each other to improve their oral reading and pronunciation. If possible, let students record their reading, then listen to themselves critically.

4. Assign the excerpt to be practiced and memorized, and then have students take turns reciting it to small groups of classmates.

5. Read the second excerpt from the Declaration of Independence aloud to students.

6. Have students work independently, in pairs, or in small groups to make predictions about what they think the colonists will do next. Ask them to write their predictions in their notebooks, then share them with the class.

HISTORICAL THINKING AND APPLICATION ACTIVITIES

1. Discuss these questions with students: *Why did the colonists think that England would never give them more freedom? Is it important for a government to have the consent (agreement) of the people that it governs? Why or why not?*

2. Ask students whether they think it is useful to memorize things in English, and what kinds of things should be memorized. Have them identify some of the things they have memorized in English (or in another language).

3. Have students from other countries work in small groups to discuss the types of things they have had to memorize in their first language. Each group should draw up a list of speeches, poems, anthems, and

documents that are frequently memorized by students in their native countries. Next to each title, students should write the reason why that particular text is considered important to "learn by heart."

4. Discuss typical July 4 celebrations and events. Ask international students if they have similar holidays in their own countries in which they celebrate independence, or if they have another day of national importance. Have them write brief descriptions of such holidays and share them with the class.

THE WAR FOR INDEPENDENCE, 1775–1783   PAGES 71–72

> **History Objective:** Study the major events and outcomes of the War for Independence.
>
> **Language Objectives:** Understand information presented in a chart and on a map; research and write a brief report.
>
> **Historical Thinking Objectives:** Use maps to build historical knowledge; explain causes; gather knowledge of time and place to construct a story or narrative (research).
>
> **Learning Strategy Objectives:** Identify the purpose of the learning strategy *using resources* and practice this strategy by finding additional information about the War for Independence using the library and the Internet.

PROCEDURES

Presentation

1. Remind students that when they scan for specific information, they should pay special attention to the words that signal the needed information. Ask them to name the learning strategy for looking for specific information (*selective attention*). In the chart on p. 71, the specific information is grouped in columns under the key words that signal important information (Event, Where, When, What Happened). Have students read through the information on the chart quickly.

2. <u>History Mystery</u> (p. 71). Have students work in pairs to read, discuss, and answer the History Mystery. You may need to describe what a *diary* is and remind students of who King George III was.

Practice and Self-Evaluation

1. **Map Skills: Battlefields of the Revolutionary War.** Have students look at the map on p. 72 to locate the eight cities where battles took place. Students should write the months and years of these events in their notebooks. Have students scan the reading on p. 69 to find the dates of the Battles of Lexington and Concord and write these last two dates in their notebooks. After writing in all eight dates, ask students to close their eyes and try to picture the map of the thirteen colonies and the location of the battles and events identified. Without looking at the map, ask them to answer questions such as, *Which battle was farther north, Saratoga or Trenton? Which two battles were closest together?*

2. <u>Gather More Information.</u> In groups of two or three, ask students to find out additional information about important events in the Revolutionary War. Have each group find additional information on one of the events listed in the chart on p. 71 and then share the information with the class.

3. **Tell what you learned.** Ask students to choose an event in the Revolutionary War that they find interesting and write about it in their notebooks.

4. **Writing a Report.** See "How to Teach Writing Lessons," p. xiii.

5. Have students write brief summaries of the information contained in the chart on p. 71 on a separate sheet of paper. Then have students work in pairs to discuss and revise these first drafts. They should ask each other (and the teacher) for additional words, spellings, and help in writing good sentences.

6. After students have evaluated and revised their short reports, have them write the final drafts in their notebooks, taking care with handwriting, spelling, and punctuation.

HISTORICAL THINKING AND APPLICATION ACTIVITIES

1. Have students discuss these questions: *Why do you think the British army at Trenton was surprised by Washington's army? Why do you think that the winter Washington's army spent at Valley Forge was important in American history? Why was it important that France entered the war?*

2. Have students generate questions they would like answered about the battles of the American Revolution. Write their questions on the board or on chart paper. Have them work in groups to find the answers to their questions in the information given

in the chart. If the information is not there, encourage students to find the information in appropriate reference books and CDs.

REVOLUTIONARY LEADERS   PAGES 73–77

A Great American Leader, pages 73–74

History Objective: Learn about the life of George Washington and his role in the founding of the United States.

Language Objectives: Read for comprehension; develop academic language; scan for specific information.

Historical Thinking Objectives: Create a time line of Washington's life; identify central questions of historical narratives.

Learning Strategy Objectives: Explicit: Practice previously introduced learning strategy *graphic organizers* to make a time line of George Washington's life. **Implicit:** Use headings to *predict* text; use context to *make inferences*; use *selective attention* to scan a text for specific information.

PROCEDURES

Presentation

1. See "How to Teach Reading Lessons," p. xi.
2. Before students open their books, ask them what they already know about George Washington. Write this information on the board. It will be confirmed or corrected after students have read p. 73.
3. Have students read aloud the headings, and then predict what information will be found in each section.
4. Have students read p. 73 silently, trying to guess at any new words from the context.
5. Have students work in small groups, and assign one or more heading to each group. Without looking at the book, ask students in the groups to develop brief oral summaries for the section(s) assigned to them. Have representatives of each group share these oral summaries with the class.
6. Go over the information written on the board, and have students confirm, correct, and add to the information about George Washington.

Practice

1. See "How to Teach Learning Strategies" on p. x. Ask students to identify the strategy used to construct a time line (*graphic organizers*) and have them explain why this strategy is useful.
2. **Understanding What You Read: Using a Time Line.** Go over the directions for completing the time line of Washington's life on p. 74.
3. Have students scan the reading selection on p. 73 to find the dates and information for at least seven events in Washington's life. Each date should be written at the appropriate place on the time line, and a complete sentence describing the event should be written next to it.
4. Have students work in pairs or small groups to compare their time lines.

HISTORICAL THINKING AND APPLICATION ACTIVITIES

1. Ask students the following questions: *Why do you think Americans call George Washington "the father" of our country? What heroes helped other countries get their independence?*
2. Have students consult a junior encyclopedia and their parents to find out about heroes in their own (or other) countries. Have each student prepare a time line depicting the major events in the life of a hero from their country. In class, have students who have written about the same hero work together to pool their information and make a joint time line, incorporating their individual information.

Developing Reports: Heroes of the War for Independence, pages 74–75

History Objective: Find information about five heroes of the War for Independence (John Paul Jones, Ethan Allen, Sybil Ludington, Patrick Henry, and Paul Revere).

Language Objectives: Read for comprehension; study a model report; research and write a report; make an oral presentation; listen to and take notes on classmates' presentations.

Historical Thinking Objective: Use research skills to gather information to construct a narrative (develop a report).

Learning Strategy Objective: Implicit: Practice the learning strategies *using resources* and *taking notes* to find information and develop a report.

PROCEDURES

Presentation

1. See "How to Teach Writing Lessons," p. xiii.
2. Have students read the model report on Sybil Ludington silently, then have them identify the following markers:

   - words that tell what the report is about
   - words that indicate a main idea
   - details that explain the main ideas
   - words that introduce the concluding paragraph

3. Discuss with students how to choose the hero for their report and help them locate reference materials such as junior encyclopedias or a multimedia encyclopedia, American history textbooks, and easy biographies.
4. As students read about the heroes they have selected, have them take notes on the important facts discovered.
5. Discuss the organization of the reports, and have students select from their notes the facts that will go in the introduction, body, and conclusion of their reports. After this initial planning, help students find additional facts and vocabulary needed for their reports.

Practice

1. Have students prepare first drafts on a separate sheet of paper, then work in pairs or groups to discuss and revise the drafts.
2. Go over the directions at the bottom of p. 75 and have students write their revised reports.

Self-Evaluation

1. As a home assignment, have students practice reading their reports at least five times. It is helpful to use a tape recorder and have students evaluate their presentations using the four questions on p. 75.
2. Divide the class into groups of four students who have each prepared reports on different heroes. Have students take turns reading their reports while the others in the group take notes on the information presented. Notes on the reports listened to should be written in their notebooks. After each presentation, group members can ask questions for clarification about the information presented.

HISTORICAL THINKING AND APPLICATION ACTIVITIES

1. Discuss the following questions with students: *What are some of the qualities of these five heroes of the War for Independence? How were they alike? How were they different?*
2. Have students work in small groups to discuss what qualities a hero should have. Ask them to make a list of the qualities each group believes to be essential. Then have students think of people of the present time who are/have been heroes, according to the list of qualities they have developed. Remind them that a hero does not have to be someone famous. Have each group share their list of heroes with the class, telling why they decided that each person has/had the qualities of a hero. You may want to keep the list to use in discussions of other figures that are discussed later in the study of U.S. history.

The U.S. Constitution, pages 76–77

> **History Objectives:** Learn about the parts of the U.S. Constitution; increase knowledge of historical concepts related to governance.
>
> **Language Objectives:** Develop academic vocabulary; read for comprehension; write answers to comprehension questions.
>
> **Historical Thinking Objective:** Analyze historical document for meaning.
>
> **Learning Strategy Objectives: Implicit:** Practice the learning strategy *predicting* by using headings to anticipate information in the reading; practice the strategy *summarizing* to make oral summaries of the reading; practice the strategy *selective attention* to scan the reading text for information to support personal preferences.

PROCEDURES

Preparation

1. **Before You Read: Vocabulary.** Go over the vocabulary words. Ask students to use *amend* and *amendment* in their own sentences to check for comprehension.
2. See "How to Teach Reading Lessons," p. xi.
3. Write the headings on pp. 76–77 on the board, and have students *predict* what type of information will be found under each heading.

Presentation and Practice

1. Have students read pp. 76–77 silently.
2. Have students work in small groups. Each student should give an oral summary in his/her own words of one section of the reading.

3. Ask students which amendment(s) are most important to them personally. Have them scan through the section on the Bill of Rights to decide, and then give reasons for their selection.

4. **Understanding What You Read: Comprehension Check** (p. 77). Have students complete this section, then work in pairs or small groups to check their answers.

HISTORICAL THINKING AND APPLICATION ACTIVITIES

1. Discuss the following with students: *Each state in the United States has its own constitution, but all states use the U.S. Constitution as the basis for their state constitutions. Why is this important?*

2. Provide students with copies of the text of the Constitution (from U.S. history textbooks, encyclopedias, large dictionaries, or a web site). Have students work in groups on three or four amendments to identify new words, look up their meanings, and write a paraphrase of the amendment in their own words.

THE U.S. GOVERNMENT | PAGES 78–79

The Three Branches of Government

History Objectives: Identify the powers of the three branches of the federal government and the checks each branch has on the others; identify the U.S. senators and representatives from your state.

Language Objectives: Read a chart with bulleted information for comprehension; develop academic oral language; write answers and complete sentences.

Historical Thinking Objectives: Gather knowledge through research; reconstruct meaning of historical documents.

Learning Strategy Objectives: Explicit: Practice the learning strategy *using resources* by finding additional information about the federal government. **Implicit:** Practice the learning strategy *using imagery* to make associations between the functions of each of the three branches of government and the physical building housing each of these functions.

PROCEDURES
Presentation

1. See "How to Teach Reading Lessons," p. xi.
2. Go over the introductory paragraph with students. Suggest that as they read about each of the three branches of government they make a mental image of the famous building in Washington where each branch works (Capitol, White House, Supreme Court). Have students skim p. 78.

Self-Evaluation

1. **Understanding What You Read: Comprehension Check.** Have students read each question, scan p. 78 for the answer, and write the answers in their notebooks.
2. After students have written answers for the Comprehension Check, have them work in small groups to compare and evaluate their answers.

Expansion

1. See "How to Teach Learning Strategies" on p. x. Remind students that when they look for information beyond their textbook, they are using the learning strategy *using resources.*
2. Find Out about Your Government. Provide reference books or Internet access, or take students to the library to do the research needed for the activity at the bottom of p. 79. After students have completed this exercise, have them discuss what they know about the president, and the senators and representatives from their own states.

HISTORICAL THINKING AND APPLICATION ACTIVITIES

1. Have students discuss the following questions: *Which branch of the government would you find most interesting to work in? What would you have to do to be prepared for this kind of job?*
2. Have students select a person who represents their district or state, find out information about that person from his or her website (www.house.gov or www.senate.gov), and prepare a short biography. The biographies should be shared with classmates and can also be used as a bulletin board display.
3. The information on the website of a member of Congress also usually provides an e-mail address so that students could write a letter. Students may wish to write a letter to their representative or senator to tell that Congressperson their opinion, ask a question, or ask for information about some topic of concern.

4. As an additional History Mystery, challenge students to find out the origin of their state's name. Ask, *Who decided the name? When was it named? Why? Does the state have a state flag? Flower? Bird?*

AMERICAN CITIES GROW   PAGES 80–81

> **History Objective:** Learn about the populations of New York, Philadelphia, Boston, and Charleston from 1730 to 1790.
>
> **Language Objectives:** Read graphs for information; develop academic language; write summaries.
>
> **Historical Thinking Objectives:** Use information from graphs to increase history knowledge; create graphs to explain events in time.
>
> **Learning Strategy Objectives: Explicit:** Practice the previously introduced learning strategy *graphic organizers* to understand line graphs and to create a line graph. **Implicit:** Practice the previously introduced learning strategy *summarizing*.

PROCEDURES

Preparation

1. See "How to Teach Learning Strategies," p. x. Have students read the description of the learning strategy, then ask them to identify its name (*graphic organizers*). In this lesson students will use a graphic organizer and also create one of their own.
2. See "How to Teach Map and Graph Skills," p. xiii.

Presentation and Practice

1. **Line Graphs.** Go over the information presented in the three line graphs on p. 80. Discuss with students the grouping of numbers for populations on the left columns (grouped by 5,000s) and the grouping of time periods across the bottom (grouped by twenty-year periods). Have students ask each other questions about the line graphs, such as, *What was the population of New York in 1770?*
2. Have students work individually to read and answer the four questions on p. 81 in their notebooks. Then have them check their answers with a partner.
3. At the bottom of p. 81, have students make a line graph for the population of Charleston, either individually or in pairs. Then have them check their work with a partner.
4. Have students look at the pictures on pp. 80–81 and choose one to write a descriptive summary of. The summaries should not name the city; students should be sure to describe the pictures as accurately as possible and also include information from the line graphs on pp. 80–81.

Self-Evaluation

Have students exchange papers, read the descriptions, try to visualize the picture without referring to the book, and identify which city it is. If necessary, students can ask the author of the summary questions for clarification.

HISTORICAL THINKING AND APPLICATION ACTIVITIES

1. Point out to students that the line graphs on p. 80 show that New York and Philadelphia were about the same size in 1730 and 1750, but then Philadelphia grew very rapidly and became larger than New York. Ask students: *From what you have studied about the War for Independence, what reasons could there be for the growth of Philadelphia?*
2. Have students look again at the pictures on pp. 80–81. Discuss the following questions: *What do you think it was like to live in that city? What do you think people might have done for a living? How are all the cities the same? How are they different?*
3. Have students make a list of three cities they have lived in or visited. Using a world atlas, have them look up population figures for these cities. Then have them write brief reports on the relative population sizes of these cities, indicating which is the largest, the smallest, larger than . . . , smaller than . . . , about the same, etc.

UNIT 4

The Nation Grows

> **History and Geography Objectives:** Identify prior knowledge about the westward expansion and growth of the United States in the first half of the nineteenth century; explain history in spatial terms by comparing maps from different time periods.
>
> **Language Objectives:** Develop academic oral language; write ideas in notebook.
>
> **Historical Thinking Objectives:** Interpret data on a time line and on maps to build historical knowledge; review names and locations; hypothesize about influences of the past.
>
> **Learning Strategy Objective: Implicit:** Identify prior knowledge (*tell what you know*) about the westward expansion of the United States.

PROCEDURES

1. See "How to Use the Unit Openers," p. ix. The illustration shows a covered wagon carrying settlers to the West. Ask students to compare the map on p. 83 with the map on p. 82. Ask, *What difficulties might travelers have in expanding the country to the west? Why is there settled territory on the west coast, but not in the middle of the country?*
2. With the book closed, ask students to recall the names of the thirteen English colonies and the bodies of water that touch the U.S. coastline. Have them locate the colonies and bodies of water on a class map. Review the spelling of the colonies and of the Atlantic and Pacific Oceans and the Gulf of Mexico.
3. Read and discuss with students the information at the top of p. 83.
4. Have students work in small groups to compare the maps on pp. 82 and 83. (Students may also refer to the map on pp. viii–ix.) Have them take turns asking each other questions about the differences in the two maps. Sample questions may include: *Maine and Vermont are not part of the original thirteen states. When did Maine and Vermont become separate states?*

(Maine: 1820, Vermont: 1791) What is the difference in the number of states? What happened to the territories? What are the names of the rivers and mountains people had to cross when they traveled west in the United States? How do people cross these rivers and mountains today? How did they cross them more than 150 years ago?
5. Have students identify the location of the state where they live on the map. Ask, *Did this state exist in 1783? Did it exist in 1853?* Repeat this for other states in which students may have lived.

HISTORICAL THINKING AND APPLICATION ACTIVITIES

1. Discuss student responses to the questions about moving to new lands. Have students think about travel in the nineteenth century. Would they travel to an unknown land? Have they done so? What dangers might they expect or did they encounter? What good things could the travel bring?
2. Use these questions to promote discussion: *If you were to travel from New York to St. Louis, Missouri, in the 1800s, how would you travel (e.g., by horse, by stagecoach, on foot)? These types of travel generally allowed one to travel no more than about fifteen miles per day. How long would it take you to get there? Today, how would you travel? How long would it take? Because travel was slower, what other things did early travelers need to think about before they left for such a long journey?*
3. Ask students to discuss the following: *Has your country (or a country named by the teacher) always been the same size that it is today? Has it been smaller or larger? What happened to change the size of the country? Was it good for the country, bad for the country, or both good and bad? Why?*
4. Have students interview their parents or other family members, or consult a reference book or CD to find out information about the growth or diminution of their country or another country. In some cases, changes may be quite recent; in others, changes in a country's size may have happened far back in history.

Students can share this information in class, either orally or in writing.

5. Discuss with students the following questions: *What possible reasons can you give for the growth of the United States after it became independent from England? Why do you think the United States grew mostly to the West? As people from the United States moved into the territories in the West and Southwest, what do you think happened to the people who were already living there?*

SETTLING THE WESTERN TERRITORIES — PAGES 84–86

Moving West, pages 84–85

> **History and Geography Objectives:** Develop historical vocabulary related to westward expansion; explain history in spatial terms by comparing maps from different time periods; increase knowledge about the movement of people westward; understand the concept of Manifest Destiny; learn about the response of pioneers to indigenous peoples.
>
> **Language Objectives:** Develop academic vocabulary; develop oral language; write sentences; read for comprehension; scan for specific information; follow written directions.
>
> **Historical Thinking Objectives:** Draw upon data from maps and photographs to build historical knowledge; identify the central questions of historical narrative; appreciate historical perspective.
>
> **Learning Strategy Objectives: Explicit:** Practice previously introduced learning strategy *using imagery* to make an association between a word and its image. **Implicit:** Practice *classifying* to understand and remember vocabulary words; practice the previously introduced learning strategy *predicting* to use headings to anticipate information in the text.

PROCEDURES

Preparation

1. See "How to Teach Vocabulary Lessons" and "How to Teach Learning Strategies" on p. x.

2. **Before You Read: Vocabulary.** Have students look at the illustrations of four of the vocabulary words and use them to identify the corresponding words. Remind them that they are *using imagery* when they use illustrations to assist understanding. Have them write the correct vocabulary words in their notebooks.

3. Have students work in small groups to go over the vocabulary words on p. 84. They should discuss what words they know or can guess the meaning of, what words are cognates with their first language (if any), and how to group the words into categories (*classifying*). The words are listed alphabetically, but can be rearranged to make them easier to learn. Possible groupings: things having to do with land or people; things having to do with trees.

4. After the discussion in small groups, ask students to work individually to write the definitions beside each word, using a dictionary or the Glossary, if necessary.

5. Have students work in pairs to check their work, compare answers, and discuss any discrepancies.

6. Have students work individually on the second exercise on p. 84. Give students sufficient time so that they can think of original sentences to contextualize each of the nine words and so that they can self-monitor as they attempt to write each sentence correctly.

7. Have students share their sentences in small groups or with the whole class.

Presentation

1. See "How to Teach Reading Lessons," p. xi.

2. Preview and discuss the headings for the reading selection. Ask students to speculate about the type of information they are likely to find under each heading (*predicting*).

3. Have students read the selection silently, writing any words or phrases that they cannot understand in their notebooks. (They should not write words which they can guess the meaning of through context clues.)

4. After reading, have students ask questions for clarification about the words or phrases each has written.

Practice

1. **Understanding What You Read: Using Maps for Comprehension.** Distribute copies of the maps on pp. 82–83 (see Teacher's Guide, p. 173). Have students use the reading text on p. 85 and the maps on pp. 82 and 83 to answer the questions.

2. Students may work in pairs or small groups to discuss and answer the questions.

3. Have students share their answers with the rest of the class. (If their answers are incorrect, direct them to look again at the reading text and at the maps on pp. 82 and 83.)

HISTORICAL THINKING AND APPLICATION ACTIVITIES

1. Ask students, *Which of the vocabulary words have similar words in your first language (or in another language that you know)? Do they mean exactly the same thing? Which words do you think are most difficult? Why? What special ways do you have for remembering difficult words?*

2. Students used the learning strategy *using imagery* with the photographs on p. 84 to help them make a visual association with new vocabulary words. Have students create their own images of other words (*guide, frontier, log, path, pioneer*). Then they can share the images with classmates and use those images to practice the new vocabulary.

3. Ask students, *Why do you think the pioneers wanted to go to new lands?* Explore with students the concept of Manifest Destiny, which is important to understanding the motivations for Americans to move to new territory and claim it. Manifest Destiny refers to the belief by people in the United States that they were destined to expand their territory from "sea to shining sea" (Atlantic to Pacific Oceans).

4. Discuss: *What qualities did pioneers have to have?* Have students make a list and discuss their lists. Combine ideas into a class list of characteristics. Have students evaluate their list after they have read about Daniel Boone. Ask, *Are there any pioneers today? Where?*

5. Provide students with reference materials such as a junior encyclopedia, U.S. history textbooks, and easy library books on pioneers. Students may also use the Internet to search for additional information about pioneers. Have students work in groups to find additional information about pioneers and the movement west. Each group should find at least five new facts. These can be shared with the whole class, either orally or in writing.

A Great Explorer, page 86

> **History Objective:** Gain knowledge about life on the frontier by learning about Daniel Boone.
>
> **Language Objectives:** Read for comprehension; check comprehension.
>
> **Historical Thinking Objectives:** Read historical narratives; compare stories of historical figures, events, and eras.
>
> **Learning Strategy Objectives: Explicit:** Decide on a good strategy to use for checking answers (*selective attention*). **Implicit:** Identify prior knowledge about Daniel Boone and life on the frontier (*use what you know*); use context to derive meanings of new words (*making inferences*).

PROCEDURES

Presentation

1. Before students open their books, find out what knowledge they already have about Daniel Boone. Write this information on the board or on a transparency.

2. **Understanding What You Read: Comprehension Check.** Have students read through the comprehension questions first. This will provide them with a preview of the information in the reading selection.

3. See "How to Teach Reading Lessons," p. xi.

4. Remind students that as they are reading they should try to guess at the meanings of any new words they encounter.

5. Have students read the biography of Daniel Boone on p. 86 silently, and then complete the Comprehension Check individually. Students should answer the statements they are sure of first, then go back to answer the more difficult items.

Self-Evaluation

1. See "How to Teach Learning Strategies" on p. x. Discuss with students why it is a good idea for them to check their own work. Ask them what learning strategy or strategies they could use to check their own work. Answers may vary, but could include the following: *selective attention, cooperation, using resources, use what you know, summarizing.* Ask students to choose the strategy or strategies they will use to check their work.

2. Let students work in pairs to check their answers by going back to the reading selection and finding the sentences that provide the information needed to determine whether each statement is *True* or *False*. (Statements marked *Not Given* will not have any sentences in the reading.)
3. Have students use the library and/or the Internet to find out whether the statements marked *Not Given* are true or false. Have them correct the false statements to make them true.

HISTORICAL THINKING AND APPLICATION ACTIVITIES

1. Ask students the following questions: *What were Daniel Boone's qualities? Explain and give reasons for your answer. Was Daniel Boone a pioneer according to your list* (from "Historical Thinking and Application Activities," Teacher's Guide, p. 44)? *If not, why not? If you think he was, but he does not fit your list, should you change your list?*
2. Discuss: *What things that Daniel Boone did were successful? What things that he did were not successful? What could be some reasons why Daniel Boone was not a good businessman? Have you ever known someone who is very good at doing some things and not at all good at doing other things?*
3. Provide reference materials such as a junior encyclopedia or CD encyclopedia, U.S. history textbooks, and library books about Daniel Boone. Have students work in small groups to find out additional information about Boone's life and to construct a time line showing the dates of important events during his life.

THE UNITED STATES ACQUIRES NEW TERRITORIES   PAGES 87–89

History Objective: Gain knowledge of history concepts by finding out about the three ways in which the United States acquired new territory.

Language Objectives: Read for comprehension; write answers to questions.

Historical Thinking Objective: Use maps to practice finding historical information.

Learning Strategy Objective: Implicit: Use a map to understand events (*using imagery*).

PROCEDURES

Presentation

1. See "How to Teach Map and Graph Skills," p. xiii.
2. Have students read the introductory paragraphs, checking to see that they understand the words *border, acquire, purchase,* and *treaty*.

Practice

1. **Map Skills: New Territories.** Have students work in pairs to answer the questions by referring to the map.
2. Call on individual students to read answers aloud. Have them make corrections as needed.

HISTORICAL THINKING AND APPLICATION ACTIVITIES

1. Ask students: *Why do you think the United States wanted to acquire more territory?* (Remind them of Manifest Destiny, if necessary.) *Can you think of any problems a country might have in acquiring new territory by purchase? By war? By treaty?*
2. Have students interview their parents or other family members (or research a country on the Internet) about territorial acquisitions and disputes in their native countries or in neighboring countries. Have them take notes on the information and then write a brief summary. The summaries can be shared with the class orally or in writing.

Land by Purchase and Treaty, pages 88–89

History Objective: Gain knowledge about how the United States expanded its territory south and west.

Language Objectives: Read for comprehension; recognize main ideas; develop academic oral language.

Historical Thinking Objectives: Use data on historical maps; identify central questions of historical narrative.

Geography Objective: Use maps and globes to report information from a spatial perspective.

Learning Strategy Objectives: Explicit: Select the learning strategy that will help distinguish main ideas from details (*selective attention*). **Implicit:** Use context clues to guess word meanings (*making inferences*); use a map to visualize different geographical areas (*using imagery*).

PROCEDURES

Presentation

1. See "How to Teach Reading Lessons," p. xi, and "How to Teach Speaking Activities," p. xii.
2. Preview and discuss the headings for the reading selection on p. 88.
3. Have students read the selection silently. Remind them to guess at the meanings of new words by using context clues.

Practice

1. **Understanding What You Read: Using Maps for Comprehension.** Have students read the directions for the exercise at the bottom of p. 88 individually. Encourage them to ask questions for clarification after they have read the directions and all eight statements. Remind them to try to visualize the different parts of the map to better understand the three areas that were acquired by purchase or treaty (*using imagery*).
2. Then have students use the maps on pp. viii–ix and on p. 87 to write the names of the correct territories in their notebooks.

Presentation

1. **Understanding What You Read: Identifying Main Ideas and Details.** Remind students that a main idea tells the most important fact in a paragraph or selection, and details provide supporting information or examples.
2. See "How to Teach Learning Strategies" on p. x. Have students read the directions, then say which learning strategy will be most useful in completing the exercise (*selective attention*). If students suggest other strategies, ask them to describe exactly how they propose to use them.

Self-Evaluation

1. Have students read the five sentences on p. 89 individually and write them in their notebooks. Ask them to mark one sentence with *M* for main idea and the other sentences with *D* for detail.
2. Have students work in small groups to discuss the five statements about the Oregon country and compare their choices for the sentence that best expresses the main idea of the reading selection on p. 88. Each student should be able to explain the reasons for his/her choice. Then have students complete the sentences at the bottom of p. 89 in their notebooks.

HISTORICAL THINKING AND APPLICATION ACTIVITIES

1. Have students each write a short paragraph about the means of transportation used by their family to come to the United States. Then ask each student to select a classmate to read and provide feedback on the paragraph. Final versions of the paragraphs can be shared with the whole class.
2. Students might also combine all of their information, seek images of various forms of transportation and build a class travel collage for the westward expansion. Use an Internet search engine with key words such as *covered wagon, Oregon Trail, early pioneers, stagecoach, horse and buggy,* or *gold rush.*

U.S. PRESIDENTS: THOMAS JEFFERSON	PAGES 90–91

Writer, Thinker, President

> **History Objective:** Gain knowledge about the life and contributions of Thomas Jefferson.
>
> **Language Objectives:** Read for comprehension; develop academic oral language; write interpretation of quotation; write summary.
>
> **Historical Thinking Objectives:** Compare different stories of historical figures, eras, and events; read historical narratives; identify central questions of historical narrative.
>
> **Learning Strategy Objectives: Explicit:** Practice the previously introduced learning strategies *predicting* by using headings to preview information, and *summarizing* to evaluate comprehension of text. **Implicit:** Practice using context clues to *make inferences.*

PROCEDURES

Preparation

1. See "How to Teach Learning Strategies," p. x. Ask students to identify the name of the learning strategy described (*predicting*). Have them explain why this learning strategy is useful for reading history or other content information (answers will vary but should be specific).
2. **Before You Read: Using Headings.** Preview and discuss the headings in the reading selection. Then

have students write in their notebooks the heading under which they expect to find the information in this exercise. Remind them not to answer the questions at this point.

Presentation

1. See "How to Teach Reading Lessons," p. xi.
2. Remind students that they should try to guess at meanings of new words by using context clues (*making inferences*). Have students read the selection about Thomas Jefferson silently. If they find words or phrases whose meaning they really cannot guess, they should write them in their notebooks.

Practice

1. Have students ask questions for clarification about the words or phrases they have identified. Encourage other students to provide the answers.
2. Have students work in small groups to answer the questions on p. 90. When each group has agreed on the correct answers, have them write an additional five questions. Groups should exchange questions and then answer them.

Self-Evaluation

1. **After You Read: Making a Summary.** See "How to Teach Learning Strategies," p. x. Remind students of why it is important to say or write summaries (they help you check on your comprehension of a text). Still working in groups, have students write brief summaries of Jefferson's life and contributions. Remind them to refer to the illustrations on pp. 90–91 for additional information. The summaries can then be shared with the whole class.
2. History Mystery. See "How to Teach the History Mysteries," p. xiv. To give students some clues about how to solve the "mystery," ask them about the term "fire bell." *How would it make you feel if you heard one? Why might it fill Jefferson with terror?* Students can think about what they know about where Jefferson lived and what he did for a living. Then they might think also about what he wrote about freedom, slavery, and rights. Students might also add seventy years to the date. The answer will not necessarily be "discovered" right away. Students should be encouraged to continue to ask questions and suggest answers.

HISTORICAL THINKING AND APPLICATION ACTIVITIES

1. Discuss with students the things that Thomas Jefferson accomplished. Ask: *Of his accomplishments,* *which is most important to your life? Why?* After discussing their individual answers, ask students to write them in a paragraph in their notebooks.
2. Provide students with reference materials such as a junior encyclopedia (text or CD), U.S. history textbooks, and easy library books about Thomas Jefferson. Have students work in groups to find out more information about Jefferson. The additional information should be added to the information in the reading, and each group should make a time line of Jefferson's life and accomplishments. The time lines can be shared with the whole class and displayed on the bulletin board.
3. Encourage students to create their own History Mysteries. These are the questions in history that make you go, "Hmm, I wonder . . ."

THE JOURNEY OF LEWIS AND CLARK

PAGES 92–93

History Objective: Examine the ways in which the Louisiana Purchase and the exploration of Lewis and Clark changed the territory of and knowledge about the United States.

Language Objectives: Develop academic oral language; listen for comprehension; write notes and summaries.

Historical Thinking Objectives: Read/listen to historical narratives; identify central questions of historical narrative; draw upon data from historical maps.

Learning Strategy Objectives: Explicit: Identify and practice the learning strategies *cooperation, selective attention,* and *taking notes.* **Implicit:** Practice the learning strategies *tell what you know, predicting,* and *summarizing.*

PROCEDURES

Preparation

1. Ask students what they already know about the Louisiana Territory and the journey of Lewis and Clark. Write the information contributed on the board. Ask them why it is useful to think about their knowledge of a topic before reading additional information on the topic.

2. Explain to students that when Jefferson bought the Louisiana Territory, the United States doubled in size—but that no one knew exactly what was in the territory that Jefferson had bought. Ask students to think about some of the things Jefferson might have wanted to know about this new part of the United States (*predict*).

3. Have students work in pairs or small groups to decide what things Jefferson might have wanted to know about the Louisiana Territory. Ask them to write their ideas in complete sentences in their notebooks.

4. **What do you think?** Still working in pairs or small groups, have students decide on the qualities and skills needed by an explorer in the wilderness. When each group has reached consensus, they should write their ideas in their notebooks. Ask: *How might this list compare with the list of qualities needed for pioneers?*

Presentation

1. **Map Skills: Describe a Route.** Go over the map on p. 93 with students as a preview to what they will hear about Lewis and Clark. Have them write a paragraph describing the route of Lewis and Clark, using the information given on the map.

2. **Listening and Taking Notes.** Tell students that they will be listening to an account of the journey of Lewis and Clark. They must *listen selectively* for information about the important moments of the journey, and record this information on the chart at the bottom of p. 93. *What Happened* is already given on the chart; they must listen for and fill in information about the *Place* and *Date* for each event.

3. Have students copy the chart on p. 93 in their notebooks.

4. Read the listening text below to the students.

Practice

Have students work in small groups to compare their notes. Then have each group write a short summary of the main points of the journey of Lewis and Clark.

Listening Text for "The Journey of Lewis and Clark"

In 1803 President Thomas Jefferson bought the Louisiana Territory from France. This purchase changed the United States and made it twice as big as it had been before. Today, you are going to hear about the exploration of this new territory. First, you will hear about two men who traveled west into this unknown land. Then you will hear about the journey and about its most exciting moments.

The two men that Jefferson sent to explore the Louisiana Purchase were Meriwether Lewis and his friend William Clark. Both men were experienced frontiersmen, and both liked the life of the wilderness. They took forty-five men with them on this expedition. Each man had a special skill that would be useful in the wilderness.

Now you're going to hear about the trip and its most important moments. Lewis and Clark began the trip in St. Louis in May of 1804. They started at the point where the Missouri River meets the Mississippi. They traveled by boat up the Missouri until late October. They met many different Native American tribes along the way. The winter came at this time, so they had to stop. They were at a Mandan village. Here Lewis and Clark's expedition built small wood houses like those of the Mandan and waited for the winter to end. They called this place Fort Mandan. This was the first important moment in their journey because they built Fort Mandan and passed a very cold (temperatures to −45°F) winter safely. In a Mandan village they met a French trader whose wife was a Shoshone (SHO SHO NEE) woman named Sacajawea (SAK uju WEE u). Sacajawea and her husband agreed to go with Lewis and Clark on their journey. Sacajawea was a good guide in the wilderness and she was also an interpreter when Lewis and Clark needed to talk to other Shoshone.

The expedition left Fort Mandan in early April, 1805. Now for the second important moment of the trip. In June, Lewis and Clark came to the Great Falls of the Missouri River. This was an enormous and beautiful waterfall. It was 80 feet high, so of course the boats could not go over it. They had to build wagons with wheels and go around the falls by land. Then Clark wrote in his notes, "We are about to enter the most difficult part of our voyage."

And this was true, because ahead were the Rocky Mountains. Crossing these mountains was the next important moment in this journey. The expedition was lucky because they met friendly Shoshone. In fact, the chief was Sacajawea's brother. She had not seen him in many years. Lewis and Clark were happy because the Shoshones showed them how to cross the Rocky Mountains. One of the explorers wrote that the Rockies were "the most terrible mountains I ever beheld; I have been as wet and cold in every part as I ever was in my life." But in August the expedition did cross the mountains, and then they traveled down the Columbia River.

Finally, at long last, Lewis and Clark reached the Pacific Ocean in November, 1805. This was surely the most exciting moment of all. Clark wrote, "Ocean in view! O! The joy!"

Of course, this was not the end of the trip. Lewis and Clark had to return and tell President Jefferson about their trip. Even though they now knew about the Rocky Mountains and the Great Falls, it took them almost a year to return to their starting point. They reached St. Louis in September, 1806. During their odyssey (long journey), Lewis and Clark kept journals that provided later explorers and settlers with very important information about the many Native American tribes they had met on the Plains, in the Plateaus of the Rocky Mountains, and in the Pacific Northwest. These tribes had provided the explorers with food, shelter, and directions. They also found out that there was no water passage across the United States—the Northwest Passage that early settlers had hoped for. With important news about the new lands that were now part of the United States, this was the last exciting moment of their trip.

HISTORICAL THINKING AND APPLICATION ACTIVITIES

1. Have students look back to p. 92. Ask if they were right about the things they said Jefferson wanted to know about the Louisiana Territory. Discuss.
2. Ask students if they were right about the skills an explorer needs to survive in the wilderness. Have them explain their answers. Then ask: *How were these skills the same as or different from those on the list you made about pioneers?*
3. There are a number of excellent websites, books and videos about the marvelous journey of Lewis and Clark (2004 was the two-hundredth anniversary of the start of their trip), such as www.pbs.org/lewisandclark/index.html. Additional information can also be found in the book *Lewis & Clark: Voyage of Discovery*, by Stephen E. Ambrose, published by National Geographic. These resources provide beautiful images and maps of Lewis and Clark's voyage that provide background about the extent of the country they explored and how the land looks today.

The Highland Regions

Geography Objective: Use maps to acquire, process, and report information about Highland Regions.

Language Objectives: Read for comprehension; answer questions; use reference materials to find additional information.

Historical Thinking Objectives: Use visual data from graphs to answer historical questions; construct a bar graph for mountain heights; research world regions.

Learning Strategy Objectives: Explicit: Practice the previously introduced learning strategy *using resources* to find additional information about world mountain ranges and heights of mountains. **Implicit:** Practice the learning strategies *tell what you know, making inferences,* and *using imagery.*

PROCEDURES

Preparation and Presentation

1. Elicit from students information they already know about mountains and Highland Regions (*tell what you know*). Ask them about these regions in their native countries and in other countries that they know. Write on the board names of mountains and mountain ranges students identify.
2. See "How to Teach Map and Graph Skills," p. xiii.
3. Have students read "The Highland Regions" silently. Remind them to guess the meanings of any new words they encounter (*making inferences*). Have them ask questions to clarify and verify the meanings they have guessed.
4. Have students examine the map on p. 94, identifying regions of the world with Highland Regions and the locations of Mt. Everest and Mt. Kilimanjaro. Remind them that when they study maps, they should try to take a mental picture of the map so that they can recall its features (*using imagery*).

Practice

1. **Understanding What You Read: Using Maps for Comprehension.** Have students read the three questions on p. 94 and follow the directions to find the answers.
2. See "How to Teach Learning Strategies" on p. x. Remind students that when they look for

information beyond their textbook, they are using the learning strategy *using resources*.

3. **Doing Research: Using an Atlas, Encyclopedia, or the Internet.** In order to complete the exercises on p. 95, students will need to consult an atlas (text or CD) or an encyclopedia. If they are not accustomed to using the school library, this is a good opportunity to start. Help them locate the reference section and encourage them to ask the librarian for needed information. Have students practice the language needed to ask for the reference materials they need before they go to the library.

4. Reference materials should be scanned for sections that contain specific information about mountain ranges. Have students recreate and complete the chart on p. 95.

Self-Evaluation

1. Ask students to use the information on the chart to create a bar graph similar to the bar graph at the bottom of p. 95.

2. Have them check their graphs by working in pairs to make sure that the information on the chart and on the graphs matches.

HISTORICAL THINKING AND APPLICATION ACTIVITIES

1. Ask students, *In the United States, are there areas of the country where it would be easier to travel by foot? By wagon? By boat? How could you answer this question by looking at a map?* Suggest to students that they might think about how flat or hilly the terrain would be for travel or where they might go if they traveled on rivers. A topographic map provides this information (see pp. viii–ix).

2. Have students think about the place where they live. Ask, *Would roads be easy or hard to build near their homes? Why do they think so?*

3. Discuss with students: *When you are climbing a mountain, why does it get colder as you climb higher? Why is it harder to breathe at the top of a mountain than at the bottom? When a road crosses a mountain range, why does it have so many curves?* Have them draw a picture to explain their answers.

4. Have students interview their parents or other family members for information about Highland Regions in their native country or have them choose another country to investigate. The information can include names of mountains, altitudes, resources, products, cities or towns nearby, and the way of life of people in the region. Have students write a short paragraph and share it with the class.

Madison and the War of 1812

> **History Objective:** Explore causes and results of the War of 1812 against Britain.
>
> **Language Objectives:** Listen for comprehension; develop academic oral language; write notes and summaries.
>
> **Historical Thinking Objective:** Explain causes in analyzing historical events.
>
> **Learning Strategy Objectives: Explicit:** Identify two learning strategies to use for comprehending an oral text (*selective attention* and *taking notes*). **Implicit:** Practice the learning strategies *cooperation* and *summarizing*.

LISTENING AND TAKING NOTES

PROCEDURES

Presentation

1. See "How to Teach Listening Comprehension Lessons," p. xi.

2. Remind students about the organization of the listening mini-lectures: statement of topic (introduction), main ideas with supporting details (body), brief summary (conclusion).

3. See "How to Teach Learning Strategies," p. x. Ask students to describe the two strategies they use for listening to important information (*selective attention* and *taking notes*).

4. Write this paragraph on the board and ask students to indicate which words can be erased without losing the meaning, and which words can be abbreviated:

Another reason why the War of 1812 happened is that Americans who lived in the Northwest Territory wanted more land. These people lived where Michigan, Illinois, and Indiana are now. Some of these people wanted to settle in Canada, but Canada was British. So they wanted to fight the British so that they could settle in Canada.

As students indicate which words are less important, erase them. Write abbreviations to replace any words that can be abbreviated (the two-letter state abbreviations are listed on p. 109). Ask students to reconstruct the passage from the words remaining.

Practice

1. Have students copy the T-list on p. 96 in their notebooks.
2. Read the following text on the War of 1812 and have students write the missing information in the blanks in the T-list in their notebooks.
3. Have students work in small groups to compare and complete their notes.
4. Have students individually write short summaries of the important points about the War of 1812 in their own words, using their completed T-lists as a guide.

Listening Text for "Madison and the War of 1812"

The topic for today is the War of 1812, which was fought between Great Britain and the new nation, the United States. As you know, the United States won its independence from the British in 1783. In 1812 the two countries went to war again. Today, I'll tell you first about some of the causes of the war. Second, you'll hear about an important battle in the war. Finally, I'll tell you how this war changed the history of the United States.

Why did a second fight start between Britain and the United States just twenty-nine years after the War for Independence? There were many reasons. One reason was that the British navy often stopped American ships that were going to Europe. The British did not want the Americans to trade with France. You see, the French and the British were also at war, and the British did not want the Americans to help their enemy. Also, when the British navy stopped American ships, they sometimes captured American sailors and made them work on British ships. The Americans certainly did not like this.

Another reason why the War of 1812 happened is that Americans who lived in the Northwest Territory wanted more land. These people lived where Michigan, Illinois, and Indiana are now. Some of these people wanted to settle in Canada, but Canada was British. So they wanted to fight the British so that they could settle in Canada.

A third reason for the war was that the Native Americans in the Northwest Territory were fighting to hold on to their land. The American settlers were trying to drive them out. The settlers thought that the British were encouraging the Native peoples to attack and kill them. The settlers wanted this to stop.

Those are three of the reasons for the War of 1812. Now let's hear about an important battle. A lot of the war was fought at sea, but the battle you'll hear about was fought on land. The British marched to Washington, D.C., the new capital of the United States. They burned many buildings, and even burned the White House, where the president lived. Then they marched to Baltimore and attacked Fort McHenry. An American who watched this battle wrote a poem about it. His name was Francis Scott Key, and later his poem was set to music and became the national anthem of the United States— "The Star Spangled Banner."

Finally, after three years of fighting, the United States and Great Britain decided to end the war by a treaty in 1814. This war, however, changed the history of the United States in two important ways. First, after the war, the United States could trade freely with other countries. This helped the new nation grow. Secondly, the United States had defended itself and its independence from the British, and this made Americans very proud of their country. They forgot about settling in Canada, which was still British. In fact, Americans felt very satisfied with their country and they wanted it to continue to grow. After this war, many people decided to move west and help settle new lands for the new nation.

In conclusion, you have heard three important reasons why the War of 1812 happened. You also know that the national anthem of the United States was written during an important battle of this war. And finally, you have learned how Americans won the freedom to trade with other nations and to live and grow within their own nation.

HISTORICAL THINKING AND APPLICATION ACTIVITIES

1. Discuss with students: *Do you think the United States was right to go to war with Britain again in 1812? Why or why not?* Write reasons on the board, then have students write their own reasons in their notebooks.
2. Provide students with copies of the words and music of "The Star Spangled Banner," and let them listen to a recording or tape of the national anthem. Have them work in small groups to read and figure out the meaning of the words. Finally, ask students to bring in copies of the words (and, if possible, the music) of the national anthem of their native countries or of another country. Ask students to compare anthems from the point of view of the ideas that are expressed in the songs, taking note of similarities and differences. Students may also want to compare dates of composition of the differing national anthems and historical events that inspired them.

The Monroe Doctrine

> **History Objective:** Examine the origins and provisions of the Monroe Doctrine.
>
> **Language Objectives:** Develop academic vocabulary; read for comprehension and identify main ideas and details.
>
> **Historical Thinking Objectives:** Increase knowledge and use of academic vocabulary related to foreign policy; reconstruct the meaning of a historic passage.
>
> **Learning Strategy Objectives: Implicit:** Practice the learning strategies *tell what you know* to identify prior knowledge, and *making inferences* to guess at word meanings from context.

PROCEDURES

Preparation

1. See "How to Teach Vocabulary Lessons," p. x.

2. **Before You Read: Vocabulary.** Have students work in pairs to discuss the meanings of the vocabulary words and check on their understanding by looking them up in the Glossary. Then have students work together to write sentences that contextualize each new vocabulary word. These can be shared with the rest of the class.

3. Discuss with students what they already know about relations between the United States and Latin American countries.

Presentation and Self-Evaluation

1. Have students read the selection on the Monroe Doctrine. Remind them to guess at meanings of words they do not know.

2. **Understanding What You Read: Identifying the Main Idea.** Have students decide which of the four statements at the bottom of p. 97 represents the main idea of the reading selection. Ask students to explain their reasons for choosing an answer.

HISTORICAL THINKING AND APPLICATION ACTIVITIES

1. Discuss the following ideas with students: *When things happen that may not be good for the country, presidents may take an action to prevent similar things from happening in the future. Just before President*

Monroe declared his doctrine, the United States had fought with Great Britain in the War of 1812. Do you think there is any connection between these two things? Why do you think so? If you think there is a connection, what might that connection be? Ask students to write their answers and discuss them with a classmate. Then have them share their ideas with the class.

2. Remind students that the Monroe Doctrine said that European countries should stay out of the Americas. Have them research instances in which the United States opposed efforts of European countries to influence events in the Americas. Then discuss whether they agree or not with each use of the Monroe Doctrine.

3. Provide students with reference materials such as a junior encyclopedia, Latin American history textbooks, and easy library books on independence in Central and South American countries. They may also use the Internet. Have students work in groups to find out how different countries in Latin America became independent from Spain or Portugal. Ask each group to prepare a brief report, which can be shared with the class either orally or in writing.

Settling the West

> **History Objective:** Explore the lure of the West and the reality of life on the frontier for varying groups of people.
>
> **Language Objectives:** Develop academic vocabulary; read for comprehension; write and support opinions.
>
> **Historical Thinking Objectives:** Expand content vocabulary; consider multiple perspectives; interrogate historical data.
>
> **Learning Strategy Objectives:** Practice the previously introduced learning strategy *cooperation* to develop vocabulary; identify the learning strategy used to guess meanings from context (*making inferences*).

PROCEDURES

Preparation and Presentation

1. **Before You Read: Vocabulary.** Go over the vocabulary words with students to be certain that they understand their meanings.

2. See "How to Teach Reading Lessons," p. xi.

3. Have students read the selection on p. 98 silently. Remind them to use context clues to guess the meanings of new words.

Self-Evaluation

1. **Understanding What You Read: Comprehension Check.** Have students write answers to the Comprehension Check on p. 99 individually in their notebooks. Then ask them to work in pairs or small groups to compare answers and to check answers by referring to the reading selection on p. 98.

2. **What do you think?** Have students work in pairs or small groups to discuss the questions. Have them work cooperatively to write the reasons for their answers in their notebooks. Pairs or groups can then share their short paragraphs with the rest of the class.

HISTORICAL THINKING AND APPLICATION ACTIVITIES

1. Ask students to pretend that they were living in 1850 and had the chance to go west with a group of people. Ask if they think they would have gone. Have students write a letter to a friend explaining why or why not.
2. The Native Americans were already living on the land in the West. Ask, *What did the Native Americans do when they met Lewis and Clark? Daniel Boone?* Have students share their ideas with the class.
3. Have students explore books in the library or a website such as the Library of Congress's American Memory collection of photographs (http://lcweb2.loc.gov/amhome.html), using such key words as *settlers, westward movement,* and *gold rush* to gain more information about the lives of people who traveled west. Ask them how they would describe life for these people (dress? housing? work?, etc.). Ask, *Would you want to go west? Why? Why not?*

REGIONS OF THE WORLD   PAGES 100–101

The Mediterranean Regions

Geography Objectives: Identify locations of certain physical features on the earth, such as the equator and latitude; compare/contrast the climate in a Mediterranean Region with that in a different region; use maps to organize and report information spatially.

Language Objectives: Read for comprehension; follow written directions; write summaries.

Historical Thinking Objective: Compare and contrast sets of ideas, values, etc.

Learning Strategy Objective: Implicit: Practice the strategy *graphic organizers* and identify this strategy.

PROCEDURES

Presentation

1. Find out if students have ever visited or lived in a Mediterranean Region. If so, elicit descriptions of climate, vegetation, and way of life.
2. Have students read the selection on the Mediterranean Regions silently. Remind them to guess the meanings of new words.

Practice and Self-Evaluation

1. See "How to Teach Map and Graph Skills," p. xiii. Discuss the map on p. 100, and have students identify cities and countries in the Mediterranean Regions around the world.

2. **Understanding What You Read: Using Maps for Comprehension.** Have students work in small groups to read and follow the directions for the exercise on p. 100.

3. **Map Skills: Latitude Lines.** Have students read the paragraphs on latitude lines silently, then discuss the vocabulary and concepts with the class. If possible, have volunteers locate the following features on a globe and on a classroom map: the equator, the North and South Poles, the northern and southern hemispheres, the Tropic of Cancer, and the Tropic of Capricorn.

4. Provide practice in reading latitude lines by having students identify the approximate latitude line where they live now, and where they used to live.

5. Have students answer the four questions about latitude lines independently, then check their answers with a friend.

6. Comparing and Contrasting. Students will need to use an almanac to complete this exercise. Review the Los Angeles climate chart with students and be sure they understand what they are to do. Let students work in small groups to find and record the needed information. Have each group construct a Venn diagram to illustrate the information they have found. Ask students to identify the learning strategy they have just used (*graphic organizers*). Each group should then

develop a written summary of the comparison/contrast between Los Angeles and a local big city (probably in a different geographic region). The summaries should be shared with the class and discussed.

HISTORICAL THINKING AND APPLICATION ACTIVITIES

1. Discuss these questions: *Why do you think that the cost of living in most Mediterranean Regions is higher than in other geographical regions? Can you think of advantages of life in a Mediterranean Region? Disadvantages?*

2. Provide students with reference materials such as junior encyclopedias, geography textbooks, atlases, or the Internet to find out more about life in Mediterranean Regions. Divide students into pairs or small groups. Have each group decide on a particular Mediterranean Region and find out information about the region through the resources provided. When groups have prepared their reports, have them share them with the class.

3. Have students use the weather website www.noaa.gov to select a place each thinks he/she would like to live based on its weather. Have them look on a map/globe to find the latitude of that location. Then each student can work with a classmate to guess each other's places based on the temperature and latitude.

| U.S. PRESIDENTS: ANDREW JACKSON | PAGES 102–103 |

A Strong Leader

History Objectives: Learn about the life of Andrew Jackson; evaluate the value of the "spoils system;" examine presidential policies toward Native Americans.

Language Objectives: Read for comprehension; develop academic vocabulary; develop academic oral language.

Historical Thinking Objectives: Read and comprehend historical narratives; identify central questions; develop opinions based on data.

Learning Strategy Objectives: Explicit: Identify two learning strategies (*making inferences* and *cooperation*) to assist in developing new vocabulary. **Implicit:** Use headings to preview and predict anticipated information (*predicting*).

PROCEDURES

Presentation

1. See "How to Teach Reading Lessons," p. xi.
2. Preview and discuss the headings for the reading selection. Ask students to speculate about the type of information they are likely to find under each heading.
3. Have students read the selection silently, listing any words or phrases that they cannot understand even by using context clues.
4. Have students work in small groups and share the words and phrases each has listed. If other members of the group know the meaning of these words, they may share this information. If no one in the group knows the meaning, they should consult a dictionary or the Glossary and decide on the most logical meaning of the words.

Practice and Self-Evaluation

1. See "How to Teach Learning Strategies" on p. x. Go over the directions to the exercise with students, then discuss with them which learning strategies can help them decide on word meanings (*making inferences* and *cooperation*).

2. **Understanding What You Read: Using Context.** Have students work in pairs on the first exercise on p. 103. Ask them to read and follow the directions, finding the six words in the reading text and copying in their notebooks the sentence in which each word occurs. Then have each pair of students work together to decide on the probable meaning of each word, write its definition in their notebooks, and then check the definition in the Glossary.

3. **What do you think?** Have students work in small groups to discuss the question at the bottom of p. 103. Ask each group to find two reasons why the spoils system was fair, and two reasons why it was unfair. When each group has decided on its reasons, have them write their reasons in their notebooks. Have them share their reasons in a class discussion.

HISTORICAL THINKING AND APPLICATION ACTIVITIES

1. Discuss the following questions with students: *What were Andrew Jackson's leadership qualities, in your opinion? What were his weak points? Why do you think that people remember a strong leader such as Jackson?*
2. Ask students: *Do you believe that the spoils system still exists? Where? Why? What evidence do you have to support your belief?*
3. Have students interview their parents or other family members to find out about strong leaders their family members remember. Ask what they think made these persons strong. Have students choose one such leader and write a short paragraph about him or her. These paragraphs can be shared with the class and displayed on a bulletin board.

NATIVE AMERICANS IN THE UNITED STATES   PAGES 104–105

Native Americans Lose Their Homelands

> **History Objective:** Learn about the effect of U.S. Native American policy on Native Americans and how they responded.
>
> **Language Objectives:** Develop academic vocabulary; read for comprehension; develop academic oral language.
>
> **Historical Thinking Objectives:** Increase content specific vocabulary; gather needed knowledge of time and place to construct a story or narrative.
>
> **Learning Strategy Objectives: Explicit:** Practice the previously introduced learning strategy *cooperation*. **Implicit:** Use headings to *predict* anticipated information; check own comprehension by *summarizing* the reading text.

PROCEDURES

Preparation

1. See "How to Teach Learning Strategies" on p. x. Discuss with students how they use the strategy *cooperation* in different classes and in their lives outside of school.
2. See "How to Teach Vocabulary Lessons," p. x.

3. **Before You Read: Vocabulary.** Have students go over the vocabulary words to find out which ones they already know and which ones they can guess the meanings of. Then have them copy the list of words in their notebooks and write the letter of each definition on the line after each vocabulary word, using the Glossary, if necessary. Have students work in pairs to check their answers.

Presentation and Practice

1. See "How to Teach Reading Lessons," p. xi.
2. Preview and discuss the headings of the reading selection. Have students look at the illustration and speculate on its meaning.
3. Provide an opportunity for students to ask questions about words and expressions they have not understood in the reading selection.
4. Have students work in small groups to develop oral summaries of the information on pp. 104–105. These group summaries can then be shared with the class.

HISTORICAL THINKING AND APPLICATION ACTIVITIES

1. Discuss the following questions with students: *How did Native American and European ideas about how to use the land differ? Why do you think that the settlers did not want to share land with Native Americans? What do you think would have happened to Native Americans if Europeans had not come to America? Why do you think that the Supreme Court's decision about the Cherokee was important?*
2. Have students examine and compare two maps of Native American tribes in the 1700s and 1800s. Ask students: *What is different about the locations of Native Americans in the two centuries? What happened to explain the differences?*
3. Have students look carefully at the painting of the Trail of Tears on p. 105. Ask them to describe what they see in the painting (expressions on faces, weather, who is in the picture, etc.). Explain that this painting was painted in 1942, long after the event it describes. Ask students: *What do you think the painter of this picture wanted to say about the removal of the Cherokee? What makes you think this?*
4. Provide students with reference materials such as U.S. history textbooks, a junior encyclopedia, and library books about the history of different Native American tribes in the United States. Have students work in groups to select one Native American tribe, and make a time line of what is known of that tribe's history. The time lines can then be shown and explained to the rest of the class.

Important Native Americans

> **History Objective:** Examine the lives of the four important Native Americans [Sequoyah (si KWOI u), Osceola (os i OH la), Black Hawk, Tecumseh (ti KUM su)] and their response to U.S. Native American policy.
>
> **Language Objectives:** Read for comprehension; research and write a biographical report; make an oral presentation; develop listening comprehension; take notes.
>
> **Historical Thinking Objectives:** Gather historical knowledge to construct an explanation of time, place, or events; develop a report; compare different stories of historical figures and eras; draw upon data from maps.
>
> **Learning Strategy Objectives:** Practice using three learning strategies to develop research reports: *using resources* to find information, *plan* with an outline or graphic organizer, and *evaluate* a draft to revise it.

PROCEDURES

Presentation

1. See "How to Teach Writing Lessons," p. xiii.
2. Discuss the four Native Americans pictured on p. 106 and have students speculate about them, using the portraits to make inferences about personal characteristics. Have students choose one of the four to write a report on. Ensure that approximately the same number of students work on each person.
3. See "How to Teach Learning Strategies" on p. x. Discuss with students the three learning strategies listed on p. 106 (*using resources, planning, evaluating*). Ask them to describe how they have used these strategies in the past and how these and other strategies have helped them with a complex task such as developing a report.
4. **Researching and Writing.** Go over the questions listed under step 1 on p. 106. Ask students to develop additional questions they would like to have answered about the Native Americans they have selected. Write these questions on the board.

Practice

1. Provide students with reference materials such as U.S. history textbooks, a junior encyclopedia, and easy library books about Native Americans. Students can also use this opportunity to investigate the school library and learn to use the online catalogue and resources to look for specific topics. Ask students to go through the reference materials to find answers to their lists of questions, taking notes on the information discovered.
2. Remind students that reports should be divided into an introduction, a body, and a conclusion. Review words and phrases that can be used to introduce a topic, indicate main ideas, cite details and examples, connect ideas, indicate contrasts, show cause and effect, and introduce the conclusion. Assist students in developing an outline or other graphic organizer that they can use to organize their report (*planning*).
3. Have students first organize the information in their notes, then write a draft report on a separate sheet of paper. Have them exchange their drafts with a classmate and review each others' reports, marking parts that are hard to understand.
4. Have students work in pairs to go over the marked reports, and ask questions about and explain the parts that were hard to understand.

Self-Evaluation

1. Have students rewrite their reports in their notebooks taking into account the suggestions developed through talking with a classmate (*evaluating*). After students have written this draft, remind them to go over it once more to check for spelling, punctuation, and grammar.
2. **Presenting an Oral Report.** As a home assignment, have students practice reading their reports at least five times. It is helpful to use a tape recorder and have students evaluate their own presentations using the four questions given at the top of p. 107.
3. **Listening and Taking Notes.** Divide the class into groups of four students who have each prepared reports on different Native Americans. Have students take turns reading their reports while the others in the group take notes on the information in their notebooks. After each presentation, another person in the group should give a brief oral summary of the information.

Practice

1. **Map Skills: Homelands.** Distribute copies of the map on p. 107 (see Teacher's Guide, p. 174).
2. Have students study the map and choose four different colors for the map key. Have them check the information in their reports and notes to find out the areas where each tribe lived. Have them try to

visualize the extent of each Native American homeland and the states it covered, then color the homelands in accordance with the map key.

HISTORICAL THINKING AND APPLICATION ACTIVITIES

1. Ask students, *How were Sequoyah, Osceola, Black Hawk, and Tecumseh similar? How were they different?* Ask them to be sure to think about how each man responded to the changes brought by the Europeans. Have students tell what they admire about each and why.

2. Have students work in pairs or small groups to investigate important indigenous peoples in Central and South America. Provide resource materials in class, or have students use the library and the Internet. Hispanic students may want to find out information about important indigenous tribes from their native countries. The information collected should be organized into brief reports that can be shared with the class.

3. Have students use images to build a story about a group of people in history. Explore George Catlin images at the following websites: www.americanart.si.edu/catlin/ and http://dorgan.senate.gov/lewis_and_clark. Students can download images that they put together in a collage to tell a story about what they think is important for others to know about these Native American people. They should give each image a title that helps tell the story.

NEW TERRITORIES   PAGES 108–109

At War with Mexico

History Objectives: Learn about the causes and results of the United States war with Mexico; acquire information about U.S. territorial acquisitions between 1803 and 1853.

Language Objectives: Read for comprehension and scan for specific information; develop academic oral language; write information on a chart, including state abbreviations.

Historical Thinking Objectives: Read historical narratives; create time lines of historical narrative; use maps to acquire historical information; use graphic information to build historical comprehension.

Learning Strategy Objectives: Explicit: Practice the previously introduced learning strategy *use what you know* to make associations between prior knowledge and new information; identify the learning strategy *selective attention* to use for scanning a text for specific information; identify and explain the learning strategy *cooperation*. **Implicit:** Use the learning strategy *using imagery* to understand information presented in a map.

PROCEDURES

Preparation

1. See "How to Teach Reading Lessons," p. xi.
2. See "How to Teach Learning Strategies," p. x. Ask students to explain how thinking about what you already know about a topic can help you add new information on that topic.

3. **Before You Read: Identifying What You Know.** Discuss with students what they already know about Mexico, and ask them why they think the United States had a war with Mexico. Write their ideas on the board, and remind them to check the accuracy of their current knowledge against the information they will read on p. 108.

Presentation and Practice

1. Have students read the selection on p. 108, then follow the directions for **Understanding What You Read: Scanning for Specific Information**. Remind students that when they scan a reading selection for specific information, such as dates, they are paying attention selectively to only one type of information (*selective attention*).

2. Have students work in pairs to check the accuracy of their answers on the reading comprehension exercise.

3. Discuss the information in the reading selection and the students' ideas written on the board. Have students resolve any discrepancies noted, and add additional information to what is on the board.

4. **Understanding What You Read: The New Territories.** See "How to Teach Learning Strategies" on p. x. Ask students to explain why *cooperation* is a useful learning strategy, and ask them to give examples of how they use this strategy in other classes and in their lives outside of school.

5. Have students work in pairs to complete the chart on p. 109. Have them refer to the reading selections listed at the top of the page. Remind them to use maps for information and to try to visualize, or make a mental picture of, the important features of a map so that they can recall it (*using imagery*).
6. Have students work cooperatively to complete the chart on p. 109. Ask them to use the state abbreviations listed in the chart at the bottom of the page.
7. Have students work together to check the facts recorded on the chart.

HISTORICAL THINKING AND APPLICATION ACTIVITIES

1. Ask students, *Can you think of any examples in modern times of two countries fighting a war over territory? Do you know the reasons why these wars have been or are being fought?*
2. Provide students with reference materials such as an encyclopedia, U.S. history textbooks, Internet resources, and library books dealing with the early history of Texas and the Mexican-American War. Have students work in groups to look through these resources and select a topic for a brief report. Topics can be biographies of historical figures of the time (Santa Anna, Stephen Austin, Sam Houston, Davy Crockett, etc.), battles (Alamo, San Jacinto, etc.), or the way of life of settlers in the Mexican territory in the early 1800s. Ask each group to write three to four paragraphs about the information discovered and share their reports with the rest of the class.
3. Discuss with students: *When one country acquires territory by war, what happens to people who are living in the territory that changes from one country to another? What happens when the languages, religions, or cultures of the two countries that have a war over territory are different?*
4. Have students interview parents or other family members to find out if their native countries have ever acquired new territory through purchase, treaty, war, or any other way, or whether all or part of their native countries have ever been acquired by another nation. Have them write brief reports on this information and share them with the class, either orally or in writing.
5. Ask students to speculate about the following scenario: *Suppose that the town in which you live wants the park land next to your home to add lanes to a highway or build an airport or sports arena. This means that you will have no place to play. How would the town get the land? What would you do? How would that change your life? How would this issue relate to what you have been studying about the expansion of the United States?*

PRESIDENTS OF THE UNITED STATES	PAGES 110–111

Ten Presidents: 1801–1850

> **History Objective:** Add to knowledge about major events occurring during ten presidencies, from 1800–1850.
>
> **Language Objectives:** Read for comprehension; recognize sequence and cause-effect; develop academic oral language; write summaries.
>
> **Historical Thinking Objectives:** Use information presented in a time line to answer historical questions and to construct chronological sequence of historical events.
>
> **Learning Strategy Objectives: Explicit:** Identify and practice two previously introduced strategies: *graphic organizers* and *selective attention*. **Implicit:** Practice the previously introduced strategy *tell what you know* to share information about presidents.

PROCEDURES

Preparation

1. See "How to Teach Learning Strategies" on p. x. Have students identify the strategy (*tell what you know*) and then write the names of the first two presidents of the United States in their notebooks (George Washington, John Adams).
2. Remind students that time lines are graphic organizers that describe a sequence of past events. They can be arranged vertically, as on p. 110, or horizontally, as in the unit openers. This time line covers a fifty-year period during which there were ten different presidents of the United States. Show students how the events are grouped next to each presidency, and remind them that grouping events and facts makes them easier to remember.

Presentation

1. Ask students to keep an image of the time line in mind as they skim through the information on p. 110 to get a general idea of the main facts. Have students

ask questions for clarification of any words they do not understand.

2. See "How to Teach Learning Strategies" on p. x. Have students identify the strategies they will use to answer the questions about the time line (answers will vary, but could include *graphic organizers* and *selective attention*).

Self-Evaluation and Expansion

1. **Understanding Time Lines.** Have students work individually to answer the questions on p. 111. After reading each question, they should quickly scan the time line to find the answer and write it in their notebooks.

2. **What do you think?** Have students work in pairs or small groups to work cooperatively on the exercise at the bottom of p. 111. After copying the chart into their notebooks, have them identify the inventions and record them with their dates in the left-hand column. Then each pair or group should discuss why each invention was probably important in American history. Encourage students to seek help from each other and from the teacher on the function of any inventions they may not be familiar with (such as the McCormick reaper), and to relate the functions of these inventions to their own background experience.

3. After the pair or group discussion, have students write brief summaries of their conclusions about the importance of each invention in the right-hand column of the chart.

HISTORICAL THINKING AND APPLICATION ACTIVITIES

1. Have students discuss and write their answers to the following questions: *What were some good things that happened between 1800 and 1850? Why were they good? What were some bad things that happened in this period? Why were they bad?*

2. Provide students with reference books, history books, and an encyclopedia (online or text) containing information about the history of their native countries or an assigned country. Have students with the same country work cooperatively to develop a time line of events in their (native) country between 1800 and 1850, using the time line on p. 111 as a model. These time lines should be shared with the class and can be displayed on the bulletin board.

3. Have students analyze the time line by dividing it into categories such as presidents, decades, leaders, wars, etc. Creating a graphic organizer built around the categories will provide students with another connection to the historical data presented in the time line.

4. As a unit review, guide students in conducting a Web Quest through the Library of Congress's site American Memory (for example, they can conduct further research on Native Americans, forty-niners, Chinese immigrants, inventions). The Library of Congress photograph collections are at: http://lcweb2.loc.gov/amhome.html.

The Civil War and Reconstruction

UNIT OPENER   **PAGES 112–113**

History Objective: Identify prior knowledge students have about the Civil War and Reconstruction periods in U.S. history.

Geography Objectives: Use maps to collect and compile geographic information; review names of states in the eastern half of the United States and identify which were Union states, Confederate states, and border states.

Language Objectives: Develop academic oral language; write ideas in notebook.

History Thinking Objectives: Interpret data presented in time lines; use historical maps.

Learning Strategy Objective: Implicit: Identify prior knowledge (*tell what you know*) about civil wars.

PROCEDURES

1. See "How to Use the Unit Openers," p. ix. The photograph shows young Confederate recruits ready to go off to war.
2. Have students work in pairs to look at the map of the United States during the Civil War. They may use the map to answer the third question on p. 112.
3. Have students identify the states that are included in the Union and Confederate areas on the map and list them in their notebooks. Ask students what names they would assign to the parts of the country that are called Union states and those that are called Confederate states. Have them share their ideas and record them on the board.
4. Students can use the time line to give them more clues about the topics that will be addressed in this unit. Ask students to develop questions they would like to have answered in this unit. Write their questions on the board. If any can be answered by other students, encourage them to do so, and write the answers (which will be confirmed or corrected as students work through the unit).

HISTORICAL THINKING AND APPLICATION ACTIVITIES

1. Using the time line, ask students to find any events that they think go together. Have them name the topic or issue.
2. Have students interview their parents or other family members to find out about civil wars in their countries or in neighboring countries. Have them find answers to these questions: *What was the war about? What happened? How was the damage repaired?*

GROWING APART   **PAGES 114–115**

The South and the North

History Objective: Examine differences in the ideas and way of living of people in the North and South.

Language Objectives: Develop academic vocabulary; read for comprehension; discuss differences; write summary notes; complete a cloze exercise.

Historical Thinking Objectives: Interpret graphs to provide data to examine differences between the North and South prior to 1860; compare and contrast sets of ideas; identify causes of a problem.

Learning Strategy Objective: Identify and practice the previously introduced learning strategy *graphic organizers* to understand the information in pie graphs.

PROCEDURES

Preparation

1. See "How to Teach Vocabulary Lessons," p. x.

2. **Before You Read: Vocabulary.** Have students work in pairs to discuss the meanings of vocabulary words,

determine which (if any) have cognates in their native languages, and then check on the accuracy of their understanding by looking up the new words in the Glossary or a monolingual dictionary.

3. Still in pairs, have students work together to develop sentences that contextualize each new vocabulary word and write the sentences in their notebooks. Remind students that a good sentence provides clues to the meaning of the vocabulary word—challenge them to develop sentences that provide enough context to explain the meaning of the word. Have students share their sentences with the rest of the class.

Presentation

1. See "How to Teach Reading Lessons," p. xi.
2. Have students look at the headings in the reading selection and speculate about the type of information that will be contained in each section.
3. Have students read the selection individually, reminding them to use context clues to guess at the meanings of new words, and to ask for clarification only if they cannot make a reasonable guess and if the unknown word is really essential for comprehension.

Presentation and Practice

1. **Understanding What You Read: Thinking about Differences.** Have students work in small groups to discuss the differences between Americans in the northern states and those in the southern states. Each group should create a graphic organizer that shows five important differences. Then students should share their graphic organizers with the class.

2. **Understanding Pie Graphs.** See "How to Teach Learning Strategies" on p. x. Ask students to name as many different types of graphic organizers as they can and to give an example of how they might use each. Draw a circle on the board and divide it to represent the percentage of boys and girls in the class. Explain that a pie graph is used to show parts of a whole, and that it is called a pie graph because it is round like a pie and the divisions remind us of slices cut from a pie. Have students suggest and draw additional pie graphs that illustrate information of interest to them (e.g., students wearing a certain color; students wearing certain kinds of shoes). Tell them that when they see pie graphs in a history, math, or science book, they should try to make a mental image of the divisions of the pie to help them remember the percentages depicted.

3. Discuss the pie graphs for 1800 and 1820, encouraging students to ask questions for clarification. Then have students work individually or in pairs to complete the pie graph for 1860.

4. Have students work individually to copy and complete the paragraph in the exercise at the bottom of p. 115, using the information from the three pie graphs.

HISTORICAL THINKING AND APPLICATION ACTIVITIES

1. The lesson focused on the differences between the North and the South. Ask, *Are there any ways in which the two areas of the United States were similar? What are they? How do you think these similarities might have affected the way the two areas made decisions after the war? Have you ever been good friends with someone, then later grown apart? What were the reasons for the change?*

2. As a class, have students brainstorm information related to the class, to the school or community, or to their parents or native countries that could be represented in a pie graph. Have students work in small groups to select one of the areas they brainstormed. Then each group will do the research necessary to find the information to develop its pie graph. Each group can then show its pie graph to the class and explain the importance of the information pictured and the process by which it was developed.

SLAVERY IN THE UNITED STATES	PAGES 116–122

Slaves and Slavery, pages 116–117

History Objective: Learn about the expansion of slavery in the United States and the differences in the attitudes of nineteenth-century Americans toward slavery.

Language Objectives: Develop academic language; discuss and create a K-W-L-H chart; read for comprehension; write vocabulary definitions.

Historical Thinking Objectives: Consider multiple perspectives; identify central questions; read historical narratives.

Learning Strategy Objective: Practice the previously introduced learning strategies *use what you know* and *making inferences* to read for comprehension.

PROCEDURES

Preparation and Presentation

1. **Before You Read: Focusing on What You Already Know.** See "How to Teach Learning Strategies" on p. x. Ask students to identify the learning strategy they will be using in the "K" column of the K-W-L-H chart (*use what you know*).

2. Discuss briefly with students the concept of slavery. Then have students sit in small groups to discuss what they already know about slavery in the United States. Each group should decide on the five most important things they already know about slavery, and write them in their notebooks (in the "K" column of the K-W-L-H chart). Then ask students to discuss and fill in the questions they want to answer (in the "W" column).

3. See "How to Teach Reading Lessons," p. xi .

4. Have students read the selection on pp. 116–117 silently. Remind them to use context clues to guess the meanings of new words.

5. See "How to Teach History Mysteries" on p. xiv. Hints to assist student thinking:

   - Encourage students to think about what the cotton gin did.
   - What group or groups of people would this invention affect and why?
   - What is the relationship of those affected to the causes of the Civil War?

Practice and Self-Evaluation

1. **Understanding What You Read: Using Context.** See "How to Teach Learning Strategies" on p. x. Ask students to identify the learning strategy they will use to guess meanings from context (*making inferences*).

2. Have students look at the vocabulary words on p. 117 and make a list of the words in their notebooks. Then ask students to find those words in the reading selection. Students should work in pairs to look for the other words in the sentence that can provide context, and make a decision about the probable meaning of the word. Have students develop sentences that illustrate the five words given on p. 117, and then write them next to the words in their notebooks.

3. **Understanding What You Read: Focusing on What You Have Learned.** Have students refer to the facts they wrote at the beginning of this lesson in the "K" column in their notebooks. Have them identify the main points of the information previously known, and ask them to contribute the most important ideas they have discovered in the reading selection.

4. Have students work in small groups to discuss the original list of facts and new facts about slavery that have emerged from the reading selection and from class discussion. Each group should decide on the five most important new facts learned through the reading, and students should write these facts as complete sentences after the K-W-L-H chart.

HISTORICAL THINKING AND APPLICATION ACTIVITIES

1. Look at the images on p. 116. Ask, *What additional information do they give you about slavery? How might you find other images?* Two Internet sites can expand student information about slaves and slavery. They are part of the New Deal's Works Progress Administration Federal Writers' Project. They are an excellent source of first-hand accounts of life under slavery: http://xroads.virginia.edu/~HYPER/wpa/wpahome.html and http://memory.loc.gov/ammem/snhtml/snhome.html.

2. Read to students from the slave narratives, and have them work in groups to create plays about life during slavery. They should be aware that there are several sides to the argument and should be encouraged to include in their plays all different perspectives (e.g., slaves, owners, children, men and women).

Free States and Slave States, page 118

> **History Objective:** Examine the role of the Missouri Compromise and its effect on the differences between the North and South.
>
> **Geography Objective:** Interpret information gained from maps to identify free and slave states.
>
> **Language Objectives:** Read for comprehension; write a summary.
>
> **Historical Thinking Objective:** Draw upon data from historical maps.
>
> **Learning Strategy Objectives: Implicit:** Practice the previously introduced learning strategies *making inferences* to guess word meanings from context and *summarizing* to create brief written summaries.

PROCEDURES

Presentation and Practice

1. See "How to Teach Reading Lessons," p. xi.

2. Have students preview the selection by reading the headings and examining the map on p. 118.

3. Have students scan the reading selection to discover which states were free states, which were slave states, and what the Missouri Compromise was. Then have students read the selection thoroughly for details. Remind students to use context clues to help them understand any new words they encounter.

4. Have students work in small groups to discuss the reading and develop brief written summaries. These summaries can then be shared with the rest of the class.

5. **Understanding What You Read: Using Maps for Comprehension.** Give students copies of the map on p. 118 (see Teacher's Guide, p. 175). Have students study the map and select two colors. Ask them to color the map to indicate which states and territories were free states and which were slave states.

HISTORICAL THINKING AND APPLICATION ACTIVITIES

1. Use these questions to promote discussion: *How many people in the United States were slaves in 1790? What percentage of the total population of the United States was enslaved in 1790?* (Look at the first two sentences on p. 118.) *Is making a compromise the best way to solve a problem? Why or why not? Give examples.*

2. Provide students with reference materials such as U.S. history textbooks, an encyclopedia, or the Internet. Have them work in groups to find out how many slaves there were in the United States just before the Civil War, and how the slaves were distributed by state. Then ask each group to prepare a bar graph to display this information.

Harriet Tubman and the Underground Railroad, page 119

> **History Objective:** Learn about the role of Harriet Tubman as a leader in the anti-slavery movement.
>
> **Language Objectives:** Read for comprehension; identify main ideas; write summaries.
>
> **Historical Thinking Objectives:** Compare different stories of historical figures; read historical narratives; gather knowledge to construct a story.
>
> **Learning Strategy Objective:** Practice the previously introduced learning strategy *summarizing* to demonstrate comprehension of main ideas.

PROCEDURES

Presentation

1. See "How to Teach Reading Lessons," p. xi.
2. Tell students that they should read this selection with special attention to the main ideas, which they will then summarize in a concluding paragraph. Remind them to use context to guess the meanings of new words as they read. Encourage them to ask questions for clarification, if necessary.

Self-Evaluation

1. **Understanding What You Read: Writing a Summary.** See "How to Teach Learning Strategies" on p. x. Ask students to describe how they decide what to include in a summary. How do they know which are the most important ideas?

2. Have students write first drafts of their summaries on a separate sheet of paper, then work in small groups to compare and discuss their summaries. After making revisions and corrections, ask students to write the final version of their summaries in their notebooks.

HISTORICAL THINKING AND APPLICATION ACTIVITIES

1. Harriet Tubman worked against slavery in two important ways—she helped other slaves escape and she gave talks to large groups of people against slavery. Ask, *Which of these two ways of working against slavery do you think was most important? Why?*

2. Harriet Tubman was also known as a leader for the rights of women. Ask students, *What did she do that would make people think about her in that way?*

3. Have students interview parents or other family members to find out about individuals in their native countries who have helped oppressed people. Ask them to find out what these people did and what the results were. Have them share this information with the class, either orally or in writing.

4. Students may be interested in exploring the Internet to find further information about the Underground Railroad. Suggest they use key words such as *Underground Railroad* and *Harriet Tubman*.

> **History Objective:** Read about a controversial historical figure (John Brown) and investigate the pros and cons of his actions.
>
> **Language Objectives:** Read for comprehension; make judgments and support opinions; develop academic oral language; draft, share, revise, and edit reports.
>
> **Historical Thinking Objectives:** Consider multiple perspectives; formulate a position and defend that position.
>
> **Learning Strategy Objectives:** Practice the previously introduced learning strategies *selective attention* to find new words, and *making inferences* to guess word meanings from context; practice the previously introduced learning strategy *using resources* to learn more about a topic.

PROCEDURES

Presentation

1. See "How to Teach Learning Strategies" on p. x. Ask students to read the directions and then identify which two learning strategies will help them comprehend the reading (*selective attention* to find new words and *making inferences* to guess word meanings from context).
2. See "How to Teach Reading Lessons," p. xi, and "How to Teach Writing Lessons," p. xiii.
3. **Before You Read: Reading Analytically.** Have students skim the reading selection on p. 120 to get the main ideas, and then go through it a second time to underline the new words.
4. Have students work in small groups to discuss the words each has copied into their notebooks, share definitions, and make guesses from context clues. Any words still unfamiliar to students should be looked up in the Glossary.
5. Have students read the selection again, making sure that they understand it completely.

Practice

1. **Understanding What You Read: Discussing and Supporting Opinions.** Explain to students that they are going to participate in a formal discussion activity that resembles a debate. Explain that in a debate two persons or two teams take opposite sides

in an argument and follow special rules to present their ideas. A good debater can argue equally well *for* or *against* a particular idea.
2. Discuss the rules for the discussion activity with students. You may want to hang these rules up in the classroom, so students can refer to them.

- Listen carefully to your classmate.
- When your classmate has finished talking, you must summarize his or her main ideas; that is, say in a few words what your classmate just said.
- The mediator will decide if your summary is complete and correct. If it is not, then you must try again.
- If the mediator says the summary is correct, then it is your turn to say your ideas about John Brown.
- Your classmate must listen to you carefully and then summarize your main ideas.
- The mediator will decide if your classmate's summary is complete and correct.

3. Be sure that students understand the role of the mediator. Divide students into groups of three, and let them discuss the pros and cons of John Brown's actions for about ten minutes.

Practice

1. **Writing a Report: Using Resources.** After the discussion, have students summarize it individually. See "How to Teach Learning Strategies" on p. x. Ask students to identify the learning strategy they will use to find additional information about John Brown in reference books and on the Internet (*using resources*).
2. After the discussion, have students write a short report on a separate sheet of paper. The report will have four short paragraphs. In the first paragraph, students briefly tell who John Brown was, what he did, and why. In the second paragraph, they write why some people think John Brown was a hero. Ask them to write some of the things they and their classmates said in favor of John Brown. In the third paragraph, students write why some people think John Brown was a criminal. Have them write some of the things they and their classmates said against him. The last paragraph is a concluding paragraph. Have students summarize the main ideas in the report.

Self-Evaluation

Have students sit in the same groups of three and compare the reports they have written. They should work cooperatively to revise and edit their reports, and then copy the final draft in their notebooks.

HISTORICAL THINKING AND APPLICATION ACTIVITIES

1. Heroes are people we admire for doing great things. Villains do things we do not like. Have students discuss the following questions: *When you think of what John Brown did, would you call him a hero or a villain? Why? John Brown acted in a violent way to make his cause known. Is there something else he could have done? Is there any other time in the U.S. history you have studied so far in which violence was used to influence people? When? How did it work? What was the result?*

2. Using some of the examples provided in the second part of the activity above, have students choose a person to interview. In the interview they should present a case (hypothetical or real) where violence is used to achieve a worthwhile objective. Then they should ask for the opinion of the person being interviewed. Notes on the interviews can be shared with the class, either orally or in writing.

The Nation Falls Apart, pages 121–122

> **History Objective:** Learn how and why the southern states seceded and the importance of the election of Abraham Lincoln in 1860.
>
> **Language Objectives:** Read for comprehension; develop academic vocabulary; write answers to map questions.
>
> **Historical Thinking Objectives:** Explain causes in analyzing historical actions; practice finding information on a map; use map skills to provide more information about the Civil War.
>
> **Learning Strategy Objective: Implicit:** Practice the previously introduced learning strategy *making inferences* to guess word meanings from context.

PROCEDURES

Presentation

1. See "How to Teach Reading Lessons," p. xi, and "How to Teach Map and Graph Skills" on p. xiii.
2. Have students read the selection individually, using context to guess the meanings of new words. As students are reading, have them list new words on a separate sheet of paper and afterwards note their probable meanings (*making inferences*).

Practice and Self-Evaluation

1. After students have read the selection and noted the new words and their meanings, have them sit in small groups to discuss their word lists and revise the meanings they have noted. If necessary, ask them to check the Glossary to confirm that they understand the new words.
2. Still in small groups, have each group develop a one-paragraph summary of the reading selection.
3. **Understanding What You Read: Using Maps for Comprehension.** Have students study the map of the United States after secession on p. 122. Tell students to try to keep a visual image of this map in mind as they work on the questions on p. 122.
4. After students have completed p. 122 individually, have them work in small groups to compare and revise their answers.

HISTORICAL THINKING AND APPLICATION ACTIVITIES

1. Have students work in groups of four. Have each student in a group pick one of the four candidates for the 1860 presidential election. They should then find information on what that person thought about the question of slavery. Each person presents to the group of four. Those four then discuss why they think Douglas, Breckenridge, and Bell did not win the election.
2. Ask students to discuss the following: *Do you think the people in one part of a country have the right to secede (break away) from the other part? Why or why not?*
3. If possible, have students interview native English-speaking students regarding their opinions about whether one part of a country should be able to secede from the main country. Ask students to develop interview questions in groups and practice the interview by role-playing it in class. After students have interviewed English speakers, have them report the results to the class, and then discuss any differing points of view they may have discovered.

A Nation Divided

> **History Objective:** Learn about the conduct of the Civil War by reading and using maps and charts.
>
> **Language Objectives:** Read for comprehension; develop academic oral language.
>
> **History Thinking Objectives:** Use visual data in graphs; draw upon data in historical maps.
>
> **Learning Strategy Objective: Implicit:** Use the previously introduced learning strategies *tell what you know* and *making inferences* to comprehend the reading selection; use the learning strategy *using imagery* to understand map locations of battles.

PROCEDURES

Presentation and Practice

1. See "How to Teach Reading Lessons," p. xi.
2. Ask students what information they already know about the American Civil War (*tell what you know*). Write their contributions on the board, and explain that their ideas will be either confirmed or corrected after reading p. 123.
3. Remind students to use the learning strategy *making inferences* by using context clues to guess meanings of new words. Have students read the selection individually. Then have students work in groups to share the most important information gleaned from the reading. Assign each section in the reading to a different group of students, and have them develop a short oral paragraph that summarizes the section assigned. Ask each group to nominate one spokesperson to share their summary paragraph with the rest of the class.
4. **Map Skills: Finding Information.** Have students examine the map on pp. 112–113. Remind them to make a mental image (*using imagery*) of the map so that they can use it to understand where different Civil War battles were fought.
5. Have students read and follow the directions for p. 124. Draw their attention to the chart of important battles in Virginia. Students should read and answer the questions on p. 124 individually.
6. After students have completed the exercise on p. 124, have them check their answers with a classmate or in a small group. Ask students individually about their progress in following directions in English correctly.

HISTORICAL THINKING AND APPLICATION ACTIVITIES

1. Have students discuss the following: *Do you think that Lincoln was right to say that South Carolina had attacked the United States? Why or why not? Why do you think that more people in the North died during the Civil War than people in the South?*
2. Have students go to the website called "Valley of the Shadow: Two Communities in the American Civil War" (http://valley.vcdh.virginia.edu). It is a huge database including maps, images, letters, diaries, newspapers, and public records. The documents all relate to two communities—Staunton, Virginia, and Chambersburg, Pennsylvania—before, during, and after the Civil War. Since the database is searchable, ask students to select a topic and find two letters: one from a southern soldier, and one from a northern soldier. Students can compare the soldiers' views of battle. They can also look for images of interest (e.g., Gettysburg or the other battles discussed in the text). Then have them report back to the class with their findings, or create a dialogue using the letters between soldiers and those they left at home.
3. Have students consult reference books and also interview parents and community representatives about battles in civil wars in their native countries. They should write brief summaries and then share them with the class.

U.S. PRESIDENTS: ABRAHAM LINCOLN   PAGES 125–126

A Man for the Common People

> **History Objectives:** Learn about the life of Abraham Lincoln and his importance to history; analyze the purpose, meaning, and importance of Lincoln's words in the Gettysburg Address and in his second inaugural address.
>
> **Language Objectives:** Develop academic listening comprehension; write a summary; develop academic vocabulary; read for comprehension; develop oral language.

Historical Thinking Objectives: Obtain historical data through listening; gather needed knowledge of time and place to construct a story; ask questions about historical data; use original historical data to expand understanding of Lincoln and his time.

Learning Strategy Objectives: Explicit: Practice using the three previously introduced learning strategies: *taking notes, cooperation,* and *summarizing* to understand and remember information about Abraham Lincoln. **Implicit:** Practice the previously introduced learning strategies *selective attention* to comprehend major ideas in historical quotations and *making inferences* to understand new vocabulary.

LISTENING AND TAKING NOTES

PROCEDURES

Presentation

1. See "How to Teach Learning Strategies" on p. x. After reading the directions, ask students to identify the three learning strategies they will use for the listening activity (*taking notes, cooperation,* and *summarizing*). Ask them to explain how they have used these strategies in previous listening activities and how the strategies help them remember important information.
2. See "How to Teach Listening Comprehension Lessons," p. xi.
3. Remind students about the organization of the listening mini-lectures: statement of topic (introduction); main ideas with supporting details (body); brief summary (conclusion).

Practice

1. Write this paragraph on the board and ask students to indicate which words can be erased without losing the meaning, and which words can be abbreviated.

Many people listened to Lincoln's ideas. Many people in the North liked what he said. But white people in the southern states did not like Lincoln. They thought that Lincoln would abolish slavery and that their plantations would be ruined without slaves to work on them.

As students indicate which words are less important, erase them. Write abbreviations to replace any words that can be abbreviated. Ask students to reconstruct the passage from the words remaining.

2. Read the following text on Abraham Lincoln and have students fill in the missing information in the blanks on the T-list in their notebooks.
3. Have students sit in small groups to compare and complete their notes.

Self-Evaluation

Have students individually write short summaries of the important points about Lincoln in their own words, using their completed T-lists as a guide.

Listening Text for "A Man for the Common People"

Today, you are going to hear about Abraham Lincoln. Abraham Lincoln was the sixteenth president of the United States. He was president during the Civil War, from 1861 to 1865.

First, you are going to hear about Lincoln's childhood and his life before he became president.

Abraham Lincoln was born in 1809 in a log cabin in Kentucky. He did not have much education because his family was poor, but he loved to read. He taught himself about the law and became a lawyer.

Lincoln was very tall and thin. He was a humble man, which means that he was not proud. He liked to tell stories and jokes.

Lincoln was very interested in politics. He wanted to serve his country. First, he was elected to political office in Illinois. Then he was elected to the United States Congress. People who liked Lincoln began to call him "Honest Abe" because he told the truth and he did what he thought was right for his country.

Lincoln made speeches that convinced people it was important for the country to be united. He believed that the country could not continue to have some slave states and some free states. He said, "A house divided against itself cannot stand. I believe this government cannot . . . endure half slave and half free." Abraham Lincoln spoke out against slavery.

Now you are going to hear about Lincoln's election as the sixteenth president of the United States.

Many people listened to Lincoln's ideas. Many people in the North liked what he said. But white people in the southern states did not like Lincoln. They thought that Lincoln would abolish slavery and that their plantations would be ruined without slaves to work on them.

In 1860, Abraham Lincoln was elected as the sixteenth president of the United States. The southern states decided that they did not want to be part of the United States under Lincoln. They decided to secede, or leave the Union. The southern states set up their own government and called it the Confederate States of America.

Now you are going to hear about Lincoln and the Civil War. You are also going to hear about a very important public statement Lincoln made, called the Emancipation Proclamation.

Lincoln loved the United States. He believed that all the states had to be part of the same country. He believed that it was worth a fight in order to keep the country together. So the war between the United States and the Confederate States of America, a civil war, began in 1861. Lincoln felt great sadness during the war because so many men died, but he still believed the war was necessary in order to save the Union.

In 1863, halfway through the Civil War, Lincoln made a very important official statement called the Emancipation Proclamation. The Emancipation Proclamation said that all slaves in the southern states were free. As Lincoln signed the Emancipation Proclamation he said, "If my name ever goes into history it will be for this act, and my whole soul is in it."

Finally, you are going to hear about the end of the Civil War and the end of Lincoln's life.

Lincoln was elected to a second term as president in 1864. In 1865, the Civil War was over. The South surrendered to the Union army, and the United States was one country again. But the great president who had fought to unite the country did not live to see peace. Five days after the war was over, President Lincoln was shot to death at Ford's Theater in Washington, DC, by an actor who was opposed to Lincoln's ideas.

In conclusion, you have heard about the life of Abraham Lincoln and learned why he was an important president. You know that Abraham Lincoln believed that all the states must continue to be part of the same country. He believed that the United States had to fight the Civil War in order to bring the southern states back into the Union. You know that during the Civil War, Lincoln signed the Emancipation Proclamation, an important statement that said that slaves were now free. Finally, you have learned that President Lincoln was shot to death five days after the war was over.

Preparation

1. Discuss the vocabulary words and definitions with students before they begin reading.
2. Explain to students that they are going to read, discuss, and interpret historical quotations from

Lincoln's speeches and stories. The language will be difficult for them to understand, but they should *selectively attend to* the most important ideas.

Presentation

1. **Understanding What You Read: Interpreting Historical Quotations.** Have students read the selections and questions silently. Remind them to use context clues to guess word meanings.
2. Have students work in pairs or small groups to discuss the selections and the questions, and cooperatively decide on the information to include in the answers.

Practice

1. Have students write answers to the questions individually.
2. Have students work in pairs or groups again to compare and discuss their answers.

HISTORICAL THINKING AND APPLICATION ACTIVITIES

1. Discuss with the class: *What do you think was the most important thing that Lincoln did? Why?*
2. Provide students with library books or American history textbooks, or direct them to a junior encyclopedia (book or CD). Have them work in groups to find out more information about Abraham Lincoln. Each group should find at least five additional facts about Lincoln and write them in a paragraph. Then have groups share their paragraphs with the class. Ask the class if their additional facts changed their ideas about the most important thing that Lincoln did. If yes, ask how the ideas changed. If not, ask why not.
3. Provide the class with copies of the Gettysburg Address or put it on an overhead in front of the class (see www.loc.gov/exhibits/gadd/gadrft.html). Read it to them, and then discuss it with the class. Let them know that this speech continues to be very important. Ask, *Do you think the speech is convincing? What made it convincing? Who do you think was most convinced by Lincoln's speech at Gettysburg? Why?*

The Gettysburg Address is a famous speech delivered by President Lincoln on November 19, 1863 at Gettysburg, PA. He presented it at the dedication of the Gettysburg National Cemetery, honoring those who died in the Battle of Gettysburg earlier that year.

The writing of the Gettysburg Address has become an American myth. The most popular version states that Lincoln wrote the address on the back of a used envelope. In fact, Lincoln wrote two drafts of the brief speech and made some changes to the text as he spoke. He subsequently wrote copies of the address that he presented.

"Fourscore and seven years ago our fathers brought forth on this continent, a new nation, conceived in Liberty, and dedicated to the proposition that all men are created equal.

"Now we are engaged in a great civil war, testing whether that nation or any nation so conceived and so dedicated, can long endure. We are met on a great battle-field of that war. We have come to dedicate a portion of that field as a final resting place for those who here gave their lives that that nation might live. It is altogether fitting and proper that we should do this.

"But, in a larger sense, we cannot dedicate—we cannot consecrate—we cannot hallow—this ground. The brave men, living and dead, who struggled here, have consecrated it, far above our poor power to add or detract. The world will little note, nor long remember what we say here, but it can never forget what they did here. It is for us the living, rather, to be dedicated here to the unfinished work which they who fought here have thus far so nobly advanced. It is rather for us to be here dedicated to the great task remaining before us—that from these honored dead we take increased devotion to that cause for which they gave the last full measure of devotion—that we here highly resolve that these dead shall not have died in vain—that this nation, under God, shall have a new birth of freedom—and that government of the people, by the people, for the people, shall not perish from the earth."

4. Ask students to think about who they think is a convincing speaker. Have students interview parents or other family members to find out about famous speakers (either present or past; in their native countries or in the United States) that they know of and why they are convincing. If possible, have them bring to class some examples of quotations from these famous speakers and explain their ideas and use of language to the rest of the class. The class can create a collage of the quotes.

DEVELOPING REPORTS   PAGES 127–129

Four Important Americans

History Objectives: Find out information about four important Americans of the Civil War period; use the words of historical figures to provide meaning to the Civil War period.

Language Objectives: Research and read for comprehension; write, share, and revise a research report; present an oral report; listen and take notes on oral presentations; read for comprehension; draw inferences; develop academic oral language; write interpretations.

Historical Thinking Objectives: Obtain historical data and knowledge through research to construct a historical narrative; compare stories of historical figures and events; formulate historical questions; practice interpreting historical quotations; interrogate historical data.

Learning Strategy Objectives: Explicit: Identify the learning strategies used to develop a research report (*using resources, cooperation, selective attention, taking notes*). **Implicit:** Practice the previously introduced learning strategy *use what you know* to match historical figures with words they said (or words that were said about them).

PROCEDURES

Presentation and Practice

1. See "How to Teach Writing Lessons," p. xiii.
2. Discuss the four persons pictured on p. 127 and have students speculate about them, using the pictures to make inferences about personal characteristics. Then have each student select one person to write a report on. An approximately equal number of students should write on each person.

3. **Researching and Writing.** Go over the questions listed under step 1 on p. 127. Ask students to develop additional questions they would like to have answered about the person they have selected. Write these questions on the board.
4. Provide students with reference materials such as U.S. history textbooks, a junior encyclopedia (text or CD), and easy biographies of Frederick Douglass, Harriet Beecher Stowe, Robert E. Lee, and Clara Barton. Students can also use this opportunity to extend their familiarity with the school library resources.
5. Have students go through the reference materials to find answers to their lists of questions, taking notes on the information discovered.
6. Remind students that reports should be divided into an introduction, a body, and a conclusion. Review words and phrases that can be used to

introduce a topic, to indicate main ideas, to cite details and examples, to connect ideas, to indicate contrasts, to show cause and effect, and to introduce the conclusion.

7. Have students first organize the information in their notes, checking to see if they know what language is needed to express their ideas and what connectors are needed to link these ideas. They can ask questions for clarification if they need language assistance to express their ideas. First drafts should be written on a separate sheet of paper, and then exchanged with a classmate who is working on the same topic. Students should review each others' reports, marking parts that are hard to understand.

8. Have students work in pairs to go over the marked reports, asking questions about and explaining parts that were hard to understand.

9. Have students rewrite their reports, taking into account the suggestions developed through the discussion with a classmate. After students have written this draft, remind them to go over it once more to check for spelling, punctuation, and grammar.

10. See "How to Teach Learning Strategies" on p. x. Ask students to identify and explain the usefulness of the learning strategies they have used up to now in researching and writing their research reports. (Possible answers: *using resources, taking notes, cooperation, selective attention,* and other learning strategies.)

Practice

1. **Presenting an Oral Report.** As a home assignment, have students practice reading their reports aloud at least five times. It is helpful to use a tape recorder and have students evaluate their own presentations using the three questions on p. 128.

2. **Listening and Taking Notes.** Divide the class into groups of three students who have each prepared reports on different topics. Have students create graphic organizers for the information they will listen to. Then have students take turns reading their reports while the others in the group take notes in their notebooks on the information presented. After each presentation, another person in the group should give a brief oral summary of the information.

Self-Evaluation

1. **Evaluating Your Notes.** Have students compare their graphic organizers to those of other students, then write in their notebooks their self-evaluation of the completeness of their graphic organizer.

2. **Understanding What You Read: Interpreting Historical Quotations.** Discuss with students the important points they have discovered about the lives and personalities of Frederick Douglass, Harriet Beecher Stowe, Robert E. Lee, and Clara Barton.

3. Have students read the first quotation silently, then discuss the answers for questions *a* and *b*.

4. Have students work on their own to read and answer the questions for the next three quotations.

5. Have students work in pairs or small groups to discuss the three quotations, ask questions for clarification about new vocabulary, and compare answers.

HISTORICAL THINKING AND APPLICATION ACTIVITIES

1. Ask the class questions that encourage them to think about these four individuals. *Which of these people would you have liked to have worked with or known? Why? What did they do that you admire most?*

2. Ask students (or have them ask their parents or other family members) about a person in the history of their state, community, or native country whose life and ideas had similarities to those of the people they have studied. Have each student choose one historical figure from the list they created and write a short report on him or her.

3. Find the words or phrases in these quotations that are difficult to understand. Ask students why are they difficult. (Hint: Expressions such as *little lady, meet the question,* and *colored men* are not generally used today.)

4. Using the reference materials collected for the reports on Frederick Douglass, Harriet Beecher Stowe, Robert E. Lee, and Clara Barton, have students work in groups to locate additional quotations. Ask each group to write two or three questions about the quotations they select. Then have them exchange the quotations and questions with other groups, who can then work cooperatively to find the answers.

Putting the Nation Back Together

> **History Objective:** Learn about the human and material cost of the Civil War and the changes that occurred during Reconstruction, including the 13th, 14th, and 15th Amendments to the Constitution.
>
> **Language Objectives:** Read for comprehension; develop academic vocabulary and oral language; summarize discussions.
>
> **Historical Thinking Objectives:** Consider multiple perspectives; identify causes and solutions to problems.
>
> **Learning Strategy Objectives: Explicit:** Identify the learning strategies needed to answer the pre-reading questions (*tell what you know* and *predicting*). **Implicit:** Use context clues to *make inferences* about word meanings.

PROCEDURES

Preparation

1. **Before You Read: Thinking about What You Have Learned.** See "How to Teach Learning Strategies" on p. x. Have students read the questions and ask them to name the two learning strategies they will need to use to answer the questions (*tell what you know* and *predicting*).
2. Have students individually answer the questions about the Civil War in their notebooks, then work with one or two classmates to discuss their answers. Share answers to questions 1 and 2 in class. Share and record the varied responses to question 3. Students will check these answers after they have read "Putting the Nation Back Together."

Presentation and Practice

1. See "How to Teach Reading Lessons," p. xi.
2. Have students read pp. 130–131 silently. Remind them to look for the important ideas and to try to guess meanings of new words by using context clues.
3. Have students work in small groups to discuss the reading selection, decide on the important ideas, and figure out the meanings of new words. Each group should develop a brief summary for each section of the reading selection. These summaries should then be shared with and discussed by the whole class.

Expansion

1. **Understanding What You Read: Thinking about Reconstruction.** Have students work in pairs or small groups to discuss and write answers to the questions. (To get students started on the first question, you might suggest that they discuss things that have had to or will have to be rebuilt in their native countries or other countries because of war.)
2. After the group has discussed each question, have one student in each group develop a brief summary (oral or written) of the group's ideas. Now have students write answers to the questions individually.

HISTORICAL THINKING AND APPLICATION ACTIVITIES

1. Discuss these questions with the class: *What do you think would be hardest to rebuild after a civil war, tangibles or intangibles? Why? Give examples from what you know about the American Civil War.*
2. Provide students with the actual text of the 13th, 14th, and 15th Amendments. Have them work in groups to identify difficult words and phrases, and to paraphrase them to make them easier to understand. Then ask groups to take turns sharing their paraphrases with the whole class.

The Life of Free Blacks, page 132

> **History Objectives:** Examine the economic and social issues faced by free blacks in the South after the Civil War; review the causes and results of a historical event.
>
> **Language Objectives:** Read for comprehension; develop academic oral language; write notes and summaries; develop academic vocabulary and oral language.
>
> **Historical Thinking Objectives:** Identify the central questions of historical narratives; read, summarize, and discuss historical narratives; use vocabulary associated with the Civil War and Reconstruction to demonstrate knowledge.

PROCEDURES

Presentation and Practice

1. See "How to Teach Reading Lessons," p. xi.
2. Have students speculate about the kinds of problems blacks might have had after slavery was ended by the 13th Amendment. Have students look at the headings of the reading selection for hints about these problems. Write their ideas on the board. Their predictions will be confirmed or adjusted after reading p. 132.
3. Have students silently read the selection individually, taking notes on the important ideas. (You may want to have them take notes on a T-list.) Remind students to guess meanings of new words by using context clues.
4. Have students sit in small groups to compare their notes, pool information, share word meanings, and complete any important points missing from individual notes.

Self-Evaluation

1. See "How to Teach Learning Strategies" on p. x.
2. **Understanding What You Read: Summarizing.** Have students identify the learning strategies they will use to write their notes in summary form (*selective attention* to main ideas and *summarizing* to write them in their own words). Have students use their revised notes to write individual summaries in their own words about the main issues faced by free blacks. If possible, have students write their individual summaries using a word processing program.
3. Have students carefully edit their summaries. You may provide an editing checklist.
4. See "How to Teach Vocabulary Lessons," p. x.
5. **Understanding What You Read: Unit Vocabulary Review.** Have students work in small groups to go over the list of vocabulary words and discuss their meanings. By sharing information that they remember from this unit, each group should be able to develop definitions for most of the words. Ask one student in each group to take notes on the definitions developed by the group.
6. Still working in groups, have students match the definitions they have developed with the clues to the crossword puzzle. Remind them to use context clues to guess meanings.
7. Distribute copies of the crossword puzzle (see Teacher's Guide, p. 177), and have students complete them individually. Remind them to check their work by making sure that each word is spelled correctly, fits the right number of spaces, and provides the right letters for intersecting words.

HISTORICAL THINKING AND APPLICATION ACTIVITIES

1. Use these questions to continue the discussion of the role of whites and blacks in the South after the Civil War: *What other things could the U.S. government have done to help solve the problems encountered by free blacks? Were there other things that whites could have done? If yes, what would you suggest? Why do you think your suggestion would or would not have worked?*
2. To apply these words to history, ask students which words they think were especially useful in their study of the Civil War and Reconstruction. Ask, *Are there some words that were very important for them to know in order to learn about this time in U.S. history? Which are the most difficult words on the list? Why are they difficult? Which words are easy? Why are they easy?*
3. Provide students with graph paper and have them work in pairs to make their own crossword puzzles. They can use words from the Glossary or from the reading selections in this unit. Have them make a key to the puzzle. Have them give the crossword a title, so that others will know the subject of their crossword. Make photocopies of the puzzles so that students can work each others' puzzles.

African Americans after the Civil War, pages 134–135

History Objective: Examine the contributions of several African Americans to understand the ways in which they laid the foundations for modern black communities.

Language Objectives: Read for comprehension; develop academic oral language; write comparisons and contrasts.

Historical Thinking Objectives: Consider multiple perspectives; compare different stories of historical figures.

Learning Strategy Objectives: Explicit: Identify the learning strategies needed to work with a classmate on a Venn diagram (*cooperation* and *graphic organizers*). **Implicit:** Use the learning strategy *taking notes;* use context to *make inferences* about word meanings.

PROCEDURES

Presentation

1. See "How to Teach Reading Lessons," p. xi.
2. Have students read p. 134 silently, taking notes on the important points. Remind students to use context clues to guess the meanings of new words.
3. Have students work in small groups to discuss the reading selection and to compare and complete the notes they have taken.

Self-Evaluation

1. **Understanding What You Read: Comprehension Check.** Have students complete the Comprehension Check on p. 135 individually, then check their work by going through the reading selection on p. 134 to look for the specific information that supports their answers.

2. **Understanding What You Read: Comparing and Contrasting.** Go over the directions with students. See "How to Teach Learning Strategies" on p. x. Have students identify the learning strategies they will need to work with a partner on a Venn diagram (*cooperation* and *graphic organizers*).

3. Have students work in pairs to go through the reading selection again to find similarities and differences between Booker T. Washington and W.E.B. Du Bois. They should draw a Venn diagram and then group the information that is similar in the overlapping space, and the information that is different in the two outer circles. Then have students plan what words and phrases can be used to compare people, and what words and phrases show differences. After planning what to write, ask them to write two short paragraphs to summarize their information about Washington and Du Bois in their notebooks. Ask them to write an additional paragraph to summarize Sojourner Truth's contribution.

HISTORICAL THINKING AND APPLICATION ACTIVITIES

1. Ask the class to think about and discuss the following questions: *Why do you think it was so difficult for African Americans to get equal rights even after the 13th Amendment was passed? How did the 14th and 15th Amendments help African Americans?*

2. Have students find information in the school library or on the Internet about other famous African Americans after the Civil War. Students can work in pairs or small groups to write a short biography of an African American who was important in U.S. history. Have students share the biographies with the rest of the class and display them on the bulletin board.

WOMEN'S RIGHTS   PAGES 136–137

Women in the United States

History Objective: Examine how the Civil War changed women's roles and status in the United States.

Language Objectives: Read for comprehension; develop academic oral language; synthesize and elaborate; make judgments.

Historical Thinking Objectives: Identify central questions of historical narrative; draw on historical maps to increase historical understanding.

Learning Strategy Objectives: Implicit: Practice the learning strategy *tell what you know* to identify prior knowledge about women's rights in the United States; use context clues to *make inferences* about word meanings; use *cooperation* to discuss analysis and interpretation; use *summarizing* to write main ideas of group discussion.

PROCEDURES

Preparation

1. See "How to Teach Reading Lessons," p. xi.

2. **Before You Read: Thinking about What You Know.** Find out what students already know about equal rights for women in the United States. In small groups, have them discuss the following question: *Do women in the United States today have the same rights as men?* Have them give examples to support their opinions.

3. Then go over the headings on p. 136 and have students speculate about the information contained under each. Write student contributions on the

board. These ideas will be confirmed or corrected as students read p. 136.

Presentation

1. Have students read p. 136 silently, reminding them to use context clues to guess word meanings.
2. After discussing the reading selection, have students make any additions or changes to the information on the board that are necessary.

Self-Evaluation

Understanding What You Read: Using Maps for Comprehension. Have students examine the map on p. 137 and answer the questions about women's right to vote in different states.

EXPANSION

What do you think? Have students work in pairs or small groups to discuss the questions at the bottom of p. 137. Then have students write brief summaries of their group's discussion in their notebooks.

HISTORICAL THINKING AND APPLICATION ACTIVITIES

1. Use the following questions for class discussion: *What is important about having the right to vote? Do you think that everybody in a country should be able to vote? Why or why not? (What kinds of people should not have the right to vote? Why?) Would you be willing to march/demonstrate for your right to vote? Do you think there should be a minimum age for voting? What age? Why?*
2. Have students interview their parents or other family members to find out what rights women have in their native countries. Ask, *Can they vote? Can they own property in their own names? Do they need someone else's permission to do certain things?* Have students discuss with the whole class.

PRESIDENTS OF THE UNITED STATES	PAGES 138–139

Six Presidents: 1850–1875

History Objective: Analyze how events between 1850 and 1875 affected U.S. history.

Language Objectives: Develop academic oral language; synthesize and elaborate; make and defend judgments.

History Objective: Analyze how events between 1850 and 1875 affected U.S. history.

Historical Thinking Objectives: Interpret data presented in time lines; create time lines.

Learning Strategy Objective: Implicit: Use the learning strategies *cooperation* and *using resources* to find out additional information about the events in one of the presidencies studied in this unit.

PROCEDURES

Presentation and Practice

Review the events listed in the time line. Ask students if they believe that any of the presidents caused or reacted to any of the events that occurred during their terms in office. Ask, *Are there any events that are not familiar to the class? Where would they find information about that event?* Share what they find with the class.

Self-Evaluation and Expansion

Understanding What You Read: Finding More Information. Divide the class into small groups and assign one of the six presidents to each group. Using the library or Internet resources, have students look for more information about their assigned president. Have them use the information to create a presidential time line. Complete the activity following the steps on p. 139.

HISTORICAL THINKING AND APPLICATION ACTIVITIES

1. After students have shared their presidential time lines, discuss the time lines with the class. Ask students: *Which president do you think was the most important? Do you think it was the person or the events that made you think this president was the most important?*
2. Have students individually make a list of the things they think are most important for a person who is going to be president. Then ask them to share their list with a classmate. Ask the pair to make one list from their two lists, discussing their individual choices and reaching agreement on the items for one list. The pairs of students can then join another pair, repeating the sharing and combining of lists— combining again, if feasible—to create one or two lists from the class. These can then be shared and posted for use in later discussions of presidents.

LAND
PEOPLE
NATION

SINCE 1865

Lesson Plans

Land, People, Nation: Since 1865

Simple directions for each exercise are included in the student books. These directions are intended for teachers as well as students. Teachers are encouraged to go over the directions carefully with students to be sure that they understand what they are to do.

The presentation of most lessons should take about 20 to 30 minutes. Additional time for expansion and review activities should be planned depending on the needs and interests of students. Longer lessons involving the development and presentation of reports can be spaced over several days.

The detailed Lesson Plans (pages 75–146) provide the following information for each lesson:

- History Objectives (and Geography Objectives, if applicable)
- Language Objectives
- Historical Thinking Objectives
- Learning Strategy Objectives
- Procedures for teaching the lesson following CALLA phases (Preparation, Presentation, Practice, Self-Evaluation, and Expansion) (most Expansion activities are included in Historical Thinking and Application Activities)
- Text for listening comprehension exercises.
- Historical Thinking and Application Activities: Expansion activities that include suggested higher order questions for developing thinking skills, class activities, projects, and assignments.

The Answer Key for *Land, People, Nation: Since 1865* is provided on pp. 154–163. The Checklist of Language, Content, and Learning Strategies Objectives is provided on pp. 166–167. This checklist can be reproduced as a progress report for each student and used to facilitate communication between the ESL and classroom teacher. A map for photocopying is on p. 176.

Industrialization and Change: 1865–1900

> **History Objectives:** Determine degree of previous knowledge students have about the Industrial Revolution and its effects on U.S. history; develop an understanding of U.S. Pacific interests.
>
> **Language Objectives:** Develop academic oral language; write ideas in notebook.
>
> **Historical Thinking Objectives:** Interpret data in time lines; draw upon data in historical maps; analyze illustrations in historical stories.
>
> **Learning Strategy Objective: Implicit:** Use prior knowledge (*tell what you know*) to predict some of the probable events in the time period of this unit.

PROCEDURES

1. See "How to Preview Each Book" and "How to Use the Unit Openers," p. ix. The top photograph shows young boys working at a West Virginia mine around 1900. The middle photograph shows a young boy working in a dingy glass factory, and the bottom photograph shows a steam locomotive next to Lake Michigan in Chicago in 1866.

2. **Tell what you think.** Have students make two lists: one of objects that are made by machine, and the other of objects made by hand. Have them speculate on the reasons why so many things are made by machine today, and why some things are still made by hand. Go over the brief definition of the Industrial Revolution and the questions that follow. Have students work in pairs or groups to discuss the questions and then write their ideas in their notebooks.

3. Explain to students that the map on p. 3 shows the lands that the United States gained in the last half of the nineteenth century. Have them compare this map with those on pp. 82–83 and 87 of the previous book (*Beginnings to 1877*). Ask how the new lands were

different from those added before 1853. Ask students to study the map and make a mental picture of the relationship of the United States to the Pacific area. Have them speculate about what the new lands would mean to the United States.

4. Have students identify U.S. possessions in 1900 (the Philippines, Hawaii, Guam, and Puerto Rico) on the map. Ask if they know which places are still possessions, which places are states, and which are independent now.

5. In pairs, ask students to look at the time line. Have them think about how many of the events are familiar. Ask students to tell the class what they know about the familiar events (*tell what you know*).

6. Ask students to develop questions they would like to have answered in this unit. Write their questions on the board. If any can be answered by other students, encourage them to do so. Then students can write the answers (which will be confirmed or corrected as students work through the unit) in their notebooks.

HISTORICAL THINKING AND APPLICATION ACTIVITIES

1. Have students consider again their list of objects made by machine or by hand. Ask, *Which is better? Why?*

2. Have students interview their parents or older family members, to find out what types of goods were factory-made when they were young or when they lived in their home country. Ask, *What things are still made by hand? Who made the handmade goods? Who made the factory-made goods?* If students have examples of handmade items from their countries, ask them to bring them to class and share them with classmates. Then have students share the information they found about manufactured and handmade goods with the class, either orally or in writing.

3. Ask students to think about the ways in which countries gain possessions such as islands or territories. Have them discuss the following

questions: *Should a country try to gain possessions? Why or why not?*

4. Have students consult an encyclopedia, reference books, or the Internet to find out if their native country now has or in the past had possessions, or if it is or has been a possession of another country. Students can also interview family members for additional information. Students should prepare brief oral or written reports to share with the class.

GROWTH AND CHANGE PAGES 4–5

The United States, 1865–1900

History Objective: Learn about major political, economic, and social changes in the United States between 1865 and 1900.

Language Objectives: Develop academic vocabulary and oral language; read for comprehension; write summary notes.

Historical Thinking Objectives: Explain causes in analyzing historical actions; reconstruct literal meaning of historical passages; identify central questions of historical narrative.

Learning Strategy Objectives: Understand the usefulness of the learning strategy *using imagery* and practice this strategy to understand and remember new vocabulary; understand the purpose of the learning strategy *summarizing* and practice using it to write the main ideas of the reading text.

PROCEDURES

Preparation

1. See "How to Teach Vocabulary Lessons," p. x.
2. See "How to Teach Learning Strategies," p. x. Ask students to describe how they have used the learning strategy *using imagery* to learn vocabulary. Do they draw pictures to illustrate words? Do they imagine a symbol for a quality or emotion (for example, a smiling face for *happy*)? Encourage students to use this strategy to help them remember the meanings of new vocabulary words.

3. **Before You Read: Vocabulary.** Have students work in pairs to discuss the meanings of the vocabulary words on p. 4, determine which (if any) have cognates in their native languages, and then write the

correct definition next to each word in their notebooks. Ask students to draw a small picture or symbol next to each word to help them remember the meaning. Have them check the accuracy of their understanding by looking up the new words in the Glossary or in a monolingual dictionary.

Presentation

1. See "How to Teach Reading Lessons," p. xi.
2. Have students look at the headings in the reading selection and speculate about the type of information that will be contained in each section.
3. Have students read the selection individually. Remind them to use context clues to guess the meanings of new words, and to consult the Glossary or dictionary only if they cannot make a reasonable guess and if the unknown word is really essential for comprehension.

Practice

1. See "How to Teach Learning Strategies" on p. x. Explain to students that the learning strategy *summarizing* helps them remember the main ideas in a reading text. Tell students that after reading it is helpful to find the main ideas and write them down in their own words.

2. **Understanding What You Read: Summarizing.** Have students work in small groups to discuss the questions on p. 5. After discussing the information required to answer each question, students should individually write summary notes to answer the four questions. Then have students work in pairs to go over their answers and modify or correct them as necessary.

3. **Understanding What You Read: Using Maps.** Ask students to turn to the map on p. 3. Have them list the U.S. possessions acquired between 1867 and 1900 in their notebooks. Then have them write the dates the United States acquired each possession and how it acquired them.

HISTORICAL THINKING AND APPLICATION ACTIVITIES

1. Ask students to discuss the following question: *What kinds of problems can happen when there is a great gap between the rich and the poor in a country?*
2. Have students consult reference books or the Internet, or interview family members to find out what happened in their native countries or another country of interest in the period from 1865 to 1900. Ask them to prepare brief written reports on this information and then share the reports with the rest of the class.

What Was the Industrial Revolution? pages 6–7

> **History Objective:** Learn about the development of four major industries (textiles, railroads, steel, and oil) during the Industrial Revolution in the United States.
>
> **Language Objectives:** Develop academic oral language; read for comprehension; practice oral reading of dates and large numbers.
>
> **Historical Thinking Objectives:** Draw upon data on historical maps; use visual and mathematical data in graphs.
>
> **Learning Strategy Objectives: Explicit:** Understand how the learning strategy *graphic organizers* is used to find or organize related factual information. **Implicit:** Discuss how to use the previously introduced learning strategies to read a text.

PROCEDURES

Presentation

1. See "How to Teach Reading Lessons," p. xi.
2. Have students work in small groups to develop a plan for reading, understanding, and remembering the information in the reading selection. Students should discuss the learning strategies that they will use as they approach this selection, how they will deal with unfamiliar words, and how they will check to make sure that they have understood the reading selection. Then ask each group to develop a brief written study plan based on the discussion.
3. Have students read the selection individually, following the study plan developed by their group.

Practice and Self-Evaluation

1. Have students work in the same groups to discuss how successful the study plan was in helping them understand the reading selection. Have them check each other's recall of the important information presented, either by asking questions or giving oral summaries of important points.
2. Discuss with students the value of developing independent study plans for content reading assignments in all classes.

Presentation and Practice

1. See "How to Teach Learning Strategies" on p. x. Explain that factual information is often organized in a chart or graph. Use the time line on pp. 2–3 as an example. Ask students to identify other types of *graphic organizers* they know. Explain that using or creating *graphic organizers* is an important learning strategy for understanding and remembering information.
2. **Understanding Bar Graphs.** See "How to Teach Map and Graph Skills," p. xiii.
3. Discuss the photographs on p. 6 of Chinese and Irish workers on the transcontinental railroad, and women working in a textile factory. Discuss the information that the pictures tell you about the two industries—railroads and textiles.
4. Have students look at the bar graph on p. 7 and practice reading information from it, such as: *In 1850 there were more than nine thousand miles of railroad track.*
5. Have students use the bar graph to answer the questions. For question 4, they will need to refer to the map on pp. x–xi to estimate the distance between San Francisco and New York City.
6. Have students work in pairs or small groups to check their answers.

HISTORICAL THINKING AND APPLICATION ACTIVITIES

1. Use the following questions to promote discussion: *How many ways can you think of that textiles affect our lives today? How do we use steel and oil? What would our lives be like without these three industries? What difference do railroads make to our lives today? Why was it necessary to have a transcontinental railroad in the United States? Why do you think so many Chinese and Irish workers worked on this railroad?*
2. Ask the school librarian to assist you in providing students with encyclopedias, atlases, and other reference books containing statistical information. Have them work in groups to find information about the growth of a particular industry in one or more countries. Have each group construct a bar graph to display the information they discover, and then make a brief oral presentation about it to the rest of the class.
3. Challenge students to find out how the Bessemer process works and why it is so important. Have students share this information with the class.

The Industrial Revolution Brings Change, pages 8–9

History Objective: Learn about the effects—positive and negative—of the Industrial Revolution on people in the United States.

Language Objectives: Read for comprehension; scan for specific information; identify cause and effect; write notes.

Historical Thinking Objectives: Compare different stories of eras and events; compare and contrast sets of ideas and values.

Learning Strategy Objectives: Understand how using the learning strategy *predicting* can help students read with greater comprehension, and practice this strategy with a reading text; practice the previously introduced learning strategy *graphic organizers* to create a study chart.

PROCEDURES

Preparation

1. See "How to Teach Reading Lessons," p. xi.

2. **Before You Read: Making Predictions.** Ask students to name some of the new inventions and industries of the Industrial Revolution. Write the list on the board. With partners or in small groups, have students use the pictures to predict how life changed with the Industrial Revolution. Ask them to write their predictions in their notebooks.

Presentation and Practice

1. See "How to Teach Learning Strategies" on p. x. Model the learning strategy *predict* by showing a text and making predictions about it. For example: *Here is a text about the Industrial Revolution. Hmm. When I see this title, I think about what I already know about the Industrial Revolution. I look at the pictures of people and things. Then I make a prediction about what this text is going to tell me. This learning strategy gets me ready to read and find out more information about the Industrial Revolution.*

2. Discuss the strategy with students. Then have them work in pairs or small groups to use the images to predict how the inventions and industries probably changed the lives of Americans. Have students write their group's predictions in their notebooks.

3. Encourage groups to share their ideas with the class.

4. Have students refer to the ideas they listed in the "Before You Read: Making Predictions" exercise. Ask them if any of the changes in lifestyle they named were mentioned in the reading selection. Then ask them to discuss other changes that were mentioned in the reading selection.

Self-Evaluation and Expansion

1. **Understanding What You Read: Completing a Study Chart.** Have students complete the study chart on p. 9 by scanning pp. 8–9 for the needed information. Remind them to write key words and phrases only.

2. **Understanding What You Read: Cause and Effect.** Have students sit in pairs or small groups to discuss the questions at the bottom of p. 9. When each pair or group has decided on what bad things and what good things came about as a result of the Industrial Revolution, students should choose two or three to write down as answers to the questions.

HISTORICAL THINKING AND APPLICATION ACTIVITIES

1. Ask students, *At what age do you think a person should start working? Why? What kinds of jobs should young people do? What kinds shouldn't they do?* Ask students to explain their answers.

2. Have students interview their parents or other family members to find out what the minimum working age was when they were young, and the types of work that children did. Then ask students to share this information with the class orally or in writing.

3. Create a Venn diagram, heading one circle "Factory Owner" and the other "Worker." For each group, begin by writing the *good effects* of the Industrial Revolution in the correct circle. Are there any items that were good for both groups? List these in the shared part of the circle. Then repeat this for the *bad effects* of the Industrial Revolution. Inform students that the perspective of a group may influence whether they see a change as good or bad.

The Grassland Regions

> **History and Geography Objectives:** Learn about Grassland Regions in the world; use map skills to identify continents and states with Grassland Regions.
>
> **Language Objective:** Read for comprehension.
>
> **Historical Thinking Objective:** Draw upon data in maps.
>
> **Learning Strategy Objectives: Implicit:** Discuss prior knowledge (*tell what you know*); use context to guess word meanings (*making inferences*).

PROCEDURES

Presentation

1. Elicit from students information they already know about Grassland Regions. Ask them about these regions in their native countries or places they have traveled (*tell what you know*). Write on the board the countries and areas identified as grasslands.
2. See "How to Teach Map and Graph Skills," p. xiii.
3. Have students read "The Grassland Regions" silently. Remind them to guess the meanings of any new words they encounter (*making inferences*). Have them ask questions to clarify and verify the meanings they guessed.

Practice

1. **Understanding What You Read: Using Maps.** Have students examine the map and identify continents with grasslands. Remind them that when they study maps, they should try to take a mental picture of the map so that they can recall its features.
2. Have students read the questions on p. 10 and use the map to find the answers.

HISTORICAL THINKING AND APPLICATION ACTIVITIES

1. Use these questions to promote discussion: *If you could choose to live in a Grassland, a Highland, or a Mediterranean Region, which would you choose? Why? What would be some of the disadvantages, in your opinion, of the regions you did not choose? Who might choose to live in the regions you did not choose? Why?*

2. Have students consult reference books and also interview their parents or other family members to find information about Grassland Regions in or near their native countries or places where they have traveled or lived. Ask students to write a short report that describes the type of grassland, how people live there, products they produce, and cities or towns in the region. Have them share their reports with the class orally or in writing.

The Cowboy

> **History Objectives:** Learn about the life and history of American cowboys; examine their importance to the westward movement.
>
> **Language Objectives:** Develop academic oral language and vocabulary; read for comprehension; write notes.
>
> **Historical Thinking Objectives:** Compare different stories of historical figures and eras; identify central questions of historical narrative.
>
> **Learning Strategy Objectives:** Understand how the learning strategy *use what you know* can be used to link prior knowledge to new information, and practice this strategy by creating the first part of a K-W-L-H chart; understand why the learning strategy *making inferences* can help in understanding new words, and practice this learning strategy by using context to make logical guesses at the meanings of new words in the reading text.

PROCEDURES

Preparation

1. See "How to Teach Learning Strategies" on p. x. Introduce the learning strategy *use what you know* by modeling how you apply your own prior knowledge to a new topic. For example, write on an overhead transparency the words *Famous Explorers*. Describe famous explorers that you know about and jot down on the transparency their names and what they did. Finish by making a comment such as, *I'm surprised that I already know a lot about famous explorers. I can use what I know to learn more about these explorers.*

This is a great learning strategy. It is called use what you know. *When I think about what I already know, it helps me to focus on new information about the same topic.* Ask students to describe how they already use this strategy and encourage them to keep on using it for academic learning in school. Explain that they will use this learning strategy with the topic of the next reading: cowboys.

2. Call students' attention to the model for the K-W-L-H chart, and ask them to reproduce it in their notebooks. In the "K" column students should use the strategy *use what you know* to write down their prior knowledge about cowboys. In the "W" column students should write what they want to find out about cowboys. The "L" and "H" columns will be completed after reading the text.

3. **Before You Read: Identifying What You Already Know.** Have students work in small groups to discuss what they already know about cowboys. Each group should decide on the most important information they know, and then take notes about it in the "K" column of their K-W-L-H chart. Still working in groups, have students ask questions about things they would like to know about cowboys and write these questions in the "W" column.

4. Have students look over the headings on p. 11 and speculate about the type of information they will find in each section.

Presentation and Practice

1. See "How to Teach Reading Lessons," p. xi. Have students first skim the reading selection to get the main ideas.

2. See "How to Teach Learning Strategies" on p. x. Introduce the learning strategy *making inferences* by modeling how you read a text and use the context to guess the meanings of new words. For example, show a transparency of a text from a high school U.S. history textbook in which you have selected two or three words that you will pretend not to know. Read the text aloud and when you get to the "new" words, underline them and say, *That's a new word for me. I'm going to read the rest of the sentence, then read the sentences that come before and after to help me figure out what this word means. Hmm, I think this new word means _____.* Ask students if they ever do the same thing when encountering new words. Tell them that this is a good learning strategy that can help with both reading and listening. Have them identify the name of the strategy (*making inferences*).

3. **Understanding What You Read: Using Context.** Have students work individually or in pairs to look at the vocabulary words on p. 12. Ask them to scan the reading selection to find the words and then guess their meanings from context. Have students work cooperatively to develop definitions for the new words, then check them in the Glossary or in a monolingual dictionary.

Self-Evaluation

1. **Understanding What You Read: Focusing on What and How You Learned.** Have students work with the same groups that they worked with to complete the "K" and "W" columns of their K-W-L-H charts. Have students refer to the facts they wrote at the beginning of this lesson in the "K" column of the chart in their notebooks. Have them identify the main points of the information previously known, and ask them to contribute the most important ideas they have discovered from the reading selection.

2. Ask each group to decide on the most important new facts they learned from the reading selection, and write these facts in the "L" column of the K-W-L-H chart. Provide an encyclopedia and U.S. history textbooks for students to consult in order to answer any questions in the "W" column that were not answered by the reading.

3. Have students identify the learning strategies that their group used to learn new information about cowboys and record them in the "H" column.

4. Have groups take turns presenting their K-W-L-H charts (or part of them) to the rest of the class.

HISTORICAL THINKING AND APPLICATION ACTIVITIES

1. Think of a recent movie or television program that you have seen about cowboys. Ask, *What things in the movie/television show were the same as the information you read about cowboys? What things were different? Why do you think there were differences?*

2. Have students interview family members to find out who looked after cattle in their native countries or in countries they have visited (now and in the past). Have students write a brief comparison between these people in other countries and American cowboys of a hundred years ago. Then have students share their reports with the class orally or in writing.

3. Ask students to think about the advertisement for barbed wire on p. 12. Ask why they think it was called "the Greatest Invention of the Age." Why do they think it was so important?

Treaties and Territories, pages 13–14

> **History Objectives:** Understand reasons why Native Americans were moved to reservations and why they resisted; find out how some Native Americans live today.
>
> **Language Objectives:** Discuss prior knowledge about Native Americans; read for comprehension; develop oral language.
>
> **Historical Thinking Objectives:** Explain causes in analyzing historical actions; draw upon data in historical maps; reconstruct literal meaning of historical passage.
>
> **Learning Strategy Objectives: Explicit:** Practice the previously introduced learning strategy *use what you know* to discuss prior knowledge about Native Americans as a pre-reading activity. **Implicit:** Practice the previously introduced learning strategies *predicting* and *making inferences.*

PROCEDURES

Preparation

1. **Before You Read: Identifying What You Already Know.** See "How to Teach Learning Strategies" on p. x. Working with a partner, have students look at the pre-reading questions. The questions are about material previously presented in *Land, People, Nation: Beginnings to 1877.* (If students have not studied this book, use the questions to elicit any prior knowledge they have about Native Americans.) Remind students that the learning strategy *use what you know* can help them understand new information on the same or a related topic.
2. Ask students to give examples of how they have used this strategy in other lessons or classes. Have individuals explain how the strategy works for them.

Presentation and Practice

1. See "How to Teach Reading Lessons," p. xi.
2. Have students look at the headings in the reading selection and speculate about the type of information that will be contained in each section (*predicting*).

Have students develop a list of questions about Native Americans that they would like to have answered.
3. Have students read the selection individually, reminding them to use context clues to guess the meanings of new words (*making inferences*), and to ask for clarification only if they cannot make a reasonable guess. Have students take notes on important points as they read.
4. Have students use the notes made during reading to write answers to the questions they developed before reading. Students can work in pairs or small groups to compare original questions and answers.

Expansion

Understanding What You Read: Identifying What You Have Learned. Ask students to work with the same partner as in the Before You Read activity. Have them discuss and take notes on the new information they learned from the reading selection. Then have partners take turns sharing what they learned with the class.

HISTORICAL THINKING AND APPLICATION ACTIVITIES

1. Ask students, *What differences do you think there would be in the United States today if Native Americans had kept their land and there were no reservations?*
2. Assist students in making contact with people in the community who have Native American ancestry. If necessary, have students work in pairs or groups to conduct their interviews and write brief summaries of the information.
3. Have students interview parents or other family members to find out if people were ever forcibly moved from one area to another in their native countries or another country and, if so, what the reasons and results were. Have them write this information in the form of notes, and then share the information in class through individual oral presentations.
4. Have students read the quote from Sitting Bull on p. 13. Ask students what that quote tells them about Sitting Bull. They can check their ideas after they have heard about Sitting Bull's life in the Listening text on the following page.

> **History Objective:** Learn about the life of Sitting Bull and why he was important in U.S. history.
>
> **Language Objectives:** Listen for comprehension; develop academic oral language; take notes and write summaries.
>
> **Historical Thinking Objectives:** Identify temporal structure of historical narrative; compare different stories of historical figures, eras, and events.
>
> **Learning Strategy Objectives: Explicit:** Understand how to use the learning strategy *selective attention* together with *taking notes* to understand and remember new information. **Implicit:** Use *cooperation* with classmates to share and complete notes.

LISTENING AND TAKING NOTES

PROCEDURES

Presentation

1. See "How to Teach Learning Strategies" on p. x. Model the two learning strategies *selective attention* and *taking notes*, if possible by playing taped information on a topic different from this listening activity. Think aloud about the tape as you listen to it and take notes on an overhead transparency. For example, say, *Okay, that sounds like something important, so I'd better write it down. What's the next important point? Oh yes, I think it's . . . So I'll write that down.* Be sure that your notes are phrases, not complete sentences. Ask students to comment on what you modeled and name the two learning strategies.

2. See "How to Teach Listening Comprehension Lessons," p. xi. Remind students about the organization of the listening mini-lectures: statement of topic (introduction); main ideas with supporting details (body); and brief summary (conclusion).

3. Write this paragraph on the board. Ask students to indicate which words can be erased without losing the meaning, and which words can be abbreviated.

In June 1876, the Sioux fought General Custer and his soldiers at Little Bighorn in the state of Montana. The Sioux followed Sitting Bull's advice and fought in a new way. They won the battle. General Custer and all his men were killed. This battle became known as Custer's Last Stand.

As students indicate which words are less important, erase them. Write abbreviations to replace any words that can be abbreviated. Ask students to reconstruct the paragraph from the words remaining.

4. Ask students to copy the T-list in their notebooks. Read the following text on Sitting Bull and have students write the missing information in the blanks on the T-list.

5. Have students work in small groups to compare and complete their notes.

6. Have students individually write short summaries of the important points about Sitting Bull and Custer in their own words, using their completed T-lists as a guide.

Listening Text for "Sitting Bull"

You are going to hear about a famous Sioux (Soo) leader named Sitting Bull. You will learn who he was and how he helped the Sioux prepare for a famous battle. You will learn what happened to Sitting Bull and his tribe after the battle. Finally, you will learn how Sitting Bull died.

Sitting Bull was born around 1834 in South Dakota. He was a member of the Sioux tribe, one of the tribes who lived on the Great Plains. Sitting Bull became a medicine man and an important leader of the Sioux tribe. Medicine men are like doctors. They help cure people when they are sick. Medicine men are also religious leaders. They lead special dances and ceremonies. They are often very wise, and people in the tribe come to them for advice.

Now you will learn how Sitting Bull helped prepare the Sioux for a famous battle. In 1874, gold was discovered in the Black Hills of South Dakota. The U.S. government wanted to buy the land from the Sioux, but the Sioux did not want to give up their land. The U.S. Army was sent to fight the Sioux and force them to leave the Black Hills and live on a reservation. The Sioux decided to fight the U.S. Army for their land. Sitting Bull led a sun dance for the Sioux people. At the dance he told the people about his plan for defeating the white men. They must change their way of fighting, Sitting Bull said. Instead of showing off to prove their bravery, the Sioux should fight to kill. Otherwise, they would lose all their lands to the whites.

In June 1876, the Sioux fought General Custer and his soldiers at Little Bighorn in the state of

Montana. The Sioux followed Sitting Bull's advice and fought in a new way. They won the battle. General Custer and all his men were killed. This battle became known as Custer's Last Stand.

Now you will hear what happened to Sitting Bull and the Sioux people after they won the battle. After Custer's Last Stand, the United States sent new forces to fight the Sioux. Sitting Bull and many of the Sioux fled to Canada. Many of them died of cold and starvation in the winter. In 1881, Sitting Bull and his tribe returned to South Dakota and moved onto a reservation.

Now you will learn how Sitting Bull died. Life on the reservation was very hard. In 1890, the Sioux became involved in a new religion. This religion promised that great herds of buffalo would return to the plains, the white settlers would leave, and the native people could return to their tribal hunting grounds and their old way of life. As part of this religion, the Sioux danced a special dance called the Ghost Dance. They danced all day and night. The U.S. Army did not understand the Ghost Dance. They were afraid that the dance meant the beginning of a new war with the Sioux. They did not understand that the new religion preached against violence and war. The government ordered Sitting Bull to stop the Ghost Dance. When the Ghost Dance did not stop, police officers were sent to arrest Sitting Bull. A fight began and Sitting Bull was killed.

Today, many Sioux still live on reservations in South Dakota. They are farmers and ranchers. Other Sioux live in cities and towns throughout the United States. The Sioux and many other Americans remember Sitting Bull as a wise and brave leader who only fought to save his people, their land, and their way of life.

Practice

1. After students have taken notes on the listening text, have them work in small groups to compare their notes. Ask them to fill in any missing information
2. Have students individually use their notes to summarize the information about Sitting Bull in their own words.

HISTORICAL THINKING AND APPLICATION ACTIVITIES

1. Use these questions for discussion: *Do you think that Sitting Bull was right to tell the Sioux to fight in a new way? Why or why not?*

2. Provide students with library books, U.S. history textbooks, or online encyclopedias with information about Custer and the Sioux. Have them find five additional details or images about the battle of Little Bighorn (Custer's Last Stand), and share this information with the whole class.
3. Have students revisit their ideas about the quote from Sitting Bull. Ask them if they would change their interpretation since they have added the new information.

REGIONS OF THE WORLD   **PAGES 16–17**

The Desert Regions

History Objective: Gain knowledge about Desert Regions and how people lived there.

Geography Objective: Examine the human and physical characteristics of places and regions.

Language Objectives: Read for comprehension; develop academic oral language.

Historical Thinking Objective: Draw upon data from maps and illustrations.

Learning Strategy Objective: Understand that working collaboratively on a task is a learning strategy (*cooperation*) that can help students learn from each other and produce a better product than an individual one.

PROCEDURES

Preparation and Presentation

1. See "How to Teach Reading Lessons," p. xi.
2. Discuss with students what they already know about Desert Regions. Write the information they contribute on the board.
3. Have students read p. 16 individually. Remind them to use context clues to guess the meanings of new words.

Practice

Understanding What You Read: Using Maps for Comprehension. Have students look at the map of Desert Regions, reminding them to try to take a mental picture of the map so that they can remember the location of Desert Regions in the world. Have students use the map to answer the three questions at the bottom of p. 16.

Presentation

1. See "How to Teach Learning Strategies" on p. x.
2. Ask students why they think you often ask them to work on a task in groups. Record their answers. Explain that *cooperation* is a learning strategy that is useful not only in school but in all aspects of life. (You may want to explain that this strategy should not be used when teachers are trying to find out what each individual student has learned, as on a test.)

Self-Evaluation and Expansion

1. **What do you think?** Ask students to imagine themselves in a desert. What would they need in order to live? After initial contributions, have students continue individually writing down in their notebooks their ideas of the ten most important things needed to live in a desert.
2. Have students work in small groups to compare and discuss their lists. As an outcome of this discussion, each student should add two more ideas to his or her individual list of what is needed in the desert.
3. Still working in groups, have students go over their lists again (which now include twelve items) and decide on the five most important items and the reasons why they are important.
4. After the group discussions, have students work individually to complete the five sentences on p. 17. These sentences should reflect the group decision on the five most important items needed in a desert.

HISTORICAL THINKING AND APPLICATION ACTIVITIES

1. Ask students, *Why do people live in Desert Regions, since life is so difficult there? Are there some ways of living that require a desert region?* (crops? natural resources?)
2. Have students find out about a Desert Region in or near their native countries, or in a place they've traveled, by consulting encyclopedias, atlases, and parents or other family members. Ask each student to prepare a brief report of the information gathered, including the location of the desert, climate, resources, cities or towns (if any), irrigation (if any), and how people live. Have students share their reports with the class orally or in writing. (Alternatively, students could research and report on the Navajo who live in a Desert Region.)

Inventions in the United States: 1792–1903

> **History Objective:** Learn about inventions in the United States and their importance.
>
> **Language Objectives:** Write prior knowledge about inventions; read a chart for specific information; write study questions; read reference materials and take notes.
>
> **Historical Thinking Objectives:** Use visual and written data in charts; gather needed knowledge to construct a story.
>
> **Learning Strategy Objective:** Practice the previously introduced learning strategy *use what you know* to identify prior knowledge about inventions.

PROCEDURES

Preparation and Presentation

1. Have students first skim the information in the chart in order to gain an overview of the inventions described, and their importance.
2. See "How to Teach Learning Strategies" on p. x. Remind students that their prior knowledge can help them understand new information on the same topic.
3. **Before You Read: Identifying What You Already Know.** After students have read the chart more thoroughly, discuss their knowledge about the inventions. Clarify the functions of inventions such as the cotton gin and the reaper, if these machines are unknown.

Practice and Self-Evaluation

1. **Understanding What You Read: Study Questions.** Have each student develop five questions pertaining to the inventions presented. Encourage them to make the questions challenging. Have them write their questions in their notebooks.
2. Have students work in small groups and take turns asking their classmates the questions they have written. When all questions have been asked and answered, students should discuss which were easy, which were difficult, and why. Then have students select the two most difficult questions. Ask them to

write the two questions with answers below their questions in their notebooks.

Expansion

1. Have students look at the graph on page 19. Ask students to work with a partner to discuss what they know about patents. Do they know the word? Do they know what patents are used for? What does the graph tell them about inventions in the United States? Why are these numbers important?

2. <u>History Mystery.</u> As with other History Mysteries, this question can be posted for students to discuss outside of class. Ask students if they have guesses about how people told time. Students' answers may allow the teacher to introduce questions about when and how watches were invented, who could afford them, how telling time in the cities where there were factories was different from in the country, where the sun was used to tell the time. The use of bells—by schools, churches, factories, and government buildings— could be introduced. Students can also examine the National Museum of American History Website and the exhibit "On Time" (www.americanhistory.si.edu).

HISTORICAL THINKING AND APPLICATION ACTIVITIES

1. Use these questions to promote class discussion: *What kind of person would make a good inventor? What inventions are needed today? How does someone become an inventor?* Students may want to look at the U.S. Patent Office website to find out how one gets a patent (www.uspto.gov).

2. Provide students with an opportunity to work in the library to find additional information about inventions in the United States or in other countries from 1903 to 1920. Have them take notes on the information, including the name of the invention, the inventor, the date of the invention, and its effect on people's lives. Then have them share their notes with the class.

3. Have students work in small groups to brainstorm an idea for an invention. (Their invention can be practical or fantastic.) Each group should develop a sketch of their invention and a description of how it would work. Then they can share their inventions with the class and display them on the bulletin board.

Reforms and Reformers

> **History Objective:** Learn about the contributions to American life by individuals who worked for reforms (Francis Cabot Lowell, Jane Addams, Jacob Riis).
>
> **Language Objectives:** Read for comprehension; develop academic oral language.
>
> **Historical Thinking Objectives:** Read historical narratives; reconstruct the literal meaning of historical passage; use visual data from photographs and broadsides; compare different stories of eras and events.
>
> **Learning Strategy Objectives: Explicit:** Practice the previously introduced learning strategy *cooperation* to develop a short group oral report. **Implicit:** Use headings to *predict* anticipated information in a reading text; use context to *make inferences* about meanings of new words.

PROCEDURES

Preparation

1. See "How to Teach Reading Lessons," p. xi.
2. Have students look at the headings and speculate about the type of information that will be contained in each section (*predicting*).

3. **Before You Read: What Would You Do?** See "How to Teach Learning Strategies" on p. x. Have students work with several classmates to share their ideas in response to the questions on page 20. Have each group prepare a short report for the whole class.

Presentation

1. Have students read the selection individually, reminding them to use context clues to guess the meanings of new words (*making inferences*), and to consult the Glossary or dictionary only if they cannot make a reasonable guess and if the unknown word is really essential for comprehension.

2. Have students work in small groups to examine the photographs, time schedule, and quote on pp. 20–21. Ask them to take notes on the relation of the visuals to the information they have read. Each group should write a brief description of at least two of the visuals, and add to the description a summary of the

information they gained from reading. Then have them take turns sharing their short reports with the rest of the class.

Self-Evaluation

1. **Understanding What You Read: Writing a Summary.** See "How to Teach Learning Strategies" on p. x. Remind students that writing a summary of what they have read is a good way to check how well they have understood a text.
2. Have students write one or two sentences that summarize each section of the reading text.
3. Have students share their summaries with a classmate to get feedback. Then ask them to revise and edit their summaries.

HISTORICAL THINKING AND APPLICATION ACTIVITIES

1. Use these questions for class discussion: *Do you know of any people today who are working on reforms? What reforms do you think are needed today? How can they be brought about?*
2. Ask students, *What do you think it would have been like to work in a factory in the early 1900s? How do you think factory work then would compare with factory work today?*
3. Have students interview their parents or other family members to find out about reforms in their native countries, or a country of their choice. Have them find answers to these questions: *Are there famous reformers? What did they do? Are there any reformers working today?* Have students develop brief written reports and then share them with the rest of the class.

IMMIGRANTS IN THE UNITED STATES PAGES 22–27

Immigration to the United States, pages 22–25

> **History Objective:** Learn about immigration in the United States and how the U.S. educational system responded.
>
> **Language Objectives:** Read for comprehension; write notes; develop academic oral language.
>
> **Historical Thinking Objectives:** Reconstruct literal meaning of historical passages; compare and contrast sets of ideas and values.

> **Learning Strategy Objectives: Explicit:** Practice the previously introduced learning strategy *selective attention* to scan a reading text to find the sections where answers to questions will probably be found. **Implicit:** *Make inferences* about word meanings by using context clues; use/create *graphic organizers* (Venn diagrams) to compare and contrast information read.

PROCEDURES

Preparation

1. See "How to Teach Reading Lessons," p. xi.
2. Ask students to define the words *immigrant* and *immigration.* Write their definitions on the board and have the class decide on a good composite definition.
3. **Before You Read: Using Headings.** See "How to Teach Learning Strategies" on p. x. Have students identify the headings on pp. 23–24. Then have them read the questions on p. 22 and write in their notebooks the heading of the section where they can expect to find the answer. Ask students to explain how the learning strategy *selective attention* can help them read with greater comprehension.
4. Have students read the quote on p. 22, then work in pairs to write the quote in their own words. Then have students look at the photo and caption, and discuss: *Why is this statue important to Americans? What does it symbolize?*

Presentation

1. Have students skim the reading selection to find the answers to the questions on p. 22, and write the answers in their notebooks as they find them.
2. Have students read pp. 23–24 thoroughly for additional information. Remind them to use context clues to guess the meanings of unfamiliar words (*making inferences*).
3. Have students look at the graph on p. 24. Ask them what the descriptions in the legend mean. Ask, *What countries are in northern and western Europe? What countries are in southern and eastern Europe? What countries are included in Asia, North America, and South America?* Ask students to work in pairs to determine the following: *In which years there were the largest number of immigrants from northern and western Europe? From southern and eastern Europe? Asia, etc.? Which area had the largest number of immigrants after the Civil War? What new information about immigrants does the graph provide?*

Practice

1. **Understanding What You Read: Comparing and Contrasting.** Have students work in pairs to complete the three Venn diagrams. You may want to work with students to complete the first one. Then, in pairs, have students draw and complete the second and third after they have copied the first in their notebooks. Ask students to identify the learning strategy they are using (*graphic organizers*).

2. **Understanding What You Read: Working with Study Questions.** Have students work in pairs to develop study questions for each section of the reading selection and write them on a sheet of paper. Remind students that study questions should ask about the most important ideas or information in a selection. Remind students to also look at the pictures to help them learn more about immigration.

3. Have students work with their partners to write answers to the study questions on a separate sheet of paper. Then ask them to exchange their questions with another pair of students. Each pair should write answers to the study questions the other pair prepared.

4. Ask each pair to correct the answers the other students wrote to their questions. Then have them compare the results and evaluate how well they answered the questions.

HISTORICAL THINKING AND APPLICATION ACTIVITIES

1. Use the following questions for class discussion: *What do you think are the biggest difficulties an immigrant to the United States has to face? What is the best way to solve these difficulties? Do you think immigration to the United States is different today than it was in 1900? Why do you think so? How is it different?*

2. Have students work in groups to discuss their ideas about the best way to learn English. Ask each group to develop a list of suggestions for learning English quickly that would be helpful for a new immigrant of their same age. These lists can be shared with the rest of the class and displayed on the bulletin board.

Developing Reports: Immigrants, pages 25–27

History Objective: Expand knowledge about immigrants and immigration to the United States.

Language Objectives: Develop academic vocabulary and oral language; research and take notes; use the writing process to develop and present a research report; listen to classmates' oral reports.

Historical Thinking Objectives: Formulate historical questions; gather needed knowledge of time and place to construct a narrative.

Learning Strategy Objectives: Understand how the learning strategy *using resources* can expand one's knowledge base through using reference materials and the Internet to conduct research, and practice this learning strategy to access additional information for a research report; practice the previously introduced learning strategy *cooperation* to get feedback from a partner.

PROCEDURES

Preparation and Presentation

1. See "How to Teach Writing Lessons," p. xiii.
2. Work with students to brainstorm the names of important or famous people they know who have come to the United States. Work with the librarian to collect resources for student use.
3. See "How to Teach Learning Strategies" on p. x. Explain the meaning of *resources* and have students brainstorm different types of resources, such as classmates, teachers, textbooks, reference books, the Internet. Explain that the learning strategy *using resources* is useful for finding additional information on a topic.

4. **Researching: Finding the Information You Need.** Review note-taking techniques and have students take notes on their chosen immigrant. Ask them to take notes on information that answers the questions in number 2 of this exercise. (Remind students that when they are taking notes on index cards, they must write the name of the author, the title of the book or article, and the date of publication in parentheses when they use a direct quote.)

Practice

1. **Writing a First Draft: Putting the Information Together.** Have students organize and plan their compositions by deciding on the structure (such as an introduction, a body, and a conclusion), and the sequence of ideas they will present. Then have them identify vocabulary, possible language markers, and any other language information that they will need in the composition.

2. Have students ask the teacher or other native English speakers to provide new words and expressions needed.

3. Have students write the first draft of their compositions. They should focus on expressing their meaning rather than on correctness at this point, as they will have opportunities to edit for spelling, punctuation, and grammar later.

Self-Evaluation

1. **Revising: Checking the Information in the Report.** Have students work in pairs to exchange compositions and critique them. The writer should have a short list of questions to ask the reader for self-evaluation purposes. Sample questions might include: *Do you understand the story? Are the ideas in the right order? Which parts could be improved? Are there any errors in spelling, grammar, or punctuation?*

2. **Editing: Checking Spelling, Punctuation, and Grammar.** Have students revise their compositions one or more times, incorporating their classmate's suggestions, if appropriate, and their own new ideas and/or corrections. Remind them to check the spelling, punctuation, and grammar. Tell them to check with the teacher if they are not sure about grammar. Then have students write the final draft on a separate sheet of paper.

Expansion

1. **Presenting an Oral Report.** Have students work in small groups and read their compositions to each other. Ask students to take notes in their notebooks as they listen to each others' compositions.

2. Have students write three important things they learned from listening to each classmate's report.

HISTORICAL THINKING AND APPLICATION ACTIVITIES

1. Use these questions in a classroom discussion: *When are members of an immigrant family no longer considered immigrants? What changes take place as immigrants become part of life in the United States? Are all of these changes good? Are all of them bad?*

2. Have students keep journals of their families' experiences as immigrants or of moving from one area of the United States to another. These can be interactive journals which are shared with the teacher and in which the teacher writes comments and also shares information about his or her family's immigration history.

3. Ask students, *How did the immigrants studied in this section get an education? How did the barriers they overcame compare with immigrant experiences today?*

Nine Presidents: 1865–1900

History Objective: Review major events occurring during nine presidencies, from 1865 to 1900.

Language Objectives: Comprehend information in a time line; develop academic oral language; write summaries.

Historical Thinking Objective: Practice using a time line to answer questions and to understand the chronological sequence of historical events.

Learning Strategy Objective: Implicit: Use the learning strategy *selective attention* to scan a time line for specific information.

PROCEDURES

Presentation

1. Remind students that time lines are a visual way of describing the sequence of past events. This time line covers a thirty-five-year period in which there were nine different presidents of the United States. Show students how the events are grouped together next to each presidency, and remind them that grouping events and facts makes them easier to remember.

2. Ask students to keep an image of the time line in mind as they skim through the information on p. 28 to get a general idea of the main facts. Have students ask questions for clarification for any words they do not understand.

Self-Evaluation and Expansion

1. **Understanding Time Lines: Comprehension Check.** Have students work individually to answer the questions. After reading each question, they should quickly scan the time line to find the answer and write it in their notebooks (*selective attention*).

2. **What do you think?** Have students sit in pairs or small groups to work cooperatively on the exercise. Each pair or group should think of as many uses as possible for telephones and electric lights. Then ask them to imagine how communication and lighting were

handled before there were telephones and electricity. After deciding on the ideas they would like to record, have students individually write brief summaries of their discussions and conclusions in their notebooks and then share their ideas with the class.

HISTORICAL THINKING AND APPLICATION ACTIVITIES

1. Ask students to think about the activities that they do most days. Ask, *How many of these activities depend on the telephone and on electricity? Could you accomplish the same number or the same kind of activities without these inventions? Why or why not?*

2. Have students work in pairs to pick one event in the time line about which they would like to know more. Have them look in encyclopedias or on the Internet to find out three facts about the event or person and why the event or person is important in U.S. history. Have students share the information with the class.

3. Have students consult reference books and interview parents or other family members to find out when telephone service and electricity were introduced in their native countries or in a country of their choice, and the extent to which they are available today. Students should share this information with the rest of the class, either orally or in writing.

Starting a New Century: 1900–1940

> **History Objective:** Identify prior knowledge about events and people at the turn of the twentieth century.
>
> **Language Objectives:** Develop academic oral language; write ideas in notebook.
>
> **Historical Thinking Objectives:** Interpret data in time lines; use visual data from photographs; formulate questions to focus inquiry/analysis.
>
> **Learning Strategy Objective: Implicit:** Use prior knowledge (*tell what you know*) and images (*using imagery*) to speculate about events in the time period 1900–1940.

PROCEDURES

1. See "How to Use the Unit Openers," p. ix. The photographs show events and inventions of the early twentieth century.

2. **Tell what you think.** Have students look at and describe the images in the collage. Elicit any prior knowledge they have about the images. Have students work in pairs or groups to discuss the images and then write their ideas about them in their notebooks.

3. Have pairs of students look at the time line. Ask them how many of the items are familiar. Then ask students to tell the class what they know about the familiar items.

4. Ask students to develop questions they would like to have answered in this unit. Write their questions on the board. If any can be answered by other students, encourage them to do so, and write the answers (which will be confirmed or corrected as students work through the unit) in their notebooks.

HISTORICAL THINKING AND APPLICATION ACTIVITIES

1. Have students look at the photographs of the inventions (automobile, bicycle, airplane, phonograph, typewriter, stove). Discuss which inventions are still in use today and which have been replaced by newer inventions (e.g., the bicycle not replaced, but changed and motorized, the coal stove replaced by electric and gas stoves, the phonograph by CD players, the typewriter by computers). Have students write their conclusions in their notebooks, using this format: *In the early twentieth century, people used* (invention) *to* (how it was used). *Today they use* (newer invention). Or: *Today they still use* (early invention), *but* (description of how it has changed).

2. Have students interview their parents or older family members to see if they recognize any of the photographs on pp. 30–31 and to describe how they used them in the past. In addition, have students find out what other inventions their parents and/or older family members used in the past (pre-1940). Students should report on their findings to the class. If students have a picture of the item described, ask them to share that as well.

A New Era

> **History Objectives:** Learn about major political, economic, and social changes in the United States between 1900 and 1920; examine how rapid growth of cities changed urban life.
>
> **Language Objectives:** Develop academic vocabulary and oral language; read for comprehension; discuss and write answers to critical thinking questions.
>
> **Historical Thinking Objectives:** Appreciate historical perspectives; explain causes and results in analyzing historical actions; use data in photographs and graphs.

PROCEDURES

Preparation

1. See "How to Teach Vocabulary Lessons," p. x.

2. **Before You Read: Vocabulary.** Have students work in pairs or small groups to go over the vocabulary words and match them to their definitions. They should write the words and definitions in their notebooks.

3. See "How to Teach Learning Strategies," p. x. Ask students to describe how they have used the learning strategy *using imagery* to learn vocabulary. Did they draw pictures to illustrate words? Did they imagine a symbol for a quality or emotion (for example, a smiling face for *happy*)? Encourage students to use this strategy to help them remember the meanings of new vocabulary words. Have them check the accuracy of their understanding by looking up the new words in the Glossary or in a monolingual dictionary.

Presentation

1. See "How to Teach Reading Lessons," p. xi.
2. Have students look at the headings in the reading selection and speculate about the type of information that will be contained in each section (*predicting*).
3. Have students read the selection individually, reminding them to use context clues to guess the meanings of new words, and to consult the Glossary or a dictionary only if they cannot make a reasonable guess and if the unknown word is really essential for comprehension (*making inferences*).

Practice and Self-Evaluation

1. Have students study the images on pp. 33–34. With a classmate, ask them to think about what information the images give them to help them answer the questions. For example, what evidence can they find about women's work? What can they say about the use of automobiles in the early twentieth century by looking at the pictures?

2. Ask students to study the graph on p. 34. Again, have students work in pairs to decide on a sentence that would describe what the graph tells them about changes in American life after the Civil War. Each pair can share their sentence with the class.

3. **Understanding What You Read: Changes in Everyday Life.** Have students work in pairs or small groups to discuss the questions on p. 34. To answer some of the questions they will need to refer back to the reading selection on pp. 32–34. For other questions they will have to draw conclusions, make applications, describe a process, and evaluate information.

4. Have students share their answers with the class and then post them on the bulletin board.

HISTORICAL THINKING AND APPLICATION ACTIVITIES

1. Ask students to calculate the percentage of change in the number of Americans living in cities from 1860 to 1920. Then have them look again at the sentences they created describing the graph. Have them think about these questions: *How can the percentage data be added to the description of the graph? Is there another way they could illustrate the information, e.g., through pictures, through another type of graphic?*

2. Have students consult reference books or the Internet, or interview family members to find out what effect the automobile and other inventions of the time period had on their native countries (or a country of their choice) in the period 1900–1920. Ask them to prepare brief written reports on this information and share it with the rest of the class.

LABOR UNIONS   **PAGE 35**

Workers' Power Grows

PROCEDURES

Preparation

1. Brainstorm with students what they have already
learned about labor unions (*tell what you know*).
Write their ideas on the board or on an overhead
transparency. Encourage them to include any personal
knowledge about labor unions. Ask if anyone in their
families belongs to a labor union and why.

2. **Before You Read: Tell What You Know.** Have students
work in small groups to discuss the questions and
then write their answers in their notebooks. Have a
designated leader in each group organize the
discussion and answers, then present the results to
the whole class.

Presentation and Practice

1. See "How to Teach Reading Lessons," p. xi.
2. Have students read the selection individually. Ask
them to write down in their notebooks any new
words they encounter.

3. **Understanding What You Read: Using Context.** See
"How to Teach Learning Strategies" on p. x. Remind
students that they can often understand new words
by using the context to *make inferences.*

4. Have students find the new vocabulary words (*join,
conditions, threaten, unsafe*) in the text, read the
context before and after each word, and write what
they think each word means in their notebooks. The
same process can be repeated with other words that
students have identified as unknown vocabulary.

5. Have students work in pairs or small groups to check
their answers in the Glossary.

HISTORICAL THINKING
AND APPLICATION ACTIVITIES

1. Discuss: *How did the information you learned from the
reading and discussion about labor in the United States
add to the knowledge you had before? What new
information do you still want to know?*

2. Ask a representative from a local labor organization
to talk to the class about his/her organization. Have
students prepare questions before the speaker arrives.
Questions might include: *What is the history of this
organization? What are the goals of the organization?
Why would people join? What plans does this
organization have for the future?*

3. Have students select a current labor organization and
look in the library or on the Internet to find out
about the history, membership, current goals, and
future goals of that organization. Ask them to report
the information to the class.

IMMIGRATION AND MIGRATION　　**PAGES 36–37**

New Opportunities

PROCEDURES

Preparation

1. See "How to Teach Learning Strategies" on p. x.
Have students tell what they already know about
immigration to the United States, including personal
stories. Discuss with students how using their prior
knowledge helps them understand new information
on the same topic. Name the strategy: *use what you*

know. Remind students that the learning strategy *tell what you know* can help them understand new information on the same or a related topic.

2. Ask students to give examples of how they have used this strategy in other lessons or classes. Have individuals explain how the strategy works for them.

3. **Before You Read: Identifying What You Already Know.** Have students work in pairs to discuss what they already know about immigration to the United States. Have them write down their prior knowledge on this topic in their notebooks and share this information with the class.

Presentation and Practice

1. See "How to Teach Reading Lessons," p. xi.
2. Have students look at the headings in the reading selection and speculate about the type of information that will be contained in each section (*predicting*).
3. Have students read the selection individually, reminding them to use context clues to guess the meanings of new words (*making inferences*), and to ask for clarification only if they cannot make a reasonable guess. Have students take notes on important points as they are reading.

Practice

1. **Understanding What You Read: Comparing and Contrasting.** Explain to students that the images on pp. 36–37 provide information that complements the text. Have them describe what information the images provide and tell why they think the images add information to the text.
2. Have students work in pairs to discuss the questions on p. 37 and write answers in their notebooks.
3. Each pair of students should construct a graphic organizer that compares and contrasts the reasons why people immigrated in the early 1900s, why people moved during the Great Migration, and why people may immigrate to the United States today. Provide additional information and resources as needed.

HISTORICAL THINKING AND APPLICATION ACTIVITIES

1. Ask students to interview a family member or friend who immigrated to the United States, or who moved from coast to coast in the United States, to find out why that person moved. Then ask students to compare those reasons with the ones they suggested in the Understanding What You Read activity.

2. Ask students to work in groups of three or four to create an illustration titled "What Immigration Means to Me." Have them share their illustrations with the class.

REFORMS IN CIVIC LIFE   PAGES 38–39

The Progressive Movement

> **History Objective:** Learn about the origins of the Progressive movement and the groups that worked together to address concerns at the local and state levels.
>
> **Language Objectives:** Develop academic vocabulary and oral language; read for comprehension; discuss the effects of new laws on different people.
>
> **Historical Thinking Objectives:** Explain causes in analyzing historical actions; compare and contrast sets of ideas and values; compare different stories of historical figures, eras, and events.
>
> **Learning Strategy Objectives: Explicit:** Practice the previously introduced learning strategy *cooperation* to develop a chart that summarizes the information in the reading selection. **Implicit:** Practice the previously introduced learning strategy *making inferences* to use context to figure out the meanings of new words.

PROCEDURES

Preparation

1. See "How to Teach Vocabulary Lessons," p. x.

2. **Before You Read: Vocabulary.** Go over the definitions on p. 38 to be sure that students understand them.

3. Have students skim the reading on pp. 38–39 to match the underlined words to the definitions and write both in their notebooks.

Presentation

1. See "How to Teach Reading Lessons," p. xi.
2. Have students read the selection individually, reminding them to use context clues to guess the meanings of new words, and to consult the Glossary or a dictionary only if they cannot make a reasonable guess and if the unknown word is really essential for comprehension (*making inferences*).

Practice

1. **Understanding What You Read: Thinking about Effects.** Have students work in groups of three or four to discuss the laws described in the reading. Have them identify the people who were affected by these laws (e.g., children, women, workers, rich and poor families).

2. Have each group construct a chart that shows how different groups of people were affected by the new laws.

3. See "How to Teach Learning Strategies" on p. x. Remind students that when they work together on an assignment they are using the learning strategy *cooperation*. Ask students to explain how this strategy helps (or does not help) them.

HISTORICAL THINKING AND APPLICATION ACTIVITIES

1. Discuss: *What laws would be important to improve the lives of school-age students?* Have students create a poster asking for support for such a law.

2. Have students create a list of laws today that address the same issues as those addressed by the Progressives, such as working conditions, drug regulation, public school safety, and building safety. Have students work in groups to research on the Internet or in the library to find out information about one of these laws. Have them report the information to the class and discuss how they think the current law is related to the laws of the Progressive era.

WORLD WAR I PAGES 40–45

"The War to End All Wars," pages 40–42

History Objective: Learn about the causes of World War I and why the United States intervened.

Language Objectives: Develop academic vocabulary; read for comprehension; scan for specific information to develop a time line; find additional information in reference materials.

Historical Thinking Objectives: Draw upon historical data on maps; interpret historical passages; create time lines.

Learning Strategy Objectives: Practice the previously introduced learning strategy *graphic organizers* to construct a time line using information in the reading text.

PROCEDURES

Preparation

1. **Before You Read: Vocabulary.** See "How to Teach Vocabulary" on p. x.

2. Have students work individually or in pairs to match words with the correct definitions and write both in their notebooks.

3. See "How to Teach Map and Graph Skills" on p. xiii.

4. **Before You Read: Studying a Map.** Have students study the map on p. 41, then write two lists in their notebooks: the countries that were the Allies and those that were the Central Powers in World War I.

Presentation

1. See "How to Teach Reading Lessons" on p. xi. Have students read the text on pp. 41–42 rapidly to get the gist.

2. Discuss the major events of World War I and have students locate the places where they occurred on the map on p. 41.

Practice

1. History Mystery. After students have read the selection "The War to End All Wars," ask them to read the History Mystery on p. 42. Ask students to interpret the quote and to write their hypotheses on a sheet of paper. Write the quote on the bulletin board and post students' guesses beside it. Reexamine students' ideas on the bulletin board when you have completed the study of World War I. (This quote might also be discussed again when students study the assassinations of President Kennedy and Martin Luther King, Jr.)

2. **Understanding What You Read: Making a Time Line.** See "How to Teach Learning Strategies" on p. x. Ask students to describe the graphic organizers they have used and how they help them learn and remember new information.

3. Have students work in pairs to construct a time line of the events described in the reading. Then have them add additional information by consulting reference materials and the Internet.

4. Have students share their expanded time lines with the class.

HISTORICAL THINKING AND APPLICATION ACTIVITIES

1. Discuss: *What is the advantage of an alliance of nations? Why would the nations of Europe build the particular alliances they did?*

2. Have students use the library or the Internet to find out more information about Armistice Day. Ask them to share what they find with the class. Encourage them to answer these questions: *Are there other days of remembrance for the military? What are they and what is their history? Are these days still celebrated? Why or why not?*

3. You may want to further explore the students' responses to the History Mystery.

The War Experience, pages 43–44

History Objective: Learn about the impact at home and abroad of the U.S. involvement in World War I.

Language Objectives: Discuss photographs of World War I and write a paragraph comparing it to today's wars; read for comprehension; scan a table for specific information; write answers to questions.

Historical Thinking Objectives: Use mathematical data from graphs; analyze illustrations in historical stories; compare and contrast values and eras; identify the central questions of a historical narrative.

Learning Strategy Objective: Implicit: Practice using context clues to *make inferences.*

PROCEDURES

Preparation

1. Before You Read: Analyzing Images. Ask students to describe what they have seen on television about today's wars in different parts of the world. Write down key words on the board, such as *bombs, fighter planes, aircraft carriers,* and *tanks.*

2. Have students study and describe the images on p. 43. Explain new vocabulary as needed. Elicit comparisons with what they have seen on television. Create a Venn or some other visual diagram to organize the ways they compare wars then with today's wars.

3. Have students write a paragraph about similarities and differences between the images of World War I and today's wars.

Presentation

1. See "How to Teach Reading Lessons" on p. xi.

2. Have students read the text on pp. 43–44. Remind them to use context clues to figure out meanings of any new words they encounter.

Practice

1. Understanding What You Read: Reading a Table. Have students study the table of World War I casualties on p. 44. Ask questions such as: *What was the total number of wounded from Portugal? How many soldiers were mobilized from Turkey?*

2. After students have had some practice finding information in the table to answer questions, have them work individually to read the four questions and write answers in their notebooks.

HISTORICAL THINKING AND APPLICATION ACTIVITIES

1. Work with the math teacher to develop questions students could answer using the data in the table, e.g., percentage wounded of total mobilized and percentage of Russians of total mobilized. With the new information, what other descriptions can students make about the casualties in World War I?

2. Ask students to create a letter home from a soldier in World War I. Have them choose a location using the map on p. 41, and a situation based on the illustrations, reading, and discussion.

The Treaty of Versailles, page 45

History Objective: Learn about the impact at home and abroad of the peace settlement that ended World War I.

Language Objective: Compare and discuss maps of Europe before and after World War I; read for comprehension; write a summary.

Historical Thinking Objective: Draw upon data in historical maps; examine cause and effect.

Learning Strategy Objective: Practice the previously introduced learning strategy *summarizing* to identify and write down the main ideas in a reading text.

PROCEDURES

Presentation and Practice

1. **Before You Read: Studying Maps.** Have students look at the map on p. 45 and compare it to the map of Europe on p. 41. Have them describe the changes.
2. Have students work in pairs to write answers to the questions about the map in their notebooks.
3. **Understanding What You Read: Summarizing.** Have students read the information about the Treaty of Versailles by paragraphs. After reading each paragraph, have them write one or two sentences in their own words that tell the main idea of the paragraph. After completing the summary for all of the paragraphs, have students work in small groups to give feedback and revise their summaries.

HISTORICAL THINKING AND APPLICATION ACTIVITIES

1. Discuss: *Do you think that the senators should have signed the Treaty of Versailles with Wilson's Fourteen Points? Why? Why not?*
2. Look up the text of Wilson's Fourteen Points in the library or on the Internet. Have students take turns reading the points. Ask them to discuss which point they think is most important to the United States today.

AFTER WORLD WAR I   PAGES 46–47

Times of Contrast

> **History Objective:** Learn about the positive and negative effects of World War I.
>
> **Language Objectives:** Read for comprehension; scan for specific information; identify cause and effect; write and answer study questions.
>
> **Historical Thinking Objectives:** Consider multiple perspectives; identify central questions, problems, and dilemmas of the past.
>
> **Learning Strategy Objective:** Practice the previously introduced learning strategy *selective attention* to find specific information in the reading text.

PROCEDURES

Preparation

1. **Before You Read: Using Headings.** See "How to Teach Learning Strategies" on p. x. Explain to students that the strategy *selective attention* can help them find main ideas in a text. Have them look at the headings and decide under which heading they will probably find the information to answer each of the four questions.
2. Have students use the strategy *selective attention* to scan each section to find the answer to the question and write it in their notebooks.

Presentation

1. See "How to Teach Reading Lessons," p. xi.
2. Have students read the text individually. Provide assistance with vocabulary as needed.

Self-Evaluation

1. **Understanding What You Read: Working with Study Questions.** Have students work in pairs to write study questions for each section of the text. They should write the answers on a separate sheet of paper.
2. Have each pair of students exchange their study questions with another pair and write answers to the questions.
3. Have students correct the answers written by other students, using their separate answer sheets.
4. Have each set of students (two pairs) compare their answers and decide which pair had the most correct answers.

HISTORICAL THINKING AND APPLICATION ACTIVITIES

1. Discuss the following questions with students: *Does intolerance of certain groups of people still exist? What examples can you give? Have you ever been intolerant of another person or group? Has anyone ever been intolerant of you or a group to which you belong? Are there groups in your area working to increase tolerance?*
2. Ask students to use the library or the Internet to find out more about the organizations and Acts mentioned in the text (KKK, NAACP, *Emergency Immigration Act*). Ask, *Do they still exist? What are their goals? Are they the same as or different than in the 1920s? Why?*

A Decade of Excess, pages 48–49

History Objective: Learn about how the United States changed from the end of World War I to the Great Depression.

Language Objectives: Discuss and write about images of the 1920s; read for comprehension.

Historical Thinking Objectives: Use visual data from photographs; identify problems and dilemmas in the past.

Learning Strategy Objectives: Practice the previously introduced learning strategies *selective attention* and *taking notes* to assist in comprehension of the text.

PROCEDURES

Preparation

1. **Before You Read: Analyzing Images.** Elicit from students what they have learned about World War I. Ask them how they think people felt once the war was over. How would they feel? Would they want to have some fun? What would they do for fun?
2. Have students examine the images on p. 48. Have them describe what people are doing in each picture.
3. Have students work in pairs to select the pictures showing things that they think are fun. Have them write what the picture shows and why they think it is fun. Then ask each pair to share their ideas with the class.
4. See "How to Teach Learning Strategies" on p. x. Tell students that they will be using two strategies that work together as they read the text on p. 49: *selective attention* to find key words and ideas and *taking notes* to write down the most important ideas (in their own words) in the reading. (They have previously used these two strategies together for listening comprehension.)
5. **Reading and Taking Notes.** Tell students that they will read about both good things and bad things that happened in the 1920s. Ask them to make a T-list in their notebooks. They should label one column "Good things in the 1920s" and the other column "Bad things in the 1920s."

Presentation

1. See "How to Teach Reading Lessons" on p. xi.
2. Have students read p. 49 individually. Ask them to take notes, writing events and situations in the correct column of their T-lists. Then have students work in pairs or small groups to compare their notes, revise them as needed, and write a summary of the text without looking at the book.

HISTORICAL THINKING AND APPLICATION ACTIVITIES

1. Have students consult reference books to find information about life in the 1920s in their native country or in a country of their choice. Have them create a Venn diagram to illustrate similarities and differences with life in the 1920s in the United States.
2. Find the book, *Having Our Say: The Delany Sisters' First 100 Years*. This book is an oral history of African American sisters, children of activist Martin Delany, who were over 100 years old when they were interviewed. Read students the section on the Harlem Renaissance, as well as other parts of their story throughout the later part of the twentieth century.

The Great Depression, pages 52–53

History Objective: Study the causes of the Great Depression and how it affected American society.

Language Objectives: Develop academic oral language and vocabulary; read for comprehension; identify cause and effect.

Historical Thinking Objectives: Use visual data from cartoons; explain causes in analyzing historical eras and events; identify the central questions of a historical narrative.

Learning Strategy Objectives: Explicit: Practice the previously introduced learning strategies *making inferences* to use context to figure out meanings of new vocabulary words and *graphic organizers* to create a graphic organizer showing causes and effects of the Depression. **Implicit:** Practice the previously introduced learning strategy *predicting* with headings and *taking notes* to write down the main ideas of each section.

PROCEDURES

Preparation and Presentation

1. **Before You Read: Using Context.** Call on students to read the vocabulary words aloud. Provide assistance with pronunciation as needed, but do not explain the meanings. Explain to students that they will use the context provided by the comic strip and the reading selection to try to figure out the meanings of these words.
2. See "How to Teach Learning Strategies" on p. x. Ask students the name of the learning strategy they will be using (*making inferences*) as they guess at word meanings using context.
3. Have students look at the drawings first, then have them read the comic strip individually to get the gist.

Practice

1. Have students work in pairs to develop definitions for the vocabulary words on p. 50. They can reread the comic strip and the reading selection as needed to clarify their understanding. Provide help as needed.
2. Ask students to describe how they used the learning strategy *making inferences* to figure out word meanings.

Presentation

1. See "How to Teach Reading Lessons" on p. xi.
2. Ask students to tell what they think the word *depression* means. If they say that it refers to feelings of sadness or hopelessness, write that definition on the board. Then explain that *depression* also has another meaning. Go over the definition in the first paragraph on p. 52. Have students compare and contrast the two meanings of the word *depression* and write their ideas in a Venn diagram on the board. Have students write their own definition of (economic) *depression* in their notebooks.
3. Have students look at the headings of "The Great Depression" on pp. 52–53. Ask students to explain the meaning of each heading, and explain any new words or concepts (for example, you can explain *speculation* by referring them back to the comic strip on pp. 50–51). Ask students to predict what kind of information they will probably find in each section.
4. Have students read pp. 52–53 individually or in pairs. Have them take notes on the main ideas in each section. Have them present the main ideas to the rest of the class, and discuss and resolve any discrepancies.

Practice

1. **Understanding What You Read: Identifying Cause and Effect.** Discuss with students some of the bad things that happened to people as a result of the Great Depression.
2. Have students work in groups of three or four to reread the text on pp. 52–53 and make a list of each of the bad things that happened, or effects of the Great Depression. Check that each group has identified all of the effects mentioned in the text.
3. See "How to Teach Learning Strategies" on p. x. Remind students that the learning strategy *graphic organizers* can help them organize and understand complicated information. Still working in the same groups, have students construct a graphic organizer that illustrates the causes and effects of the Depression. Have them work with their list of effects first and then find a cause for each. They may have to reread earlier information in this unit.
4. Have each group show and explain their graphic organizer to the class.

HISTORICAL THINKING AND APPLICATION ACTIVITIES

1. Have students work in small groups to dramatize the comic strip. They can add additional characters and lines to the basic story line. Have students present their role plays to the class.
2. Have students use the library or the Internet to find out about economic depressions during the 1920s and 1930s in other parts of the world.

THE 1930s   **PAGES 54–55**

Franklin Delano Roosevelt

History Objectives: Learn about the first two terms of President Franklin Delano Roosevelt; examine how life changed during the 1930s.

Language Objectives: Discuss prior knowledge about the early twentieth century; read for comprehension.

Historical Thinking Objective: Identify problems and identify solutions chosen.

PROCEDURES

Preparation

1. See "How to Teach Learning Strategies" on p. x. Elicit from students what they can recall from this unit. Remind students that focusing on their prior knowledge (*use what you know*) is a good way to prepare to learn additional information on a related topic. Explain that this learning strategy often works together with the strategy *predicting* to make a logical prediction of what events might happen next (linking causes to possible effects). Ask students to give examples of how they have used these strategies in other lessons or classes. Have individuals explain how the strategies work for them.

2. **Before You Read: Identifying What You Know and Predicting.** Have students first work individually to write down what they can remember about the important events in U.S. history from 1900 to 1931. Then ask them to compare their list with a classmate and revise as necessary.

3. Have each pair of students work with their combined lists to predict events that could come about as a result of earlier events. They should keep their list of predictions to use at the end of the unit on p. 61.

Presentation

1. See "How to Teach Reading Lessons," p. xi.
2. Have students read the selection individually, reminding them to use context clues to guess the meanings of new words (*making inferences*), and to ask for clarification only if they cannot make a reasonable guess.

Practice

1. **Understanding What You Read: Making a Graphic Organizer.** See "How to Teach Learning Strategies" on p. x. Ask students how the learning strategy *graphic organizers* helps them understand new information. Have them write their answers in their notebooks.

2. Have students work in pairs or groups of three to create a graphic organizer of the Alphabet Soup Agencies and their functions. Ask each group to explain their graphic organizer to the rest of the class.
3. Discuss with students how this strategy helps them understand and remember new information.

HISTORICAL THINKING AND APPLICATION ACTIVITIES

1. Use these questions for discussion: *What do you think life was like for children in the Depression? Why do you think so?* Images from the Library of Congress's American Memory collection of WPA photos of the Depression would assist this discussion (www.memory.loc.gov).
2. Read sections from the Studs Terkel book, *Hard Times,* to the class. These interviews provide first-hand accounts from a broad range of people (by region, age, occupation, experience). Or the shorter interviews or excerpts could be read aloud or performed as role-plays.
3. Have students, working in groups of three or four, select one of the Alphabet Soup Agencies for further research. Ask students to find out if the agency was particularly beneficial to a particular group (e.g., women, children, immigrants) and if the agency was operating in their region.

| ELEANOR ROOSEVELT: WOMAN OF VISION | PAGE 56 |

LISTENING AND TAKING NOTES

PROCEDURES

Presentation

1. See "How to Teach Learning Strategies" on p. x. Remind students that they will be using the same two learning strategies that they used for the reading on p. 49 (*selective attention* and *taking notes*).

2. See "How to Teach Listening Comprehension Lessons," p. xi. Remind students about the organization of the listening mini-lectures: statement of topic (introduction); main ideas with supporting details (body); and brief summary (conclusion).

3. Write this paragraph on the board and ask students to indicate which words can be erased without losing the meaning, and which words can be abbreviated.

Eleanor was born in New York City in 1884, before the twentieth century began. Her father was the younger brother of another President Roosevelt, Theodore, so he was her uncle. Her mother died when she was only eight, and her father, whom she adored, died when she was ten. She lived with her grandmother until she went to a boarding school in England. She was a very shy and awkward girl, but at the school she gained much self-confidence.

As students indicate which words are less important, erase them. Write abbreviations to replace any words that can be abbreviated. Ask students to reconstruct the paragraph from the words remaining.

4. Have students copy the T-list in their notebooks. Read the following text on Eleanor Roosevelt and have students fill in the missing information in the blanks on the T-list.

Listening Text for "Eleanor Roosevelt"

Eleanor Roosevelt was not only the wife of the thirty-third president of the United States, but also a social activist, author, lecturer, and representative to the United Nations. The story of her life gives us a lot of information about the life of women in the first half of the twentieth century and about the major events of that time period. She was personally involved in many of these events, and she worked to make life better for many people.

Eleanor was born in New York City in 1884, before the twentieth century began. Her father was the younger brother of another President Roosevelt, Theodore, so he was her uncle. Her mother died when she was only eight, and her father, whom she adored, died when she was ten. She lived with her grandmother until she went to a boarding school in England. She was a very shy and awkward girl, but at the school she gained much self-confidence.

She returned to New York where she did social work and met Franklin Roosevelt. She married him in 1905 and they had six children. (One child died in infancy.) At that time, she said, "I suppose I was fitting pretty well into the pattern of a fairly conventional, quiet, young society matron." But that did not last long.

In 1910, Franklin was elected to the state senate in New York and began a long political career. Eleanor was determined to help him, but also to have interests of her own. She became involved in politics also by becoming active in the Democratic Party and in the League of Women Voters and the Women's Trade Union League. After Franklin became ill with polio, she became his constant helper. From his position as Governor of New York State in 1928, to his election to the presidency in 1932, to his death in 1945, she worked with him, advised him, and informed him. She was referred to as his "eyes and ears." When they traveled on official visits, she was the one who could go into the neighborhoods and talk to the people about the issues that concerned them. She also campaigned for him and with him.

She became the official greeter at the White House during the twelve years that her husband was president. But she again branched out and did things on her own. She gave speeches, held press conferences (with only women in attendance), and gave lectures and radio broadcasts. She also began writing a newspaper column called "My Day." She wrote it six days a week from 1936 to 1962! She wrote about her ideas on issues as varied as her views on current events, on race, and on women's roles. She reached millions of readers with her views.

One incident for which she is well known was when she resigned from an organization called the Daughters of the American Revolution in 1939 because they refused to allow the famous singer, Marian Anderson, to perform in their auditorium because she was African American. Eleanor wrote, "I am in complete disagreement with the attitude taken in refusing Constitution Hall to a great artist. . . . You had an opportunity to lead in an enlightened way and it seems to me that your organization has failed." She then arranged for Marian Anderson to sing instead at the Lincoln Memorial in Washington,

DC. Seventy-five thousand people attended this concert. She was also active in many social causes, such as investigating working conditions, supporting the anti-lynching campaigns, and seeking fair housing for minorities. She also encouraged her husband to appoint the first woman, Frances Perkins, to a position in his cabinet.

Throughout the long years of World War II, she visited soldiers around the world and convinced the Army Nurse Corps to admit black women. In 1945, just before the end of the war, her life changed again when her husband, President Roosevelt, died. She was out of the public spotlight for about a year, but then returned to her active life. She was chosen by President Truman to lead the United Nations Human Rights Commission where she helped draft the Declaration of Human Rights. She continued to be involved in the Democratic Party and to write her newspaper column. She died in 1962 in New York City.

In one of her "My Day" columns near the end of her life she wrote: "I could not, at any age, really be contented to take my place in a warm corner by the fireside and simply look on." She certainly didn't. Eleanor Roosevelt is remembered by so many people for her active, caring, smiling presence throughout very significant times in U.S. history.

Practice

1. After students have taken notes on the listening text, have them work in small groups to compare their notes. Ask them to fill in any missing information
2. Have students individually use their notes to summarize the information about Eleanor Roosevelt in their own words.

HISTORICAL THINKING AND APPLICATION ACTIVITIES

1. Use these questions for class discussion: *What do you think is the most important thing that Eleanor Roosevelt did? Why do you think so?*
2. There were many women who met Eleanor Roosevelt or worked with her. Ask students to select someone such as Marian Anderson or Frances Perkins and find out more about their lives. Have them find answers to the following questions: *How were these women important to the life of Eleanor Roosevelt? How was she important to their lives?* Have students share their information with the class.

DEVELOPING REPORTS　**PAGES 57–59**

Important People of the Early Twentieth Century

History Objective: Expand knowledge about figures important to the development of the United States in the first forty years of the twentieth century.

Language Objectives: Develop academic vocabulary and oral language; research and take notes; use the writing process to develop and present a research report; listen to classmates' oral reports.

Historical Thinking Objectives: Formulate historical questions; gather needed knowledge of time and place to construct a narrative; analyze the interests and values of various people; compare different stories of historical figures, eras, and events.

Learning Strategy Objectives: Practice the previously introduced learning strategy *using resources* by using reference materials and the Internet to conduct research; practice the learning strategy *cooperation* to work with a classmate on revising a research report.

PROCEDURES

Preparation and Presentation

1. See "How to Teach Writing Lessons," p. xiii.
2. Brainstorm with students the names of people in the early twentieth century that they have read about in this unit. For each name suggested, identify the category of that person's contributions (e.g., artist, aviator, business person). Explain any new words as needed. Have students choose a person, or you may assign a person.
3. Following are some suggested individuals from this period that students can research: Charles Lindbergh (aviator); Tarbell, Riis, Sinclair (reformers); Wilson, Hoover, Roosevelt (presidents); Ida Wells, W.E.B. DuBois (activists); Babe Ruth, Satchel Paige (athletes); figures of the Harlem Renaissance, etc. Students may find other people of interest as they research.
4. Work with the librarian to collect resources for student use.

5. **Researching: Finding the Information You Need.** See "How to Teach Learning Strategies" on p. x. Remind students that the strategy *using resources* is used whenever we look for additional information on a topic.

6. Review note-taking techniques and have students take notes on their chosen individual. They should take notes on the information listed on p. 57. Remind students that when they are taking notes on index cards, they must write the name of the author, the title of the book or article, and the date of publication in parentheses when they use a direct quote.

Practice

1. **Writing a First Draft: Putting the Information Together.** Have students organize and plan their compositions by deciding on the structure (such as an introduction, a body, and a conclusion), and the sequence of ideas to be presented. Then have them identify vocabulary, possible language markers, and any other language information that they will need in the composition.

2. Students should ask the teacher or other native English speakers to provide new words and expressions as needed.

3. Have students write the first draft of their compositions. They should focus on expressing their meaning rather than on correctness at this point, as they will have opportunities to edit for spelling, punctuation, and grammar later.

Self-Evaluation

1. **Revising: Checking the Information in the Report.** Have students work in pairs to exchange compositions and critique them. The writer should have a short list of questions to ask the reader for self-evaluation purposes. Sample questions might include the following: *Do you understand the story? Are the ideas in the right order? Which parts could be improved? Are there any errors in spelling, grammar, or punctuation?*

2. Have students revise their compositions one or more times, incorporating their classmate's suggestions, if appropriate, and their own new ideas and/or corrections.

3. See "How to Teach Learning Strategies" on p. x. Ask students to identify the learning strategy they were using as they gave and received feedback on their reports (*cooperation*). Ask them to describe other ways in which they use this learning strategy.

Practice and Self-Evaluation

1. **Editing: Checking Spelling, Punctuation, and Grammar.** Go over the directions at the top of p. 59 with students. Have them check their reports for spelling, punctuation, and grammar. Then have them write their final draft on a separate sheet of paper.

2. Presenting an Oral Report. Have students work in small groups and read their compositions to each other. Have students take notes in their notebooks as they listen to each others' compositions.

3. Then ask students to write three important things they learned from each report.

HISTORICAL THINKING AND APPLICATION ACTIVITIES

1. After listening to the reports of other classmates, ask students which individual they believe was the most important in U.S. history. Ask why they think so. Encourage students to share their ideas in a class discussion.

2. The teacher may want to explore the PBS video series, *Jazz*, seeking the sections that address the 1920s and 1930s. By using sections of the video, students will get a chance to hear the music and acquire a context for understanding the era.

3. Invite a speaker to class who is familiar with the era of the Great Depression in your community. This might be an individual from the local library, historical society, or college or university.

PRESIDENTS OF THE UNITED STATES	PAGES 60–61

Eight Presidents: 1900–1940

History Objective: Review major events occurring during eight presidencies, from 1900 to 1940.

Language Objectives: Comprehend information in a time line; develop academic oral language; research for additional information; write predictions.

Historical Thinking Objective: Practice using a time line to answer questions and to understand chronological sequence of historical events.

Learning Strategy Objectives: Understand how the learning strategy *classifying* can be used to remember information, and practice this strategy by determining categories for the events in the time line; practice the previously introduced strategy *predicting* to speculate what might happen next in each event category.

PROCEDURES

Preparation and Presentation

1. Remind students that time lines are a visual way of describing the sequence of past events. This time line covers a forty-year period in which there were eight different presidents of the United States. Call on students to explain why there were only eight different presidents in this period of forty years.
2. Show students how the events are grouped together next to each presidency, and remind them that grouping events and facts makes them easier to remember.
3. Ask students to keep an image of the time line in mind as they skim through the information on pp. 60–61 to get a general idea of the main facts. Have students ask questions for clarification of any words they do not understand.

Practice and Expansion

1. **Understanding What You Read: Classifying Events.** Have students work in small groups to decide how the different events affected particular groups of people. Students will need to do library and/or Internet research to find out more information about the events on the time line.
2. See "How to Teach Learning Strategies" on p. x. Model the strategy *classifying* by using the time line to demonstrate how events have been classified under different presidencies. Explain that using this strategy can help students remember important information and relationships.
3. As each group discovers more information about each event on the time line, have them decide on a category for the event. More than one event will fit into a category. Each group should make a chart that shows their categories and the events for each category.
4. See "How to Teach Learning Strategies" on p. x. Have each group use their charts to *predict* what might happen next in each event category.

HISTORICAL THINKING AND APPLICATION ACTIVITIES

1. Challenge students to think of a different way to classify the events in the time line. Have them work in groups of three or four to create a time line covering the same period, but categorizing the items in a different way. Have them share the new categories. When all have shared, ask students which way they prefer to remember events in this time period.
2. Have students work in pairs to pick one event in the time line about which they would like to know more. Have them look in encyclopedias or on the Internet to find three facts about the event or person, and why the event or person is important in U.S. history. Have students share the expanded knowledge with the class.

The United States Becomes a World Leader: 1940–1960

....

UNIT OPENER PAGES 62–63

History Objective: Examine the extent of students' prior knowledge about effects of the Depression and the war in Europe on life in the United States.

Language Objectives: Develop academic oral language; write ideas in notebooks.

Historical Thinking Objectives: Interpret data in time lines; use data from photographs, paintings, and drawings; formulate questions to focus inquiry and analysis.

Learning Strategy Objectives: Implicit: Use prior knowledge (*tell what you know*) and images (*using imagery*) to speculate about events in the time period 1940–1960.

PROCEDURES

1. See "How to Use the Unit Openers," p. ix. The images illustrate events of the mid-twentieth century.

2. **Tell what you think.** Have students look at and describe the images in the collage. Elicit any prior knowledge they have about the images. Have students work in pairs or groups to discuss the images and their ideas about the questions. Then have them write their ideas in their notebooks. Discuss if and how the images helped them answer the questions.

3. Have students work in pairs to look at the time line. Ask them how many of the items are familiar. Ask students to tell the class what they know about the familiar items.

4. Ask students to develop questions they would like to have answered in this unit. Write their questions on the board. If any can be answered by other students, encourage them to do so, and write the answers (which will be confirmed or corrected as students work through the unit) in their notebooks.

HISTORICAL THINKING AND APPLICATION ACTIVITIES

1. Have students look at the photographs and place them in a time line. Ask them what other images they might add to represent the events of this time period.

2. Have students interview their parents or older family members to see if they recognize any of the photographs on pp. 62–63. Students should report their findings to the class. Students may be able to bring in photographs from family members or friends that will add to the time line. Create a class time line with copies of the images brought into the class. Students can also explore the question: *How are the images related to each other? Do some depict the same event? Era? Location?*

THE AFTERMATH OF WORLD WAR I PAGES 64–66

From Depression to War

History Objectives: Learn about the international background to World War II; analyze the factors contributing to the rise of fascism, nazism, and communism in the interwar period.

Language Objectives: Develop academic oral language; expand academic vocabulary and concepts; read for comprehension; discuss and write a summary of the reading text.

Historical Thinking Objectives: Compare different stories of historical figures and

---

events; identify the central questions of a historical narrative; explain causes in analyzing historical actions.

Learning Strategy Objectives: Explicit: Practice the previously introduced learning strategy *use what you know* to link prior knowledge to new information and create the first part of a K-W-L-H chart; practice the previously introduced learning strategy *summarizing* to write the main ideas of the reading text. **Implicit:** Look at headings to practice the learning strategy *predicting*; use context to practice the strategy *making inferences.*

PROCEDURES

Preparation

1. See "How to Teach Learning Strategy Lessons" on p. x. Remind students of the learning strategy *use what you know* and how it can help them learn new information on a related topic. Ask students to describe how they already use this strategy and encourage them to continue using it for academic learning in school. Explain that they will use this learning strategy with the topic of the next reading.

2. Call students' attention to the model of the K-W-L-H chart, which they will reproduce in their notebooks. In the "K" column, students should use the strategy *use what you know* to write down what they have already learned about World War I. In the "W" column, students should write what they want to find out about what happened after this war. The "L" and "H" columns will be completed after reading the texts on pp. 64–66 and 67–68.

3. **Before You Read: Identifying What You Already Know.** Have students sit in small groups to discuss what they already know about World War I. Each group should decide on the most important information they know, and then make notes about it in the "K" column of their K-W-L-H chart. Still working in groups, have students ask questions about what they would like to know about the aftermath of World War I, and write these questions in the "W" column.

4. Have students look over the headings and pictures on pp. 64–66. Have them speculate about the type of information they will find in each section (*predicting*).

Presentation

1. See "How to Teach Reading Lessons," p. xi. Have students first skim the reading selection to get the main ideas.

2. Remind students to use context to guess the meanings of new words (*making inferences*).

Practice and Self-Evaluation

1. See "How to Teach Learning Strategies" on p. x. Remind students that the learning strategy *summarizing* is a good way to review a reading (or listening) selection and check on how well one has understood it.

2. Have students work individually to reread the selection on pp. 64–66 and write one or two sentences that give the main idea of each section.

3. Assign pairs to check each others' summaries, using the seven-item checklist on p. 66. Have students revise their summaries

4. <u>History Mystery.</u> See "How to Teach the History Mysteries," p. xiv. This mystery requires that students think about the policies that Hitler proposed regarding the people he did not like. Have students list those people they suspect Hitler would target. Talk about the Olympics and its goals, and who participates. As with other History Mysteries, students can hypothesize about the answer to the question and post their answers or write them in their notebooks. As a non-Aryan, Jesse Owens would have been on Hitler's list had he lived in Germany.

HISTORICAL THINKING AND APPLICATION ACTIVITIES

1. Have students create a chart that compares the ideas of Hitler, Mussolini, Franco, Hirohito, and Lenin. Have them find answers to these questions: *Why might they be allies? In what areas might they disagree?* Ask them to think about what each nation had to gain by working with the other.

2. Have students talk to a family member or a neighbor who remembers World War II. Have students ask them what they remember about the Axis leaders. Then students can report what they find to the class.

> **History Objective:** Learn about World War II from 1939 until the entrance of the United States in 1941.
>
> **Language Objectives:** Develop academic vocabulary; read for comprehension; discuss what has been learned and how it was learned.
>
> **Historical Thinking Objectives:** Use data from maps; identify the central questions of a historical narrative; read historical narratives.
>
> **Learning Strategy Objectives: Implicit:** Look at headings to practice the learning strategy *predicting*; use context to practice the strategy *making inferences*.

PROCEDURES

Preparation

1. See "How to Teach Vocabulary Lessons," p. x.

2. **Before You Read: Vocabulary.** Have students work in pairs or small groups to go over the vocabulary words and find their definitions in the Glossary. Have them write the words and definitions in their own words in their notebooks.

Presentation

1. See "How to Teach Reading Lessons," p. xi.
2. Have students look at the headings in the reading selection and speculate about the type of information that will be contained in each section (*predicting*).
3. Have students read the selection individually, reminding them to use context clues to guess the meanings of new words, and to consult the Glossary or a dictionary only if they cannot make a reasonable guess and if the unknown word is really essential for comprehension (*making inferences*).

Practice

1. **Understanding What You Read: Using Maps.** See "How to Teach Map and Graph Skills" on p. xiii.
2. Give each student a copy of the map on p. 69 (see Teacher's Guide, p. 176). Have them read the directions and complete the map as instructed. Ask students to focus on the amount of territory that was

conquered in a little over two years. What conclusions can students draw about the Axis and about the Allies? What information does the map give students about World War II that they could not get from the text?

Self-Evaluation

1. **Understanding What You Read: Focusing on Your Learning.** Have students work in the same groups that they worked in to complete the "K" and "W" columns of their K-W-L-H charts on p. 64. Have students refer to the facts they wrote at the beginning of this lesson in the "K" column in their notebooks. Have them identify the main points of the information previously known, and ask them to contribute the most important ideas they have discovered in the reading selection.
2. Each group should decide on the most important new facts learned from the two readings on pp. 64–69, and students should write these facts in the "L" column of the K-W-L-H chart. Provide an encyclopedia and U.S. history textbooks for students to consult in order to answer any questions in the "W" column that were not answered by the reading.
3. Have students identify the learning strategies that their group used to learn new information about the aftermath of World War I and record them in the "H" column.
4. Have each group present their K-W-L-H chart (or part of it) to the rest of the class.

HISTORICAL THINKING AND APPLICATION ACTIVITIES

1. Assist students in finding other maps covering the same time period (1936–1941) in other texts, encyclopedias, or on the Internet. Have them compare the information on the maps. Ask, *How are the maps different? How are they alike? What new information can you add about the movement of Axis and Allied armies?*
2. Have students consult reference books and the Internet, or interview family members to find out what happened in their native countries (or a country of their choice) in the period during World War II. Encourage them to find out what happened to different groups of people such as civilians, children, and soldiers. Then ask them to prepare brief written reports on this information and share them with the rest of the class.

World War II and the United States, pages 70–73

> **History Objectives:** Recognize the reasons for American isolationism and entry into World War II; examine the effects of World War II on the home front.
>
> **Language Objectives:** Develop academic vocabulary and oral language; read for comprehension; write descriptions of images.
>
> **Historical Thinking Objectives:** Read historical narratives; use visual data from photographs, images, and cartoons; explain causes in analyzing historical actions.
>
> **Learning Strategy Objectives:** Use the previously introduced learning strategy *use what you know* to review what is already known about World War II and to predict reasons for the United States entry into this war (*predicting*); practice the learning strategy *using imagery* to study images to gain an understanding of how World War II affected the lives of Americans.

PROCEDURES

Preparation

1. See "How to Teach Learning Strategies" on p. x. Ask students to name the strategy they use when they are recalling their prior knowledge on a topic (*use what you know*). Ask them to explain how this strategy helps them learn new information.

2. **Before You Read: Making Predictions.** Have students work with partners to discuss the questions and then write their answers in their notebooks. Ask them to name and explain the learning strategy they will use (*predicting*).

Presentation

1. See "How to Teach Reading Lessons," p. xi.
2. Have students read the selection on pp. 70–71 individually. Have them write in their notebooks any new words they encounter.
3. Ask students to identify which of the Four Freedoms is illustrated in the painting on p. 70 (freedom of worship). Ask students how they might illustrate the other three freedoms?

Presentation and Practice

1. **Winning the War.** Have students work in pairs to study and describe the photographs on pp. 72–73, and to read their captions.
2. See "How to Teach Learning Strategies" on p. x. Remind students that they can gain a great deal of information through studying photographs and other images of a particular period in history (*using imagery*).

Self-Evaluation

1. **Understanding What You Read: Using Images.** Have students continue to work in pairs to list the different kinds of experiences that people had during World War II. Then have them share their descriptions with another pair of students and revise as needed.
2. Ask students to describe how the learning strategy *using imagery* helped them understand what life was like in the United States during World War II.

HISTORICAL THINKING AND APPLICATION ACTIVITIES

1. Download the complete text of the speech President Roosevelt delivered to Congress on December 8, 1941 (www.ourdocuments.gov). Ask students to read the text or listen to it read. Use these questions for class discussion: *As a member of Congress, how would you have responded? Why? Why did President Roosevelt ask Congress for permission to go to war?* (See U.S. Constitution, art. 1, sec. 8, Powers of Congress.)
2. Ask students to build their own collage of life at home during World War II with a special focus on their state, city, or town. Check with the librarian or the local historical society to gather information.

WORLD WAR II, 1941–1945   PAGES 74–75

The United States Joins the Allies, page 74

> **History Objective:** Learn about the reasons why the United States entered World War II and the effects of that action on the war.
>
> **Language Objectives:** Read for comprehension; discuss and write answers to map questions.

Historical Thinking Objectives: Explain causes in analyzing historical actions; draw upon data in historical maps; reconstruct the literal meaning of a historical passage.

Learning Strategy Objectives: Implicit: Practice the previously introduced learning strategies *making inferences* to understand new words and *selective attention* to identify map locations and answer questions.

PROCEDURES

Presentation

1. See "How to Teach Reading Lessons," p. xi.
2. Have students read the selection individually, reminding them to use context clues to guess the meanings of new words (*making inferences*), and to ask for clarification only if they cannot make a reasonable guess.

Practice

1. **Understanding What You Read: Using Maps.** Have students work in pairs to discuss the maps on pp. 74 and 149, answer the questions, and write the answers in their notebooks.
2. Call on students to share their answers with the class.

HISTORICAL THINKING AND APPLICATION ACTIVITIES

1. Discuss: *How do maps help you learn about a time period in history? What information is found on a map that can not be found in a typed page of text?*
2. Examine additional maps of World War II from an atlas or the Internet. Have students compare the maps. Ask them what additional information about the conduct of the war they gain by looking at other maps. Ask them to write the new information in their notebooks.

The Code Talkers, page 75

History Objective: Learn about a group of Native American men who helped in the war effort with special skills and abilities.

Language Objectives: Listen for comprehension; develop academic oral language; take notes and write summaries.

Historical Thinking Objectives: Identify the temporal structure of a historical narrative; compare different stories of historical figures, eras, and events.

Learning Strategy Objectives: Explicit: Practice using the previously introduced learning strategies *selective attention* together with *taking notes* to understand and remember new information. **Implicit:** Use *cooperation* with classmates to share and complete notes.

LISTENING AND TAKING NOTES

PROCEDURES

Preparation

1. See "How to Teach Learning Strategies" on p. x. Remind students that they will be using the same two learning strategies that they used for the listening exercise on p. 56 (*selective attention* and *taking notes*).
2. See "How to Teach Listening Comprehension Lessons," p. xi. Remind students about the organization of the listening mini-lectures: statement of topic (introduction); main ideas with supporting details (body); and brief summary (conclusion).
3. Write this paragraph on the board and ask students to indicate which words can be erased without losing the meaning, and which words can be abbreviated:

The Navajo marines were a very select group and they were highly trained. They knew English and Navajo and they actually created the code from their language. They learned how to work all of the radios and telephones they would need to communicate and they learned how to repair them. They also went through basic training for the Marine Corps and were excellent shots.

As students indicate which words are less important, erase them. Write abbreviations to replace any words that can be abbreviated. Ask students to reconstruct the paragraph from the words remaining.

Presentation and Practice

1. Have students copy the T-list in their notebooks. Read the following text on the Code Talkers and have students fill in the missing information in the blanks on the T-list.

2. After students have taken notes on the listening text, have them work in small groups to compare their notes. Ask them to fill in any missing information.
3. Have students individually use their notes to summarize the information about the Code Talkers in their own words.

Listening Text for "The Code Talkers"

This is a story about a very special group of men who fought in World War II. These men were known as Code Talkers. Before 1968, very few people knew about the Code Talkers because what they did was kept secret for twenty-three years. To begin with, in 1942, only twenty-nine men were a part of this group, but by the end of the war in 1945, over 400 men had become members. One member of this group said, "our language was our weapon."

The Code Talkers were Navajo from the southwestern part of the United States. The Navajo language, like many Native American languages, is learned orally. There is no written language, so only those who were Navajo knew the language. This fact would be very important in the fighting of World War II because the soldiers fighting the war had to talk to each other when they were attacking. They did not want the enemy to hear what they were planning, so they put all of their messages in code. The enemy did the same thing, but many experts in the United States, working together, did break both the German and Japanese codes. Thus, the United States knew what the Japanese were planning in the Pacific, but they did not want the Japanese to know about U.S. plans.

Philip Johnston, a civil engineer who had grown up on a Navajo reservation and knew the Navajo language, had an idea. He suggested that the Navajo language itself could be used as a code because so few people knew it. His idea was accepted by the U.S. Marine Corps and in November of 1942 they ran a contest with new Navajo marines serving as communication specialists. The contest was between a pair of Navajo marines and a pair of regular marines communicating between two camps using code. Because the Navajo were speaking to each other in their own language, they could send and receive messages much more quickly. The other marines had to use a codebook to translate what they heard. This took them much longer.

The Navajo marines were a very select group and they were highly trained. They knew English and Navajo, and they actually created the code from their language. They learned how to work all of the radios and telephones they would need to communicate, and they learned how to repair them. They also went through basic training for the Marine Corps and were excellent shots.

The Navajo language did not have words for airplanes or battleships or for the locations in the Pacific Ocean where they were fighting. So the Navajo marines created new words and they memorized all of them, over 200, so that they would not have to use a code book that might be captured by the enemy. They often used animal words. An "iron fish" was a submarine; a "shark" was a destroyer; a "hummingbird," a fighter plane. Battleships were "whales"; bombers were "buzzards," dive-bombers were "chicken hawks." They also gave code words to the letters of the alphabet so they could spell out names, such as *Guam.*

In battle in the Pacific, the Navajo Code Talkers were very important for the United States. The messages they sent were often intercepted by the Japanese, but they were never able to break the code. The Navajo marines were sometimes mistaken for Japanese and one was even captured by the U.S. Marines before they discovered who he was. After that, each Navajo Code Talker was assigned white marine body guards. One Navajo marine tells of walking by mistake into a Japanese camp. They thought he was Japanese and he was able to walk back to his unit unharmed.

In all, over 400 Navajo Code Talkers served in World War II. These Code Talkers fought with great bravery and some died, but their special code helped the Allies win the war against the Japanese, island by island, in the Pacific. When the Navajo Code Talkers were discharged from the U.S. Marine Corps in 1945, they were asked to keep the code a secret, and they did until 1968 when the code was declassified (no longer secret). Until that time, we did not know their story.

The Code Talkers returned to their homes and became community leaders, teachers, and businessmen after the war. A reunion in 1969 at the Fourth Marine Corps Division first recognized the special things the Code Talkers had done. August 14 was declared by Congress as National Code Talkers Day in 1982. In December 2000, a bill was passed by Congress to honor the Code Talkers with congressional gold and silver medals. The medals were awarded in the summer of 2001 in a ceremony in Washington, D.C.

Said one Navajo Code Talker, "Our language was our weapon and we developed a code the Japanese would never break."

1. Use the video, *Navajo Code Talkers: The Epic Story* to provide students with additional information about the Code Talkers, as told by some of the surviving members.
2. Discuss: *How is knowledge of another language helpful in time of war? In what other instances might it be an advantage? How many ways can you think of that a second language could be an advantage?*

THE END OF WORLD WAR II — PAGES 76–78

The Axis Powers Are Defeated

> **History Objective:** Learn about the effects of the end of World War II outside of the United States.
>
> **Language Objectives:** Develop academic vocabulary and oral language; read for comprehension; identify cause and effect.
>
> **Historical Thinking Objective:** Explain causes in analyzing historical periods; analyze illustrations in historical stories; compare and contrast ideas and values.
>
> **Learning Strategy Objectives: Explicit:** Practice the previously introduced learning strategy *selective attention* to scan for specific information in the reading text. **Implicit:** Use the learning strategy *cooperation* to work with a classmate to develop a chart that identifies causes and effects of events in World War II; practice the previously introduced learning strategy *making inferences* to use context to figure out the meanings of new words.

PROCEDURES

Preparation

1. See "How to Teach Learning Strategies," p. x. Ask students to give examples of how they have used *selective attention* in previous lessons and in other ways.
2. **Before You Read: Using Headings.** Go over the five questions in Before You Read and the headings in the reading on pp. 76–77. Ask students to tell the heading

under which they would expect to find the answers to the questions.
3. Have students copy the headings in their notebooks. Then have them use *selective attention* to scan the reading to find the answers to the questions. Have them write the answers in their notebooks.

Presentation

1. See "How to Teach Reading Lessons," p. xi.
2. Have students read the selection individually, reminding them to use context clues to guess the meanings of new words, and to consult the Glossary or a dictionary only if they cannot make a reasonable guess and if the unknown word is really essential for comprehension (*making inferences*).

Practice

1. **Understanding What You Read: Identifying Cause and Effect.** Discuss cause and effect using examples familiar to students. For example: *You go to a movie with a friend and get home late. You don't do your homework. What is the cause? What is the effect? Could the effect become the cause of another event?* Explain that events in history usually have one or more causes and that the effects themselves often become the causes of future events.
2. Have students work in pairs to discuss the events in the chart on p. 78. Ask them to copy the chart in their notebooks.
3. Without looking back at the reading, have students try to recall the causes and effects that are missing in the chart and write them in the appropriate cells in the chart.
4. Have students check and correct their work by rereading pp. 76–77.
5. Think about It. Ask students what other words have been used in this book to mean Russia or Russians (e.g., the Soviet Union, Soviets). Ask them to speculate on why this is so. Direct them to reread earlier units, if necessary. After discussion, have students write answers to the questions in their notebooks.

HISTORICAL THINKING
AND APPLICATION ACTIVITIES

1. Discuss: *What was the most important result of World War II? Explain.*
2. Ask students to look at a headline from a local newspaper. Read the headline and ask students to think about whether the headline represents a *cause* (something will result, e.g., "Hurricane Isabel Headed

Toward Land") or an *effect* (the result is identified in the headline, e.g., "Devastated Town Begins to Rebuild"). Practice with multiple headlines and ask students if they can create a strategy for identifying causes and effects.

3. Have students look at a map of the world in 1945 and a map of the world in 2000. Ask, *Are there countries other than the Soviet Union that have changed their names? What have they become? Do you know why the names have changed?* Encourage students to look in an encyclopedia or on the Internet to find the answers.

LIFE IN THE UNITED STATES AFTER WORLD WAR II   PAGES 79–80

Boom Times, page 79

> **History Objectives:** Learn how World War II affected people's lives in the United States and the extent and impact of economic changes in the postwar period; learn how social changes of this period affected various Americans.
>
> **Language Objectives:** Develop academic oral language; write predictions and reflections; read for comprehension.
>
> **Historical Thinking Objectives:** Ask questions about historical data; use data from historical maps; identify causes of a problem or dilemma.
>
> **Learning Strategy Objectives: Implicit:** Practice the previously introduced learning strategies *predicting* to link causes to possible effects and *selective attention* to scan for specific information; practice the previously introduced learning strategy *making inferences* to use context to figure out the meanings of new words.

PROCEDURES

Preparation

1. **Before You Read: Think and Make Predictions.** Explain the word *boom* as applied to a sudden increase in something. If possible, provide an example that relates to students' lives (e.g., *There seems to be a boom in scary movies right now. Many new movies are scary.*).

2. Have students work in groups of three or four to discuss and list changes that might have taken place in the United States after World War II. Have each group share their ideas and predictions with the class (*predicting*).

Presentation

1. See "How to Teach Reading Lessons" on p. xi. Have students read the text on p. 79 individually, using *selective attention* to find out how many different kinds of booms are mentioned.

2. Provide assistance with any new vocabulary as needed.

Practice

1. **Understanding What You Read: Checking Your Predictions.** Have students work in groups again to discuss the booms they found in the reading and check their predictions.

2. Students should correct any mistaken predictions in their notebooks and explain why their prediction was incorrect (this is important in developing analytical thinking). Reassure students that predictions are often incorrect, but that using this learning strategy helps them think more deeply about what they are learning.

3. **Understanding What You Read: Thinking about Effects.** Briefly describe the baby boom after World War II. Define *baby boomer*, if necessary.

4. Have students work in small groups to discuss and write answers to the questions about baby boomers. Have each group share their ideas with the class.

Presentation

1. See "How to Teach Reading Lessons" on p. xi. Ask students to give examples of prejudice that they have read about earlier in this book.

2. **Prejudice Follows the Soldiers Home.** Have students read the selection on p. 80 individually or in pairs, using the learning strategy *making inferences* to figure out the meanings of any new words.

Self-Evaluation

1. Think about It. Ask students to define the word *prejudice* and to give examples.

2. Have students work in pairs to discuss examples in history where one group of people held prejudices against another. Students familiar with the history of other countries may draw examples from their knowledge.

3. Have students work individually to write in their notebooks their personal ideas about ways that prejudice could be reduced. Have them share their ideas with the class.

HISTORICAL THINKING AND APPLICATION ACTIVITIES

1. Ask students to think about the effect of booms on the 1950s. List the effects. Use these questions for classroom discussion: *Are there areas in the United States today where you think there are booms? How are they like the booms of the 1950s? Will they have similar or different effects?*

2. If you wish to pursue the study of prejudice, there are excellent teaching and learning materials from Teaching Tolerance, a project of the Southern Poverty Law Center (www.splcenter.org).

THE COLD WAR ERA   PAGES 81–84

A New Kind of War, pages 81–82

History Objective: Learn about how Cold War policies influenced domestic and international politics.

Language Objectives: Develop academic oral language; write predictions; read for comprehension.

Historical Thinking Objectives: Hypothesize about influences of the past; identify central questions of historical narrative.

Learning Strategy Objectives: Explicit: Practice the previously introduced learning strategy *predicting* to link causes to possible effects. **Implicit:** Practice the previously introduced learning strategy *making inferences* to use context to figure out the meanings of new words.

PROCEDURES

Preparation

1. **Before You Read: Making Predictions.** Ask students to describe what they have learned about the events in World War II. Have them tell what the effects of each event might be on the United States' relationships with other countries, or on its foreign policy.

2. See "How to Teach Learning Strategies" on p. x. Ask students to identify the learning strategy they were using when they were telling what the effects of each event in World War II might be (*predicting*).

3. Have students work in groups of three or four to write their ideas about possible effects of the events of World War II on U.S. foreign policy.

Presentation

1. See "How to Teach Reading Lessons" on p. xi.

2. Have students look at the map on p. 81. Ask them to compare this map with the map on p. 69. Ask, *How are the two maps different? Why are there differences?* Encourage students to use the information from the map to help them with their predictions about the reading selection.

3. Have students read the selection on pp. 81–82. Remind them to use the strategy *making inferences* from context clues to figure out meanings of any new words they encounter.

Practice

1. **Understanding What You Read: Checking Your Predictions.** Have students work in the same groups they were in before reading pp. 81–82 to check and correct their predictions.

2. Remind students that predictions are often incorrect, but they nevertheless help the reader understand the text better. Tell them that it is important to correct any incorrect predictions.

HISTORICAL THINKING AND APPLICATION ACTIVITIES

Discuss the U.S. policy of containment. Ask students to define it by asking how they might contain a pet in their house or contain a fuel spill. Ask, *What does it mean to "contain" communism?* Ask students how they can use the map on p. 81 to explain what the United States meant by containing communism as a policy after World War II.

Cold War Fears, pages 83–84

History Objective: Learn about how Cold War policies influenced domestic and international politics.

Language Objectives: Develop academic oral language; write summaries; read for comprehension.

Historical Thinking Objectives: Identify the central questions of a historical narrative; use visual data from photographs and drawings.

Learning Strategy Objectives: Explicit: Practice the previously introduced learning strategies *use what you know* to apply prior knowledge to a related topic and *summarizing* to identify and write down the main ideas in a reading text. **Implicit:** Practice the previously introduced learning strategy *making inferences* to use context to figure out the meanings of new words.

PROCEDURES

Preparation

1. **Before You Read: Identifying What You Already Know.** Have students copy the words and phrases listed on p. 83 in their notebooks. Then ask them to quickly write down what they can remember about each word or phrase from earlier lessons in this unit.
2. Have students compare lists with a classmate and pool information. Then have them share their lists with two other classmates.
3. See "How to Teach Learning Strategies" on p. x. Ask students to name the learning strategy they have just used (*use what you know*) and give examples of how they have used it in other learning tasks.

Presentation

1. Have students read the text on pp. 83–84. Remind them to use the strategy *making inferences* from context clues to figure out meanings of any new words they encounter.
2. Have students look at the two photographs at the top of p. 84 and describe what they see. If any students have seen an air raid shelter or have had school safety drills in a country threatened by war, you might consider having them describe their experiences and feelings (unless the experiences have been highly traumatic).

Practice

1. **Understanding What You Read: Summarizing.** Have students look at the three headings in the reading selection and describe the main idea under each heading.
2. Have students write a summary of the reading selection by writing the main idea for each section. Remind students to use their own words, not to copy from the text.

3. See "How to Teach Learning Strategies" on p. x. Ask students to name the learning strategy they use when they write down the main ideas of a text (*summarizing*).
4. **Understanding What You Read: Using Images.** Have students look at the movie poster at the bottom of p. 84. Ask, *Is it scary? Why or why not?*
5. Have students read the information about people's fears of the atomic bomb and radioactivity. Have them discuss how an image such as the poster might increase those fears. Have them write their ideas in their notebooks.

HISTORICAL THINKING AND APPLICATION ACTIVITIES

Use these questions for class discussion: *What are today's scary movies? What events in the real world might make them especially scary? Give examples.*

NEW DIRECTIONS IN THE 1950s   **PAGES 85–86**

Social and Technological Changes

History Objectives: Learn how social changes of the postwar period affected various Americans; understand how postwar science augmented the nation's economic strength and transformed daily life.

Language Objectives: Develop academic vocabulary; read for comprehension; scan for specific information to identify causes and potential effects; write definitions and predictions.

Historical Thinking Objectives: Hypothesize about influences of the past; read a historical narrative; appreciate historical perspectives; use data from historical images and paintings.

Learning Strategy Objectives: Explicit: Practice the previously introduced learning strategy *making inferences* to use context to guess meanings of new words. **Implicit:** Practice the previously introduced learning strategy *predicting* to link causes to possible effects.

PROCEDURES

Preparation

1. **Before You Read: Using Context.** See "How to Teach Vocabulary Lessons" on p. x.
2. Have students work in pairs to discuss the vocabulary words, using what they know about similar words in English or in another language to make a preliminary guess about each word's meaning. For example, if students know that the prefix *un-* in front of a word makes the meaning the opposite, or *not + word,* they should be able to figure out at least two of the words.
3. See "How to Teach Learning Strategies" on p. x. Ask students to name the learning strategy they use to figure out the meanings of new words from context clues (*making inferences*).

Presentation

1. See "How to Teach Reading Lessons" on p. xi.
2. Have students scan through the text on pp. 85–86 to find each new vocabulary word, read the surrounding sentences, and guess its meaning from context.
3. Ask students to describe how the learning strategy *making inferences* helped them understand the vocabulary words. Have them revise the definitions they developed for the vocabulary words in Before You Read.
4. Have students reread pp. 85–86 carefully, this time focusing on the events described during Eisenhower's presidency.

Practice

1. **Understanding What You Read: Making Predictions.** Have students work in groups of three or four. Each group should discuss and define each of the four events listed, rereading pp. 85–86 if necessary. Have them describe the events in their own words and write them in their notebooks.
2. Have the groups speculate about how each event might affect the United States in the 1960s. Ask them to write their predictions in their notebooks and then share them with the class.

HISTORICAL THINKING AND APPLICATION ACTIVITIES

1. Discuss with students questions such as the following: *What technological change was the most important for people of that time period? Why do you think so? Think about your perspective. Are you answering differently because you live more than fifty years after this time and you have the benefit of knowing more than people did then?*
2. Use the sections from the PBS video series *Eyes on the Prize* that illustrate events leading up to the *Brown v. Board of Education* decision, and the part that President Eisenhower played in the integration of Little Rock High School to introduce students to the beginnings of the civil rights movement. Discuss the role/feelings of President Eisenhower, Thurgood Marshall, the students who integrated Little Rock High School, and the students who opposed the integration. Ask students to think about the role of the courts in guaranteeing civil rights.

DEVELOPING REPORTS   **PAGES 87–89**

Inventors and Scientists of the Mid-Twentieth Century

History Objective: Through research, gain knowledge about individual scientists and inventors of the mid-twentieth century.

Language Objectives: Develop academic vocabulary and oral language; research and take notes; use the writing process to develop and present a research report; listen to classmates' oral reports.

Historical Thinking Objectives: Formulate historical questions; gather needed knowledge of time and place to construct a narrative.

Learning Strategy Objectives: Practice the previously introduced learning strategy *using resources* by using reference materials and the Internet to conduct research; practice the learning strategy *cooperation* by working with a classmate to revise a research report.

PROCEDURES

Preparation and Presentation

1. See "How to Teach Writing Lessons," p. xiii.
2. Have students examine the photographs and read the major accomplishments of each of the scientists and inventors pictured on p. 87.

3. Additional scientists and inventors from this period that you may want to add to this assignment include the following: Howard Aiken, computer pioneer; Bette Nesmith Graham, inventor of Liquid Paper correction fluid; Mies van der Rohe, architect. Others may be found by looking in an encyclopedia or on the Internet.

4. Work with the librarian to collect resources for student use.

5. **Researching: Finding the Information You Need.** See "How to Teach Learning Strategies" on p. x. Remind students that the strategy *using resources* is used whenever we look for additional information on a topic.

6. Help each student choose an important inventor or scientist to research. Review note-taking techniques and have students take notes on their chosen individuals. They should take notes on the information listed on p. 88. Remind students that when they are taking notes on index cards, they must write the name of the author, the title of the book or article, and the date of publication in parentheses when they use a direct quote.

Practice

1. **Writing a First Draft: Putting the Information Together.** Have students organize and plan their compositions by deciding on the structure (such as an introduction, a body, and a conclusion), and the sequence of ideas to be presented. Then have them identify vocabulary, possible language markers, and any other language information they will need in the composition.

2. Students should ask the teacher or other native English speakers to provide new words and expressions as needed.

3. Have students write the first draft of their compositions. Have them focus on expressing meaning rather than correctness at this point, as they will have opportunities to edit for spelling, punctuation, and grammar later.

Self-Evaluation

1. **Revising: Checking the Information in the Report.** Have students work in pairs to exchange compositions and critique them. The writer should have a short list of questions to ask the reader for self-evaluation purposes. Sample questions might include the following: *Do you understand the story? Are the ideas in the right order? Which parts could be improved? Are there any errors in spelling, grammar, or punctuation?*

2. Have students revise their compositions one or more times, incorporating their classmate's suggestions, if appropriate, and their own new ideas and/or corrections. The final draft should be written or typed on a separate sheet of paper.

3. See "How to Teach Learning Strategies" on p. x. Ask students to identify the learning strategy they were using as they gave and received feedback on their reports (*cooperation*). Ask them to describe other ways in which they use this learning strategy.

Practice and Self-Evaluation

1. **Editing: Checking Spelling, Punctuation, and Grammar.** Go over the directions on p. 89 with students. Have them check their reports for spelling, punctuation, and grammar. Then have them write their final draft on a separate sheet of paper.

2. **Presenting an Oral Report.** Have students sit in small groups and read their compositions to each other. Have students take notes in their notebooks as they listen to each others' compositions.

3. Then ask students to write three important things they learned from each report.

HISTORICAL THINKING AND APPLICATION ACTIVITIES

1. Discuss: *Which person had the greatest impact on your lives today? Explain your answer.*

2. Have students create a class collage titled "Inventors of the Mid-Twentieth Century" using information and pictures from all of their reports.

3. Have students make a list of the inventors and their inventions. Ask students to present the list to several class members and ask them who they think had the greatest impact on life today. Compile the answers from all class members and make a chart representing the results.

Three Presidents: 1940–1960

> **History Objective:** Review major events occurring during three presidencies, from 1940 to 1960.
>
> **Language Objectives:** Comprehend information in a time line; develop academic oral language; research for additional information; write predictions.
>
> **Historical Thinking Objective:** Practice using a time line to answer questions and to understand the chronological sequence of historical events.
>
> **Learning Strategy Objective: Implicit:** Practice the learning strategies *using resources, taking notes,* and *graphic organizers* to find additional information about one president and to create a detailed time line.

PROCEDURES

Preparation and Presentation

1. Remind students that time lines are a visual way of describing the sequence of past events. This time line covers a twenty-year period in which there were only three different presidents of the United States. Call on students to explain why there were only three presidents in this period. (Roosevelt was elected for four terms.)
2. Show students how the events are grouped together next to each presidency, and remind them that grouping events and facts makes them easier to remember.
3. Ask students to keep an image of the time line in mind as they skim through the information on p. 90 to get a general idea of the main facts. Have students ask questions for clarification for any words they do not understand.

Practice and Expansion

1. **Understanding What You Read: Using a Time Line.** Have students work in small groups to select one of the three presidents for further study.
2. Have students use the library and/or the Internet to research more information about the president they are studying. Ask them to look up new information on the presidential time line so that they understand each event. Remind them to look for information about technology and inventions.
3. As each group discovers more information about events and inventions during the time period selected, have them develop a detailed time line and then present it to the class.

HISTORICAL THINKING AND APPLICATION ACTIVITIES

1. Ask students to classify the events from the selected presidency by the following categories: those issues/events that had to do with the economy, with politics, or with society (people). Use these questions for class discussion: *Are there some presidents who spent more time with economic or political issues, or who focused on social issues? Who are they? Provide evidence to support your answer.*
2. Have students work in pairs to pick one event in the time line about which they would like to know more. Have them look in encyclopedias or on the Internet to find out three facts about the event or person and why the event or person is important in U.S. history.
3. Ask students to look at the titles they gave to the pictures of life in the 1950s on p. 91. Ask, *What story do those descriptions tell you about the 1950s?* Have students look in the library or on the Internet to find out more information about the United States in the 1950s. Are there other pictures that might be added to the collage of life in the 1950s?

Eras of Protest: 1960–1980

> **History Objective:** Identify prior knowledge about people and events from 1960 to 1980.
>
> **Language Objectives:** Develop academic oral language; write ideas in notebook.
>
> **Historical Thinking Objectives:** Use visual data; interpret data in time lines.
>
> **Learning Strategy Objective: Implicit:** Use prior knowledge (*tell what you know*) and images (*using imagery*) to speculate about events in the time period 1960–1980.

PROCEDURES

1. See "How to Use the Unit Openers," p. ix.

2. **Tell what you think.** Have students look at and describe the posters on the opening pages. Elicit any prior knowledge they have about the images on the posters.

3. Have pairs of students study and answer the questions on p. 92. Ask them to write their ideas in their notebooks. Then ask the students to share their ideas with the class. Ask students how the posters might help explain the title of this unit.

4. Have students look at the events listed on the time line. Ask them to make a web that shows how they think these events might be connected to each other and to the posters. Have them copy their webs in their notebooks. Then have them check their webs as they learn about events in the unit.

HISTORICAL THINKING AND APPLICATION ACTIVITIES

1. Develop historical research capabilities by asking students to think about historical events (hypothesize) that led to the creation of these poster campaigns. Have students make a list of people or events that they think might be behind such a campaign. Ask students to be detectives and look very carefully at the posters. Ask, *What evidence do you find to support your hypothesis?* Have students share the information with the class.

2. Have students interview family members or community members who were alive in the 1960s and 1970s to find out as much information as possible about their involvement with or opinion of any civil rights groups at the time. Ask students to share this information in class, either orally or in writing. Note that some of these movements have a reach outside the United States. Students may find information about involvement of family members in civil rights movements in other countries.

A New Frontier, page 94

> **History Objectives:** Develop content vocabulary related to the early 1960s; learn about the New Frontier.
>
> **Language Objectives:** Develop academic vocabulary; read for comprehension.
>
> **Historical Thinking Objectives:** Build historical comprehension; read historical narratives.
>
> **Learning Strategy Objective: Implicit:** Practice the previously introduced learning strategy *selective attention* to identify new vocabulary words.

PROCEDURES

Preparation

1. **Before You Read: Vocabulary.** See "How to Teach Vocabulary Lessons" on p. x.

2. Have students work in pairs to study the words in the word bank. Students in each pair should first use the

learning strategy *selective attention* to identify the new words and then copy them in their notebooks.

3. Have students look up each new word in the Glossary and read the definition. Then have them write the definition in their own words next to each new word in their notebooks.

4. Finally, have students define orally the words that were not identified as new words.

Presentation

1. See "How to Teach Reading Lessons," p. xi.
2. Preview and discuss the title of the reading.
3. Have students read "A New Frontier." Or have students do paired reading in which they take turns reading a section aloud and discuss it with their partner.
4. Have students summarize the main ideas in the reading orally.

Practice

1. **Understanding What You Read: What Do You Think?** Discuss the definition of *frontier* and ask students to work in pairs or groups of three to respond to the question, writing their ideas in their notebooks. Have students refer back to the reading for clues. Then have each group share their ideas with the class.

2. Read the quotation by President Kennedy aloud. Have students answer the following questions in their notebooks and discuss them with the class: *What do you think President Kennedy meant by* freedom? *Who is he talking to? What do you think he wants the audience to do?* Discuss the answers with the class.

HISTORICAL THINKING AND APPLICATION ACTIVITIES

1. Have students work in groups of three to five to select one word from the vocabulary list that they find to be a powerful word. Have students make a collage of images relating to that word. Have students share the collage with the class and explain why they picked the images they did. They can use magazines, newspapers, or computer images to create the collage.

2. Have students interview friends or family members to ask them what they think of when they hear the word *frontier*. Discuss with the class: *How many different answers did you hear?* (Record the answers.) *Were the answers different from older people than from younger people? From people new to the United States versus those who had lived in the United States for a long time? What did you find out about the word*

frontier? Did people understand frontier *as a history word or a science word?*

3. Play students the audio of President Kennedy delivering his Inaugural Address in 1961 (www.jfklibrary.org) or read aloud a section of the speech. Ask students what they notice about the words he uses. Ask them why they think people thought that he could "change things for the better."

The Cold War Intensifies, pages 95–98

> **History Objectives:** Examine events and policies, both domestic and foreign, during the presidency of John F. Kennedy; evaluate the results of those policies.
>
> **Language Objectives:** Develop academic oral skills; write answers to questions about prior knowledge; read for comprehension; analyze the results of the Cold War and explain reasons why each was positive or negative.
>
> **Historical Thinking Objectives:** Explain continuity and change over time; draw upon data in historical maps.
>
> **Learning Strategy Objectives:** Practice the previously introduced learning strategy *use what you know* to recall prior knowledge about the Cold War; use the learning strategy *graphic organizers* to analyze the results of the Cold War.

PROCEDURES

Preparation

1. See "How to Teach Learning Strategies" on p. x. Remind students that recalling known information related to a new topic helps them increase their understanding of the topic. Ask students to identify the strategy they are using.

2. **Before You Read: Identify What You Already Know.** Have students work with a partner to complete the questions about the Cold War. Then ask students to share the information they record with the class.

3. Ask students to share ideas about how they think the Cold War might get more intense.

Presentation

1. See "How to Teach Reading Lessons," p. xi. Have students read pp. 95–96 silently or share the reading with a classmate.

2. After they have read those pages, ask students how the Berlin Wall and the Cuban crises made the Cold

War worse. Have students write their conclusions in their notebooks and share them with the class.

3. In pairs, have students study the maps on p. 96 and answer the following questions. *What does the information in the bottom map tell you about the Bay of Pigs? What does it add to your knowledge about the event? What do the two maps tell you about the missile crisis? Why were people in the United States afraid of the Soviets? How do the maps add to the story?* Ask students to write their ideas in their notebooks.

4. Have students, silently or in pairs, read pp. 97 and 98. Again, ask students to summarize the main points of the reading. Ask, *How do you think knowing about the race into space and the Peace Corps adds to the information you know about the Cold War? How was the Soviet Union involved in both? How do the pictures on pp. 97 and 98 add to your knowledge of the space race and the Peace Corps?*

Practice

1. **Understanding What You Read: Comparing and Contrasting.** Remind students of the strategy they are using in working with the chart (*graphic organizers*).

2. Working in pairs, have students create a chart from the information in the reading selections and the photographs. The last column asks students to provide evidence for their decisions—an excellent way to build historical thinking.

3. Each pair should share their chart with the class, allowing students to change or add information.

HISTORICAL THINKING AND APPLICATION ACTIVITIES

1. Ask students to work in pairs or groups to create a graphic organizer that illustrates how the events of the New Frontier were related to containment. Have them explain their graphics to the class. You may also have students display their graphics and use them for review. For advanced discussion, use these questions to discuss the policy of containment: *Was it the best policy for the Cold War? Why do you think so? If not, what might have been a better policy? Why?*

2. Have students ask family members about their recollections of the Cold War. Ask them to find out where family members were living and what happened there. Then have students share this information orally with the class.

3. Discuss these questions with students: *Why would President Kennedy want to start the Peace Corps? (Think about a "war of influence.") How did the Peace Corps help the United States?* Ask students to look on the Internet to find out about the Peace Corps today. Ask, *Is its purpose the same today as it was in the 1960s?*

4. Show students clips from the movie *Thirteen Days,* especially sections where the discussions are about how the United States responded to the Soviet Union. Ask students to write down what they believe is accurate, and why they think so. This provides students with an opportunity to analyze historical movies.

| **CONTINUING THE FIGHT FOR EQUALITY** | **PAGES 99–107** |

The Civil Rights Movement, pages 99–101

> **History Objectives:** Identify prior knowledge about the civil rights movement; describe the relationship between goals, methods, and results.
>
> **Language Objectives:** Develop academic oral language; write about prior knowledge of civil rights and about additional information students would like to learn; read for comprehension, recognizing the main ideas and details; develop a summary chart of information read.
>
> **Historical Thinking Objectives:** Identify causes of a problem or dilemma; analyze illustrations in historical stories; formulate historical questions; read historical narratives imaginatively.
>
> **Learning Strategy Objectives: Explicit:** Identify and practice the previously introduced learning strategy *use what you know* to recall prior knowledge about civil rights. **Implicit:** Practice the learning strategy *graphic organizers* to complete a chart that summarizes information about the civil rights movement.

PROCEDURES

Preparation

1. See "How to Teach Learning Strategies" on p. x. Ask students which strategy they use when they think about previous knowledge (*use what you know*). Discuss with students how this strategy assists them in learning new material.

2. Call students' attention to the model of the K-W-L-H chart, which they will reproduce in their notebooks. In the "K" column, students will use the strategy *use what you know* to write down what they have already learned about the civil rights movement in the 1960s. In the "W" column, students will write what they want to find out about it. The "L" and "H" columns will be completed after reading the text.

3. **Before You Read: Identifying What You Already Know.** Have students work in small groups to discuss what they already know about the civil rights of different groups of Americans. Each group should decide on the most important information they know, and then take notes about it the "K" column of their K-W-L-H chart. Still working in groups, have students ask what they would like to know about the civil rights movement in the 1960s and write these questions in the "W" column.

Presentation

1. See "How to Teach Reading Lessons," p. xi.

2. Preview and discuss the headings of the reading selection on pp. 99–101. Have students also examine the pictures and guess which of the headings the pictures illustrate. Ask, *What information do pictures give that words do not?*

3. Provide an opportunity for students to ask questions about words and expressions they have not understood in the reading selection.

4. Have students work in small groups to develop oral summaries of the information on pp. 99–101. Then have them share their group summaries with the class.

5. Show students sections of the PBS video series *Eyes on the Prize* (the "Montgomery Bus Boycott" and "Freedom Summer" sections are particularly appropriate). Ask students what new information they learned that they could add to their summaries.

Practice

1. **Understanding What You Read: Making a Chart.** Go over the directions for completing the chart titled "African Americans and Civil Rights," on p. 101. Have students copy the chart in their notebooks, leaving space for adding information after 1954–1956.

2. Have students look back over the reading on pp. 99–101 and also pp. 85–86 in Unit 3 to find the dates that are important in the movement by African Americans for civil rights. Have students fill in the names of the most important people involved in each event. You could expect such dates as 1960 (integrate restaurants), 1964 (freedom summer, voting rights), and 1968 (Martin Luther King, Jr., assassinated).

3. Have students work in pairs or small groups to compare their charts.

HISTORICAL THINKING AND APPLICATION ACTIVITIES

1. Using the "W" column from the chart on p. 99, ask students to brainstorm what resources they could use to answer their questions. Have them record the list in their notebooks. Ask students to consider perspectives. Ask them whose views they would like to hear in answer to their questions and ensure that they have a balanced picture of the past.

2. Ask students to look again at their data chart from p. 101. Discuss: *In which years did the results actually match the goals? What influence do you think the method had on the result? Based on your chart, which method was more successful? How do you know?*

3. Make use of excerpts from the PBS video series *Eyes on the Prize* to provide visual evidence of the activities of various African American civil rights groups, actual footage of protests, speeches, and other events.

Martin Luther King, Jr., page 102

History Objective: Analyze the leadership and ideology of Martin Luther King, Jr., and evaluate his legacy.

Language Objectives: Listen for comprehension; develop academic oral language; write notes and summaries.

Historical Thinking Objectives: Identify central questions of narrative; consider multiple perspectives; compare different stories of historical figures, eras, and events.

Learning Strategy Objectives: Explicit: Identify and practice using the previously introduced learning strategies *selective attention* together with *taking notes* to understand and remember new information. **Implicit:** Use *cooperation* with classmates to share and complete notes.

LISTENING AND TAKING NOTES

PROCEDURES

Preparation

1. See "How to Teach Learning Strategies" on p. x. Ask students to identify the two learning strategies they will use to listen to the biography of Martin Luther King, Jr. (*selective attention* and *taking notes*).
2. Ask students to share with the class what works best for them in deciding on the main ideas.
3. Give students time to copy the T-list in their notebooks.

Presentation

1. See "How to Teach Listening Comprehension Lessons," p. xi.
2. Remind students that there is organization to the listening mini-lectures. Ask students about how they will use the T-list to record information.
3. Write this paragraph on the board and ask students to indicate which words can be erased without losing the meaning, and which words can be abbreviated:

To carry out his work of increasing freedom for African Americans, Dr. King helped begin the Southern Christian Leadership Conference. This group was responsible for the non-violent protests, the marches, the sit-ins, and the boycotts. Many people besides blacks joined the group, such as Jewish activists and white Protestant ministers in the North.

As students indicate which words are less important, erase them. Write abbreviations to replace any words that can be abbreviated. Ask students to reconstruct the passage from the words remaining.

Practice and Self-Evaluation

1. Have students copy the T-list on p. 102 in their notebooks. Read aloud the following text on Martin Luther King, Jr., and have students fill in the missing information in the blanks on the T-list.
2. Have students work in small groups to compare and complete their notes.
3. Have students individually write short summaries of the important points about Martin Luther King, Jr., in their own words, using their completed T-lists as a guide.

Listening Text for "Martin Luther King, Jr."

In 1983, the Congress of the United States made the third Monday in January a national holiday. This holiday is close to the birthday of a special man in U.S. history and in the struggle for people's rights. His name is the Reverend Dr. Martin Luther King, Jr. In his life, he was involved in events that would change history; his death caused riots across the United States.

Martin Luther King, Jr., was born in Atlanta, Georgia, in 1929. His father and his grandfather were both ministers, so people thought that the young Martin Luther King would also be a minister. But he thought he wanted to be a doctor. He changed his mind, though, when he was eighteen years old, and he was ordained as a Baptist minister.

By this time, he had already had a lot of schooling. Because of segregation, he attended segregated schools. But Martin Luther King was very bright and he finished high school when he was fifteen. He graduated from college by the time he was nineteen and went to a seminary to learn more about preaching. He went to Boston University where he developed a reputation as a great speaker. He also received his doctorate in 1955.

In 1953, Dr. King married a music student he met while he was studying in Boston, Ms. Coretta Scott. They would have four children.

Dr. King's ideas about religion and about life came from studying and from listening. While he was in college, Dr. King read about Mohandas Gandhi of India. Gandhi wrote about and practiced non-violent protest. This idea became very important to Dr. King. He was also influenced by the sermons he heard and read from white ministers preaching against racism and black ministers preaching against segregation. His first church job was at the Baptist Church in Montgomery, Alabama. It was 1954. He was twenty-six years old.

Martin Luther King, Jr., had not been in town very long before he was asked to lead the group that was carrying out the bus boycott in Montgomery. If you remember, blacks in Montgomery decided to walk or carpool rather than ride the buses, to protest the arrest of Rosa Parks.

Rosa Parks had refused to give up her seat on the bus to a white man. Dr. King believed this kind of non-violent protest was right. Some protesters were injured and Dr. King's home was fire-bombed.

To carry out his work of increasing freedom for African Americans, Dr. King helped begin the Southern Christian Leadership Conference. This group was responsible for the non-violent protests, the marches, the sit-ins, and the boycotts. Many people besides blacks joined the group, such as Jewish activists and white Protestant ministers in the North.

Dr. King organized marches and demonstrations in several Southern cities—always set to be non-violent. When he encouraged teenagers and children to join the march in Birmingham, they did. They marched down the streets singing. But the police wanted to stop the marchers. They attacked the peaceful marchers with fire hoses and dogs. They arrested many people, including Dr. King. From his jail cell, Dr. King wrote a famous letter that explained how people have the right to disobey unjust laws. (He was actually writing some of the ideas expressed in the Declaration of Independence.) The television news cameras also filmed the attacks on peaceful marchers. People outside the South were shocked.

Now more people joined the struggle Dr. King was leading. A huge rally in Washington, DC, in the summer of 1963 attracted 250,000 supporters. The speech that some of you may have heard, called the "I Have a Dream" speech, was given there.

Not all blacks thought that non-violence was the way to get more rights. People such as Stokely Carmichael and Malcolm X believed that African Americans could gain more by responding to the attacks and not just letting people hurt them. They also thought that blacks might do better if they worked by themselves without help from whites. These ideas led to some rioting, but also to the growth of the Black Power movement that focused on helping poor people.

Dr. King continued to organize marches. His marchers were often attacked, but this gained them more support. He received the Nobel Peace Prize in 1964, in recognition of his work for racial justice through peaceful means. At this time, he also became involved in protests against the Vietnam War, which shifted some of the work of his organization away from civil rights to anti-war efforts.

Martin Luther King, Jr., also changed some of his goals and began to work on gaining economic equality for blacks. He wanted to use the same non-violent methods on a Poor People's Campaign. He was in Memphis, Tennessee, in April 1968 to support workers striking for better wages when he was assassinated.

His murder shocked the world. In the United States, there were riots in more than one hundred cities. People were angry and frustrated that Martin Luther King, Jr., was gone. Many people felt they had lost their great leader.

The fact that the Congress declared a national holiday for Dr. King tells you that many people believed he was a great man. His ideas of non-violent change made a difference. The civil rights laws that gave voting rights to more African Americans, and the laws that integrated more schools, stores, and transportation were a result of the leadership of the Reverend Dr. Martin Luther King, Jr.

HISTORICAL THINKING AND APPLICATION ACTIVITIES

1. Have students think about cause and effect. Ask, *What happened in Martin Luther King's early life that made him choose to (1) fight for civil rights and (2) use non-violence?*

2. Divide students into two groups. Provide students with encyclopedias or Internet references to find out more information about Martin Luther King, Jr., and Malcolm X. Then create mixed groups where each group has some students who have information about each of the figures. Have students make a Venn diagram about the similarities and differences of the two men. Then ask students to summarize the ways in which the two men agreed and the ways in which they disagreed.

3. Ask students what they thought of Martin Luther King, Jr., when they saw him speaking in the video clips. Use these questions for class discussion: *Would you have joined his cause? What was it that he said or did that would make you want to follow him or not?*

4. Discuss with the class: *Are there still civil rights issues in the United States today? What are they? Are there groups of people working to make changes? Who are they? What are their methods? Would you try to make change in the same way?*

5. Provide students with a copy of Martin Luther King's "I Have a Dream" speech below. Have students listen to the video clip from *Eyes on the Prize* as they read the text.

> *I have a dream that one day this nation will rise up and live out the true meaning of its creed [beliefs]: "We hold these truths to be self-evident, that all men are created equal."*
>
> *... I have a dream that my four little children will one day live in a nation where they will not be judged by the color of their skin, but by the content of their character.*
>
> *... So let freedom ring from the prodigious hilltops of New Hampshire, let freedom ring from the mighty mountains of New York, let freedom ring from the heightening Alleghenies of Pennsylvania, let freedom ring from the snow-capped Rockies of Colorado, let freedom ring from the curvaceous slopes of California. But not only that. Let freedom ring from Stone Mountain of Georgia, let freedom ring from Lookout Mountain of Tennessee, let freedom ring from every hill and molehill of Mississippi. From every mountainside, let freedom ring.*
>
> *And when this happens and when we allow freedom to ring, when we let it ring from every village and every hamlet, from every state and every city, we will be able to speed up that day when all God's children, black men and white men, Jews and Gentiles, Protestants and Catholics, will be able to join hands and sing in the words of the old Negro spiritual: "Free at last. Free at last. Thank God almighty, we are free at last."*

Others Struggle for Equality, pages 103–107

History Objective: Analyze the agendas, strategies, and effectiveness of various groups of people (Hispanic Americans, Native Americans, Asian Americans, women) involved in the civil rights movement.

Language Objectives: Develop academic oral language; scan reading for specific information to write answers to questions; read for comprehension; write about what was learned.

Historical Thinking Objectives: Use visual data from photographs and graphs; gather needed knowledge of time and place; compare and contrast goals and ideas.

Learning Strategy Objectives: Explicit: Identify and practice the previously introduced learning strategy *selective attention* to scan for specific information. **Implicit:** Practice the previously introduced learning strategies *using resources* to find additional information about the topic, and *graphic organizers* to record the main ideas in the reading selection; identify the learning strategies used to understand and recall the information in these readings.

PROCEDURES

Preparation

1. **Before You Read: Using Headings.** Have students work in pairs to look at the photographs and charts on pp. 103–106. Ask them to answer the eight questions on p. 103 in their notebooks. Ask, *What information do the photographs and charts provide? Do they help you answer any of the questions? What evidence do they provide?*
2. See "How to Teach Reading Lessons," p. xi.

Presentation

1. Have students read each section individually, reminding them to use context clues to guess the meanings of new words, and to consult the Glossary or a dictionary only if they cannot make a reasonable guess and if the unknown word is really essential for comprehension.
2. Ask students to stop at the end of each section. Have them talk to their partners to decide on the main ideas in the section. Then ask them to write their ideas in their notebooks under the correct heading.

Practice and Self-Evaluation

1. **Understanding What You Read: Focusing on Your Learning.** Ask students to return to the groups in which they developed the K-W-L-H chart on p. 99. Have them work as a group to answer questions 1–3 on p. 107. Encourage students to use an encyclopedia or the Internet to look for answers to questions that still need to be answered. Ask students to copy the chart at the bottom of the page in their notebooks. Have groups complete the chart with the new information they found.

2. Have students share their K-W-L-H charts with the rest of the class and discuss the strategies they used to finish them. Following discussion, encourage students to make any needed changes in their charts.

HISTORICAL THINKING AND APPLICATION ACTIVITIES

1. Have students formulate a hypothesis about why a particular civil rights group chose to use a certain strategy (e.g., sit-ins). Ask, *Do you think that group might make a different decision today? Why? Why not?*

2. Use these questions to promote class discussion: *If the class wanted to change a policy, what policy would that be? Who would you have to convince to change? What strategy do you think would be the most effective? Why?*

3. Have students work in pairs and choose one civil rights leader or organization to research further using the Internet or book sources. Have students make a brochure or poster about that leader or organization. Then have them take turns sharing what they learned with the class.

AFTER THE NEW FRONTIER PAGES 108–109

End of an Era

History Objectives: Identify prior knowledge about Kennedy's presidency; understand the roles of Presidents Kennedy and Johnson in trying to improve American society.

Language Objectives: Develop academic oral language; write and share ideas; read for comprehension; write a summary of the main ideas in the reading selection.

Historical Thinking Objectives: Identify problems and dilemmas of the past; identify central questions of historical narrative.

Learning Strategy Objectives: Identify and practice the learning strategies *use what you know* to recall prior knowledge about Kennedy; use *summarizing* to write the main ideas in the reading.

PROCEDURES

Preparation

1. See "How to Teach Learning Strategies" on p. x.

2. **Before You Read: Identifying What You Already Know.** Have students read the directions aloud. Ask them what learning strategy they need to use for the discussion (*use what you know*). Ask students to give examples of when they have used this strategy and how it has helped them.

3. Have students work in small groups to discuss what they already know about John F. Kennedy. They should think about what they have heard about President Kennedy's life, his ideas, and his goals. Ask them to write these ideas in their notebooks along with questions they have about President Kennedy.

4. Have students look at the headings, the quotes, and the pictures. Ask them what information they might expect to learn about Presidents Kennedy and Johnson in this reading.

Presentation

1. See "How to Teach Reading Lessons," p. xi.

2. Have students skim the reading to get the main ideas and then reread each section to understand the details.

Practice and Self-Evaluation

1. **Understanding What You Read: Summarizing.** See "How to Teach Learning Strategies" on p. x. Have students explain how the learning strategy *summarizing* helps them understand and remember the main ideas of a reading.

2. Have students work individually to write answers to the four questions on p. 109. Then have them use those answers to write a summary. Remind them that they should use their own words, not copy the words from the reading.

3. Have students work with a partner to compare and contrast their summaries. Did they answer all the questions in their summaries? If they are uncertain about the answers, discuss them as a class. Students should add new information to the summaries in their notebooks.

4. History Mystery. Students may have already read the Martin Luther King, Jr., quote by the time they completed the reading. If not, have someone read the quote to the class. Ask students to think about why Martin Luther King, Jr., would be interested in what President Johnson was doing in Vietnam. (This may also be a good lead-in to the next section in which the Vietnam War is discussed.) As with the other

History Mysteries, have students speculate about the answer. Have them write their ideas in their notebooks. Ask students to respond to the same question again after they have completed pp. 110–112. Ask them to compare this answer with their first guesses. The discussion can include how government dollars are spent; how presidents make policy decisions; and choices that presidents make and their impact on Americans.

HISTORICAL THINKING AND APPLICATION ACTIVITIES

1. Have students choose one of President Kennedy's accomplishments or challenges to research further. Have them write a paper that tells 1. why they were interested in this topic; 2. new or interesting facts they learned about this topic; and 3. how the topic links to events or policies today.
2. Have students work in pairs to research one of the programs enacted under President Johnson's Great Society. The research should be presented as a poster that supports the adoption of the program, highlighting the benefits of the program for people in American society.
3. Discuss with the class: *What program in the Great Society is most beneficial to you and your family? Why do you think so? What programs would you want to pass if you were able to make the laws? Why?*

THE VIETNAM WAR   PAGES 110–112

The United States in Vietnam

History Objectives: Examine the reasons for and conduct of the Vietnam War; learn about the foreign and domestic consequences of the Vietnam War.

Language Objectives: Develop academic oral language; write, check, and revise predictions; read for comprehension; write and answer study questions.

Historical Thinking Objectives: Draw upon data in historical maps; formulate questions to focus inquiry and analysis; read historical narratives.

Learning Strategy Objective: Implicit: Study a map and practice the previously introduced learning strategy *predicting* to answer questions about the Vietnam War.

PROCEDURES

Preparation

1. **Before You Read: Using Maps to Make Predictions.** Working in pairs, have students examine the map and answer the questions. Ask students to write their predictions in their notebooks. While giving students practice making predictions, this activity will also help them enhance their map skills and review what they know about the regions of the world (question 4) and their locations relative to other nations (questions 1–3). It will be helpful for students to refer to a world map to locate this region of the world.
2. Have students share their answers with the class and make necessary corrections or add information. Discuss question 6 with students and ask them to share their ideas.

Presentation

1. See "How to Teach Reading Lessons," p. xi.
2. Have students work in small groups to develop a plan for reading, understanding, and remembering the information in the reading selection. Have students discuss the learning strategies that they will use as they approach this selection, how they will deal with unfamiliar words, and how they will check to make sure that they have understood the selection. Ask each group to develop a brief written study plan based on the discussion.
3. Have students read the selection individually, following the study plan developed by their group.
4. Have students work in the same groups to discuss how successful the study plan was in helping them understand the reading selection. Have them check each other's recall of the important information presented, either by asking questions or giving oral summaries of important points.
5. Discuss the value of developing individual reading plans to study content.

Practice

Understanding What You Read: Checking Predictions. Have students work with the same classmates that they worked with to make predictions before reading. Ask them to talk about their predictions to see if they were correct and to correct them, if necessary. If the information was not in the reading, have students check the school library or the Internet to find the information.

Self-Evaluation

1. **Understanding What You Read: Writing and Working with Study Questions.** Ask students to work in pairs to develop study questions. You may want to review the directions on p. 112, reminding students to put their questions on a separate sheet of paper from the answers they create. Students will create both questions and answers, and respond to the answers of others.
2. Discuss with the class: *What questions were most difficult? Why? Which questions were easiest? Why? Were there strategies that you used to find answers? Remember answers?*

HISTORICAL THINKING AND APPLICATION ACTIVITIES

1. Find a National Geographic video on Vietnam so students may visualize the climate and terrain there. (If you have a student who has lived or traveled in a tropical region, he or she can expand on class knowledge of the landscape and weather in the region.) Ask students how weather and terrain might affect the war. Ask who would be advantaged by this weather and terrain, and why.
2. Have students interview family members or community members who fought in Vietnam or protested the war. Have students identify the perspective of the speaker and brainstorm a list of different perspectives that people could have had regarding a war.
3. The time line in the Unit Opener indicates that the Vietnam War began in 1959 and ended in 1975. Have students create a time line of the Vietnam War to help them think chronologically about the war. They may need to check an (Internet) encyclopedia to find some of the information. Have them answer these questions: *How long was the United States in Vietnam? When did protests start? Why did the United States leave Vietnam?*

THE ENVIRONMENTAL MOVEMENT — PAGES 113–114

Protecting the Environment

> **History Objectives:** Learn about the environmental movement; examine the importance of music in the protest movements.
>
> **Language Objectives:** Develop academic vocabulary; read for comprehension; write and edit a short essay; discuss, interpret, and write ideas about song lyrics.
>
> **Historical Thinking Objectives:** Identify problems and dilemmas in the past; formulate historical questions; use visual data.
>
> **Learning Strategy Objective: Implicit:** Use the previously introduced learning strategy *making inferences* to use context to guess word meanings.

PROCEDURES

Preparation

1. **Before you Read: Using Context.** Have students work individually or in pairs to look at the vocabulary words on p. 113, then scan the reading selection to find them and guess their meanings from context (*making inferences*).
2. Have students work cooperatively to develop definitions for the new words. Then ask them to check their definitions in the Glossary. Have students look at the poster in the photograph on p. 113. Ask, *What does the poster say? How does it make you feel? What does the poster tell you about the environment? How do you think the artist felt about the environment?*

Presentation

1. See "How to Teach Reading Lessons," p. xi.
2. Have students skim the reading to get the main ideas. Have students work in pairs to take turns reading p. 113 aloud and writing down the main ideas.

Practice and Self-Evaluation

1. **Understanding What You Read: What Do You Think?** Have students work with the same partner to answer

the questions on p. 114. Have students write their paragraphs individually in their notebooks.

2. Lead a class discussion about students' ideas about pollution.

Expansion

1. <u>Understanding Songs of Protest.</u> This era, more than many others, is noted for the use of music to express feelings about issues of importance to large numbers of people. The activity can best be done in groups of three or four students. If possible, play the music to add more richness to the activity. Lyrics and recordings of many protest songs of the 1960s are available on the Internet.

2. Have students read the lyrics to one another before answering the questions.

3. Ask groups to share their responses with the whole class.

HISTORICAL THINKING AND APPLICATION ACTIVITIES

1. Discuss why the environmental movement occurred at the same time as the Vietnam War and civil rights movement. Compare and contrast the methods, message, and results of this movement with other civil rights movements.

2. Have students draw a poster using two words of their choice from the vocabulary list on p. 113.

3. Have students think about the form of pollution that is most threatening to their community today. Use these questions for class discussion: *Are there any groups who have organized to address this issue? Are there things that you could do to help?*

4. Have students brainstorm a list of current songs of protest. Ask, *What is the song protesting? How does it make you feel?* Have students share the song, lyrics, and analysis with the class.

5. Have students think about what other art forms can be used as a means of protest (dance, plays, movies). Have them find another example of art as protest from the1960s forward. Ask them to share it with the class.

DEVELOPING REPORTS	PAGES 115–117

Leaders of Change

History Objective: Research to learn more about the lives of important leaders of the civil rights era.

Language Objectives: Develop academic vocabulary and oral language; research and take notes; use the writing process to develop and present a research report; listen to classmates' oral reports.

Historical Thinking Objectives: Formulate historical questions; gather needed knowledge of time and place to construct a story.

Learning Strategy Objectives: Identify and practice the previously introduced learning strategy *using resources* by using reference materials and the Internet to conduct research; identify and practice the learning strategy *cooperation* to work with a classmate on revising a research report.

PROCEDURES

Preparation and Presentation

1. See "How to Teach Writing Lessons," p. xiii.

2. Work with students to select the individual they will research. Any individual they choose should be from the 1960s and 1970s and should have been involved in the civil rights movements. Work with the school librarian to collect resources for student use.

3. See "How to Teach Learning Strategies" on p. x. Remind students that the strategy *using resources* is used whenever we look for additional information on a topic.

4. **Researching: Finding the Information You Need.** Review note-taking techniques and have students take notes on their chosen leader. They should take notes on the information listed on p. 115. Remind students that when they are taking notes on index cards, they must write the name of the author, the title of the book or article, and the date of publication in parentheses when they use a direct quote.

Practice

1. **Writing a First Draft: Putting the Information Together.** Have students organize and plan their compositions by deciding on the structure (such as an introduction, a body, and a conclusion), and the sequence of ideas to be presented. Then have them identify vocabulary, possible language markers, and any other language information that they will need in the composition.

2. Students should ask the teacher or other native English speakers to provide new words and expressions as needed.

3. Have students write the first draft of their compositions. Have them focus on expressing meaning rather than on correctness at this point, as they will have opportunities to edit for spelling, punctuation, and grammar later.

Self-Evaluation

1. **Revising: Checking the Information in the Report.** Have students work in pairs with a classmate to exchange compositions and critique them. The writer should have a short list of questions to ask the reader for self-evaluation purposes. Sample questions might include the following: *Do you understand the story? Are the ideas in the right order? Which parts could be improved? Are there any errors in spelling, grammar, or punctuation?*

2. **Editing: Checking Spelling, Punctuation, and Grammar.** Have students revise their compositions one or more times, incorporating their classmate's suggestions, if appropriate, and their own new ideas and/or corrections. The final draft should be written on a separate sheet of paper.

3. See "How to Teach Learning Strategies" on p. x. Ask students to identify the learning strategy they were using as they gave and received feedback on their reports (*cooperation*). Ask them to describe other ways in which they use this learning strategy.

Practice and Self-Evaluation

1. **Presenting an Oral Report.** Have students work in small groups and read their compositions to each other. Have students take notes in their notebooks as they listen to each others' compositions.

2. Then ask students to write three important things they learned from each report.

Expansion

1. Have students work in pairs to select one of the reports on which they took notes and create a graphic organizer showing the main ideas.

2. Have partners take turns sharing their graphic organizers with the rest of the group.

HISTORICAL THINKING AND APPLICATION ACTIVITIES

1. Have students work in groups to compare their stories and identify similarities and differences

between leaders in methods they used, how they organized, their experiences, and the outcomes of their efforts. Then have students summarize these similarities and differences for the class.

2. Have students interview a family member or community member who was in the United States in the 1960s and 1970s. Have them find answers to these questions: *What do they remember about this era of protest in the United States? Were they involved in any protests? Why? Why not?*

3. Ask students, *What protests have you heard about? Would you get involved? Why? Why not?*

THE POST-JOHNSON ERA | PAGES 118–119

Presidents Nixon, Ford, and Carter

> **History Objective:** Examine domestic and foreign policies from Presidents Nixon to Carter.
>
> **Language Objectives:** Develop academic vocabulary; read for comprehension; write main ideas on a chart.
>
> **Historical Thinking Objectives:** Compare and contrast sets of ideas and values; build historical comprehension.
>
> **Learning Strategy Objectives: Implicit:** Practice the previously introduced learning strategies *predicting* to predict content from section headings, *making inferences* to use context to guess word meanings, *selective attention* to identify main ideas for each president, *graphic organizers* to show the main ideas, and *summarizing* to write the main ideas in students' own words.

PROCEDURES

Preparation

1. See "How to Teach Vocabulary Lessons," p. x.

2. **Before You Read: Vocabulary.** Have students write the list of words on p. 118 in their notebooks. Ask them to work in pairs to discuss the meanings of the each word and to determine which words (if any) have cognates in their native languages. Then have students write the definition next to each word. Have them check the accuracy of their understanding by looking up the new words in the Glossary.

Presentation

1. See "How to Teach Reading Lessons," p. xi.
2. Have students look at the headings in the reading selection and speculate about the type of information that will be contained in each section (*predicting*).
3. Have students read the selection individually, reminding them to use context clues to guess the meanings of new words (*making inferences*), and to consult the Glossary or a dictionary only if they cannot make a reasonable guess and if the unknown word is really essential for comprehension.

Practice

1. **Understanding What You Read: Developing a Study Chart.** Have students work in pairs to complete the chart on p. 119. They should first copy the blank chart in their notebooks.
2. Have students reread pp. 118–119 in pairs to identify the main ideas for each president (*selective attention*). Then have them write the main ideas in the appropriate boxes in their chart (*graphic organizers*).
3. When they have filled in the information about each president, ask students to individually write a paragraph summary of each president in their own words (*summarizing*).

HISTORICAL THINKING AND APPLICATION ACTIVITIES

1. Work with students to brainstorm a list of words that come to mind when they think of President Nixon. Record the words on chart paper or on an overhead transparency. Have students work in pairs to construct a web that connects the words. Alternatively, you may ask students to use the words from the vocabulary list to create a story of the Nixon to Carter years.
2. Have students interview people who were alive at the time of the Watergate scandal. Ask them to find answers to these questions: *What do they know about Watergate? How did they feel about it? Did it change their confidence in the government? How have their opinions about the U.S. government changed in the last thirty years? Why?*
3. Discuss: *Which issue addressed in the presidencies of Nixon, Ford, and Carter do you believe is the most important? The least important? Why? Were these issues resolved or have other presidents had to address them as well?*

Five Presidents: 1960–1980

History Objective: Examine the events of five presidencies.

Language Objectives: Comprehend information in a time line; develop academic oral language; research for additional information; make an oral presentation to the class.

Historical Thinking Objectives: Use time lines; create time lines.

Learning Strategy Objectives: Implicit: Practice the learning strategies *classifying* and *using imagery* to understand a time line; apply the strategies *using resources, taking notes,* and *graphic organizers* to find additional information about one president and use it to create a detailed time line.

PROCEDURES

Preparation and Presentation

1. Remind students that time lines are a visual way of describing the sequence of past events. This time line covers a twenty-year period in which there were five different presidents in the United States. Show students how the events are grouped together next to each presidency, and remind them that grouping events and facts makes them easier to remember (*classifying*).
2. Ask students to keep an image of the time line in mind as they skim through the information on pp. 120–121 to get a general idea of the main facts (*using imagery*). Have students ask questions for clarification of any words they do not understand.

Practice and Expansion

1. **Understanding What You Read: Constructing a Time Line.** Have students work in small groups to review the time line and then select one of the presidents. Ask each group to follow the directions on p. 121 as they construct their presidential time lines (*using resources, taking notes,* and *graphic organizers*). Have groups make their time lines on chart paper.

2. Have students present their group's time line and also listen to the time line presentations of the other groups. Ask them to take notes about the other presidencies.

HISTORICAL THINKING AND APPLICATION ACTIVITIES

1. Have students look at all of the time lines together. Discuss what events, policies, and problems are the same in more than one presidency. Ask students why that might be the case. This provides an opportunity to talk about continuity and change in history.

2. Have students add graphics to their time lines. They can use magazines, newspapers, the Internet, or clip art. Be sure to have them properly credit sources with a caption.

UNIT 5

The American Identity: 1980 to the Present

UNIT OPENER | PAGES 122–123

History Objective: Identify prior knowledge about people and events from 1980 to the present.

Language Objectives: Develop academic oral language; write ideas in notebook.

Historical Thinking Objectives: Use visual data; interpret data in time lines.

Learning Strategy Objectives: Implicit: Use prior knowledge (*tell what you know*) and images (*using imagery*) to speculate about events in the time period from 1980 to the present.

PROCEDURES

1. See "How to Use the Unit Openers," page ix.

2. **Tell what you think.** Have students look at and describe the photographs on the opening pages. Elicit any prior knowledge they have about the images in the photos. Ask them to identify the learning strategies they are using (*tell what you know* and *using imagery*).

3. Have pairs of students study the images on the opening pages and the items on the time line and answer the first question in the "Tell what you think" activity: *What do you know about the events pictured here?* Have students write their ideas in their notebooks. Then ask students to share their ideas with the class.

4. Still in pairs, have students answer the second question by making a list of events. Have them share their lists with the class. You may want to compile the different lists of events so students can use them as topics for further research.

HISTORICAL THINKING AND APPLICATION ACTIVITIES

1. Ask students to talk about how the images might help explain the title of this unit.

2. Have students look at the events listed on the time line. Ask them to make a web that shows how they think these events might be connected to each other and to the images on the opening pages. Ask them to copy their web in their notebooks and check it as they learn about events in the unit.

3. Have students interview family members or community members about events that they considered important in the period from 1980 to the present. Have students share what they found with the class and expand or confirm the list the class created.

CHANGES INSIDE THE UNITED STATES | PAGES 124–125

Jobs Change; People Move

History Objectives: Learn how economic changes affect the movement of people; examine the consequences of the shift of the labor force from manufacturing to service industries; explore the continuing population flow from cities to suburbs and from "rustbelt" to "sunbelt," and their social and political effects.

Language Objectives: Develop academic oral language; write and share prior knowledge; read for comprehension; develop academic content vocabulary related to changing demographics.

Historical Thinking Objectives: Build historical comprehension; read historical narratives; use graphs and images to develop meaning.

Learning Strategy Objectives: Identify and practice the previously introduced learning strategies *use what you know* to recall prior knowledge about the causes of the movement of people from one part of the country to another, and *making inferences* to figure out the meanings of new words from context.

PROCEDURES

Preparation

1. **Before You Read: Identifying What You Already Know.** Have students identify the learning strategy they will be using to answer the two questions on p. 124 (*use what you know*).
2. Have students work in pairs to answer the two questions about moving. Not only do these questions allow students to think back over U.S. history, but they can also allow the teacher to talk about the push/pull features of migration. Ask, *What are the factors that encourage people to move to a particular place* (pull: jobs, climate, freedom) *as opposed to those factors that encourage them to leave* (push: war, lack of freedom, poverty)?
3. Have partners share their ideas with the class.

Presentation

1. See "How to Teach Reading Lessons," p. xi.
2. Preview and discuss the title of the reading, "Jobs Change; People Move." Have students individually write down in their notebooks how the two parts of the title are related.
3. Have students read pp. 124–125 individually or as a paired reading in which they take turns reading a section aloud and discussing it with their partner.

Practice

1. Have students discuss the graph (p. 124) and the image (p. 125). Ask, *What information do these two images provide to help better understand the movement of people?*
2. See "How to Teach Vocabulary Lessons" and "How to Teach Learning Strategies" on p. x.
3. **Understanding What You Read: Using Context.** Have students work in pairs to study the words in the word

bank. Remind students that they are using the learning strategy *making inferences* as they develop word meaning based on what they just read.
4. Have students look up each new word in the Glossary and read the definition. Then have them write the word and definition in their own words in their notebooks.
5. Finally, have students define orally any other words that were not identified as new words.

Expansion

1. **After You Read: Finding Out More Information.** Ask students in groups of three or four to respond to the questions in this exercise. Bring in recent newspapers for students to examine to help them answer the questions.
2. Ask groups to create a chart of high- and low-skill jobs, and the skills or education that are needed for each. Then have them share their charts with the class.

HISTORICAL THINKING AND APPLICATION ACTIVITIES

1. Ask students to look back at their notes on why people move. In pairs, ask them to create a chart that categorizes the factors by "Push" (reasons to leave a place) and "Pull" (reasons to move to another place). Students can ask family members or community members if they have moved in the past five years and why they moved. Have them add any new information to their charts and share it with the class.
2. Examine the public transportation system in your city or town. Ask students, *How do people get to and from work? School? Stores? Would a different system make it easier for people to move around the city or town? What changes would a different system of transportation make for the community?*

| U.S. SCHOOLS | PAGES 126–127 |

Schools Meet America's Changing Needs

History Objectives: Examine the role of schools and schooling in the twentieth century; find out about local and state governments' roles and responsibilities to citizens.

Language Objectives: Develop academic oral language; write answers to questions about the students' own school; read for comprehension; interview school personnel; report to the class.

Historical Thinking Objectives: Explain continuity and change over time; use images; develop research capabilities.

Learning Strategy Objectives: Explicit: Identify the learning strategies used to find out about the state government (*using resources*), and to create a poster that illustrates how the state government functions (*graphic organizers*). **Implicit:** Practice the previously introduced learning strategy *use what you know* to recall prior knowledge about the students' own school.

PROCEDURES

Preparation

1. **Before you Read: Identifying What You Already Know.** Working in pairs, have students discuss their own schools and answer the four questions on p. 126.
2. Have students record the answers to the questions in their notebooks. This may also be a good time to invite a senior member of the school staff to talk to students about the history of their school or school system.

Presentation

1. See "How to Teach Reading Lessons," p. xi. Have students read the selection on p. 126 silently or share the reading with a classmate.
2. After they have read the selection, ask students if they think there should be changes in the curriculum or facilities at their school. Ask students to write their conclusions in their notebooks, and then share them with the class.

Practice

1. **Understanding What You Read: Investigating Your Own School.** Remind students of the learning strategy they will use to investigate their school (*using resources*).
2. Have students work in groups of three to five, dividing up the questions on p. 126 and searching for the answers. Students may benefit by brainstorming other ways they might find the answers. Have them consider the following: *Who is the person to ask? What books might have the answers? Is there a website?*

3. Have each group share its report with the class, allowing students to change or add information. Students should also share the sources of their information.

Expansion

1. <u>Find Out about Your State's Government.</u> Working in groups, have students find the basic information about their own state's government. Work with the librarian to provide students with books and websites or tourism materials that will provide them with the information.
2. Have students use the information to create a poster that shows how their state's government works. Groups can take turns sharing their posters with the class. Ask them to add any information that was missing from their posters.
3. Review learning strategies, asking students which ones they used to research and to create posters (*using resources, graphic organizers*).
4. <u>History Mystery.</u> This is a complex quote because it assumes knowledge about democracy. However, it also provides an opportunity to review what students know about the U.S. government. Students may begin to decipher the meaning of the History Mystery quote by working as a class to define *democracy*. The discussion can then be tied back to the way state and local governments are organized. Students may also think about other forms of government, such as dictatorship, monarchy, and parliamentary. Encourage students to write what they think Churchill meant and hand it in without sharing it with the class. Use students' responses to guide a discussion about why Churchill might have said what he did about democracy. The following is one possible answer: Because so many people have a say, the system is not "neat," but it is more effective in hearing many voices and pleasing more people.

HISTORICAL THINKING AND APPLICATION ACTIVITIES

1. Ask students to brainstorm a list of the jobs in their school. Help them make a chart of the jobs, and the roles and responsibilities of each job. Then have students make a video about the school by interviewing the people who do the different jobs in the school.

2. Encourage students to make a poster that illustrates the history of their school. Have them share it with the rest of the school.

3. Have students form small groups, each with one student who has lived in another state. Ask each group to answer the same questions about the second state. Have them create a poster, similar in format to the one of their own state, and share the information with the class. Then have the whole class compare the states. Ask, *How are their governments similar? In what ways are their governments different?*

4. Extend the History Mystery to a comparative government chart activity, especially if there are students in the class who have experienced other forms of government.

HOW GOVERNMENT IS CHANGING   PAGE 128

The Sánchez Sisters

History Objectives: Develop an understanding of the changing role of women in U.S. politics; understand how individuals can participate as citizens.

Language Objectives: Listen for comprehension, recognizing the main ideas and details; develop academic oral language; write notes and summaries.

Historical Thinking Objectives: Identify the central questions of a historical narrative; compare different stories of historical figures, eras, and events.

Learning Strategy Objectives: Explicit: Identify and practice using the previously introduced learning strategies *selective attention* together with *taking notes* to understand and remember new information. **Implicit:** Use *cooperation* with classmates to share and complete notes.

LISTENING AND TAKING NOTES

PROCEDURES

Preparation

1. See "How to Teach Learning Strategies" on p. x. Remind students how to use the learning strategies *selective attention* and *taking notes* before they listen to the story of the Sánchez sisters.

2. Ask students to share with the class what works best for them in deciding on the main ideas.

3. Give students time to copy the T-list in their notebooks.

Presentation and Practice

1. See "How to Teach Listening Comprehension Lessons," p. xi.

2. Remind students that there is organization to the listening mini-lectures. Ask students how they will use the T-list to record information.

3. Write this paragraph on the board or on an overhead transparency and ask students to indicate which words can be erased without losing the meaning, and which words can be abbreviated:

The older sister, Loretta, earned a bachelor's degree in economics in 1982 and a master's degree in business administration (MBA) in 1984. Her jobs for the next ten years combined the two areas of business and economics—advising companies and towns about financial issues. She was elected to Congress in 1994 from the 47th Congressional District serving southern California (Orange County). She was reelected for her fourth two-year term in 2002.

As students indicate which words are less important, erase them. Write abbreviations to replace any words that can be abbreviated. Ask students to reconstruct the passage from the words remaining.

4. Read aloud the text on the Sánchez sisters and have students fill in the missing information in the blanks on the T-list in their notebooks.

Self-Evaluation

1. Have students work in small groups to compare and complete their notes.

2. Have students individually write short summaries of the important points about Loretta and Linda Sánchez in their own words, using their completed T-lists as a guide.

Listening Text for "The Sánchez Sisters"

Election night, November 5, 2002, brought special excitement to California, and especially to one family. The Sánchez family of Orange County declared victory—twice! For the first time in U.S. history, two sisters were elected to the House of Representatives. They are Loretta Sánchez, reelected to her fourth term, and Linda Sánchez, elected for her first term. When did they become interested in politics? Why did they run for office? What were their lives like before they ran for office, and how did things change after they were elected? What do they hope to do in Congress?

To explain a bit about their backgrounds, Loretta Sánchez was the second, and Linda the sixth, of seven children of immigrants from Mexico. All seven of the children attended college, because their parents wanted their children to take advantage of the chances they had not had when they grew up.

The older sister, Loretta, earned a bachelor's degree in economics in 1982 and a master's degree in business administration (MBA) in 1984. Her jobs for the next ten years combined the two areas of business and economics—advising companies and towns about financial issues. She was elected to Congress in 1994 from the 47th Congressional District serving southern California (Orange County). She was reelected for her fourth two-year term in 2002.

In Congress, Loretta Sánchez has been most interested in laws that have to do with education, crime reduction, economic development, and security. Two words used by others to describe Loretta are *accessible* and *collaborative.* She serves on a number of committees (the House Armed Services Committee, the Select Committee for Security, and the Committee on Education and the Workforce), and she likes to work with others to benefit those voters in her district.

She and her family have lived in Orange County, California, all of her life. She is married and travels home from Washington, DC, to California almost every weekend to spend time with her husband and to take part in community events and listen to those people she represents.

The younger sister, Linda, received a law degree from UCLA in 1995 after completing a B.A. in Spanish literature with an emphasis on bilingual education. She was a civil rights lawyer and a labor activist before she ran for Congress. Her first term as a congresswoman began on January 7, 2003. As you might guess, Linda is interested in working in Congress on laws that focus on education, health care, public safety, and the economy. She also is married, and she returns often to her home in Lakewood, California, to visit her family, and to keep in touch with those Californians she represents.

Both sisters are thrilled to be in Congress. They campaigned on the same core issues—education, health, and the economy, including jobs—in their districts. When Congress is in session, Loretta and Linda are both in Washington, DC. After some searching, they bought a house on Capitol Hill that they share. They looked for a while to find a house that they both liked. It had to be close enough to their offices and to the Capitol so that they could get there in fifteen minutes if they needed to cast a vote on a law before the House of Representatives.

The Sánchez sisters entered politics because they believed they could help people, especially people like their parents, who are working to achieve success. In response to a question about what someone can do to make things better, Loretta replied that everyone can do something—whether it be voting, getting others to vote, or, as she did, running for Congress. Linda added, "We were brought up with the same values, in a household where 'working-people issues' were important." And in response to a reporter's question, Linda said, "Everything is always better for me when I share successes, or even failures, with my family. I think it is good to come home to somebody who understands how difficult it can be to do the work here in Washington, and can appreciate the mini-victories or help with the mini-failures." Both Linda and Loretta continue to work hard at a job they believe will help others.

You can find out more about the Sánchez sisters and the kinds of things they do in Congress by visiting their Websites:

http://www.house.gov/sanchez/aboutloretta.html

http://www.house.gov/lindasanchez/about_linda.shtml

HISTORICAL THINKING AND APPLICATION ACTIVITIES

1. Building on the previous study of state governments, ask students to examine the history of one of the representatives from their state. If students are in the District of Columbia, have them examine the life of the "shadow" representative. Tell students that all representatives and senators have Websites. You can

direct students to the Website of their representative, found on www.house.gov. They can scroll down the list to find the appropriate person. If they research a senator, then the Websites are listed on www.senate.gov. Have students report their findings to the class.

2. Invite a local councilperson or city or state official to visit the class and talk to students about his or her job, why he or she chose to run for office, what he or she hopes to do, and what he or she thinks are the most important issues to be decided.

ENVIRONMENTAL ISSUES — PAGES 129–130

Environmental Concerns Increase

History Objective: Understand how a democratic society debates social issues and mediates between individual and group rights and the common good.

Language Objectives: Develop academic oral language; write ideas; read for comprehension; summarize graphically.

Historical Thinking Objectives: Compare and contrast goals and ideas; identify the causes of a problem or dilemma; gather data to formulate a position or course of action.

Learning Strategy Objectives: Implicit: Practice the previously introduced learning strategies *tell what you know* and *predicting* to reflect on hypothetical questions and draw conclusions, *making inferences* to figure out word meanings from context, and *selective attention* and *graphic organizers* to summarize the main ideas on a chart or poster.

PROCEDURES

Preparation

1. **Before You Read: Think about It.** Have students work in pairs to discuss a hypothetical situation. Ask students what learning strategy or strategies will be useful in deciding on an answer to this type of question (*tell what you know* and *predicting*). Ask students to share their ideas with the class. Ask, *Why did you decide on the answer you did? What prior knowledge were you using?*

2. Have each pair write their ideas in their notebooks, then share them with the class.

Presentation

1. See "How to Teach Reading Lessons," p. xi.
2. Have students read each section individually, reminding them to use context clues to guess the meanings of new words (*making inferences*), and to consult the Glossary or a dictionary only if they cannot make a reasonable guess and if the unknown word is really essential for comprehension.
3. Ask students to stop at the end of each section and talk to a partner about the main ideas in that section. Have them write their ideas in their notebooks under the correct heading.

Practice and Self-Evaluation

1. **Understanding What You Read: Environmental Issues in Your Community.** Ask students to work in pairs to develop a graphic organizer or illustrated poster from the notes they took on each section as they read.
2. Have students share their graphic organizers or posters with the rest of the class and discuss the strategies they used to complete them (*selective attention* and *graphic organizers*). Then have students make any needed changes to their work.
3. Ask students to brainstorm ideas about what they think are important environmental issues in their community. Once they have a list of issues, ask students to decide what they think are the top two or three issues. Ask, *Why did you select these items?*

Expansion

1. Have students explore recent newspapers, the library, and the Internet to get information about the views of others, such as environmentalists and businesses, on these issues.
2. Ask students to work together to make another graphic organizer or illustrated poster that shows the most important environmental issues in their community. Remind them to include information about how environmentalists and businesses are addressing these issues.
3. Finally, have students work in groups to make an action plan. Ask them to write down at least three things they can do to help their own environment. Have students share their ideas.

HISTORICAL THINKING AND APPLICATION ACTIVITIES

1. Have students act on class decisions about environmental issues in their communities.

2. Have students research Earth Day on the Internet. Ask them to make their own Earth Day posters for the next Earth Day.

3. Have students research the *Clean Air Act* or other environmental legislation. Ask, *How long has the Act been in effect? What has it done to make the air cleaner? Has the law changed since it was first passed?*

4. Create a class definition of "global warming." Discuss the following question: *Do you believe that global warming will have any influence on your life?*

MODERN TECHNOLOGY   PAGES 131–133

Inventions Change Our Lives Again

> **History Objective:** Explore how scientific advances and technological changes, such as robotics and the computer revolution, affect the economy, the nature of work, and the lives of people in the United States.
>
> **Language Objectives:** Read for comprehension and specific information; write answers to questions; develop a report on an invention and present it to the class.
>
> **Historical Thinking Objectives:** Use visual data; gather knowledge of time and place to construct a story, explanation, or narrative.
>
> **Learning Strategy Objectives: Explicit:** Practice the previously introduced learning strategy *selective attention* to scan for specific information. **Implicit:** Practice the previously introduced learning strategy *using resources* to find additional information about an invention.

PROCEDURES

Preparation

1. Have students look at the images on pp. 131–133. Use these questions to promote class discussion: *What do you already know about the items pictured there? Have you ever seen these items? When? Where? Is there more than one use for any of the items pictured?*

2. See "How to Teach Reading Lessons," p. xi.

3. **Before You Read: Looking for Specific Information.** Ask students to copy the chart in their notebooks. Provide one example of how the chart can be completed, for example, write *hybrid car* in the "Travel" column. Then model how to answer the questions regarding the hybrid car.

Presentation and Practice

1. Now ask students to work in pairs, taking turns reading each section. Have them pause after reading each section to fill in the appropriate portion of the chart for questions 1, 2, and 3. Encourage them to look back at the other units for additional information.

2. After they have finished the reading, have them talk about questions 4 and 5, and use their ideas to complete the chart.

3. Have students work in small groups to compare and contrast their answers. If they are uncertain about the answers, discuss them as a class.

Expansion

1. **Understanding What You Read: Finding More Information.** Have students work individually to research one of the inventions on pp. 131–133. They may use an encyclopedia or the Internet. The four questions on p. 133 will provide the outline for the report. Have students refer to the guidelines on pp. 88–89 to help them develop and present their reports.

2. Have students read their reports to the class. Classmates should take notes on the information presented.

HISTORICAL THINKING AND APPLICATION ACTIVITIES

1. Ask students to think about how some inventions could not have happened without other inventions coming first, e.g., *How could you have a space shuttle without computers?* Have students work in small groups to create a graphic organizer, such as a web, that explains how the new inventions on pp. 131–133 are related to each other.

2. Invite a community expert to your class to demonstrate how the Global Positioning System works. It is used extensively in geography for setting boundaries and for exploring locations.

3. Have students explore the U.S. Patent Office website (www.uspto.gov). When searching the website, remind students that they will need to identify items by a specific name, e.g., *Edison phonograph*, not just *phonograph*, because so many items will be listed. Ask them to find an invention that they think might be the "wave of the future," and share it with the class. Have students explain why they think the invention will be important in the future.

Information Explosion

> **History Objectives:** Examine the influence of the media on contemporary American culture; explore the international influence of American culture.
>
> **Language Objectives:** Develop academic oral language; read for comprehension; write a brief report evaluating the accuracy of different media.
>
> **Historical Thinking Objectives:** Use data on graphs; obtain historical data; interrogate data; formulate a position.
>
> **Learning Strategy Objectives: Implicit:** Practice the previously introduced learning strategies *use what you know* to conduct a survey of the class, and *graphic organizers* to interpret two graphs; select the learning strategies needed for a study plan.

PROCEDURES

Preparation

1. **Before You Read: Identifying What You Already Know.** Remind students about the way the words *media* and *medium* are used when we talk about television, radio, etc. Working with two or three classmates, have students complete the activity on p. 134. Ask each student to make a copy of the chart in his or her notebook. Have them begin by gathering the data about themselves (*use what you know*). Go over the example, so students have a clear idea about how to proceed to gather the needed information.
2. Have students in each group share and compile their individual information. Then work with students to add together the information from all the groups to make a class chart on chart paper or on an overhead transparency.
3. Have students add the class information to their charts, using a different color pen/marker, or put class data in parentheses.
4. Ask students what conclusions they can draw from the class data. Where do students get most of their information? What kinds of information predominate? Do they gather any information about current events? If so, from which medium?

5. Ask students how they might describe the class use of the media. Have students copy the class conclusions in their notebooks.

Presentation and Self-Evaluation

1. See "How to Teach Reading Lessons," p. xi.
2. Have students work in small groups to develop a plan for reading, understanding, and remembering the information in the reading selection. Students should discuss the learning strategies that they will use as they approach this selection, how they will deal with unfamiliar words, and how they will check to make sure that they have understood. Each group should develop a brief written study plan based on the discussion.
3. Have students read the selection "Information Explosion" individually, following the study plan developed by their group.
4. Have students work in the same groups to discuss how successful the study plan was in helping them understand the reading selection. Have them check each other's recall of the important information presented, either by asking questions or giving oral summaries of important points. Ask students to summarize the information under each heading.
5. Discuss the value of developing individual reading plans to study content.

Expansion and Practice

1. **Understanding What You Read: Evaluating Information Sources.** Using the same media categories, assign a medium to each group of three or four students. Ask them to choose two samples from the medium area, e.g., two television shows, two days' newspapers, or two magazines. Have students work with their groups to answer the questions in this exercise. Ask each individual in the group to write down the responses of all group members. Then have groups present their conclusions to the class.
2. After all groups have reported their conclusions, ask the class to consider which medium they believe presents the most accurate information about the United States. Ask students why they think so.
3. **Understanding What You Read: Using Graphs.** Have students work in pairs to study the graphs on p. 135, and to answer the questions at the bottom of p. 135 (*graphic organizers*). Have pairs share their responses with the class. Ask, *What information do the graphs provide that add to the information you read in the reading selection? Could that information be presented in another way? In what other way could it be presented? Which way is more effective in helping you understand the topic?*

Historical Thinking and Application Activities

1. Have students interview family members or community members to find out how they got information when they were children. If the person interviewed grew up outside of the United States, have students find out if that person had the same access to information as people who grew up in the United States. Ask students to find out why there might be a difference. If the person interviewed grew up outside of the United States, have students find out where that person got information about the United States.

2. Consult the librarian at your school to find out if the library has old newspapers or recordings of early radio shows. Consult a video store to see if they have early television news shows. Have students listen or watch these shows and analyze them for the message they provide about the United States. Ask, *Is it different from the message today? How?*

| **PRESIDENTS OF THE UNITED STATES** | **PAGES 136–140** |

Four Recent Presidents

History Objective: Examine domestic and foreign policies from Ronald Reagan to George W. Bush.

Language Objectives: Develop academic vocabulary; write sentences; read for comprehension; write and answer study questions; analyze and discuss political cartoons.

Historical Thinking Objectives: Identify problems and dilemmas in the past; compare and contrast sets of ideas and values; interrogate historical data; use visual data from cartoons.

Learning Strategy Objectives: Implicit: Practice the previously introduced learning strategies *making inferences* to determine the meaning of new words by using context clues, and *summarizing* to write the main ideas in the reading.

Procedures

Preparation

1. See "How to Teach Vocabulary Lessons," p. x.

2. **Before You Read: Vocabulary.** Have students copy the list of vocabulary words into their notebooks. Then have students work in pairs to discuss the meaning of each word. Have them determine which (if any) have cognates in their native languages, and then write the correct definition next to each word. Have students check the accuracy of their understanding by looking up the new words in the Glossary or in a monolingual dictionary.

Presentation

1. See "How to Teach Reading Lessons," p. xi.

2. Read the three introductory paragraphs of this reading selection (p. 136) as a class. Discuss what kinds of information students can expect to learn about each president, e.g., how one president's policies influenced the next president, and what decisions each president made in domestic and foreign policy. Make sure students can distinguish between foreign and domestic decisions, and understand how the two relate.

3. Have students create a chart in their notebooks with the following columns: "Domestic Policy," "Foreign Policy," and "Other Information."

4. Have students read one section of the reading selection at a time individually. Remind them to use context clues to guess the meanings of new words (*making inferences*), and to consult the Glossary or a dictionary only if they cannot make a reasonable guess and if the unknown word is really essential for comprehension.

5. Ask students to study the pictures and quotes on pp. 137–138. Ask them what other information the pictures and quotes provides.

Practice

1. Have students consult with a classmate to decide on several sentences to summarize the domestic and foreign policy decisions of each president (*summarizing*).

2. Have students share the information with the class.

3. **Understanding What You Read: Study Questions.** Working in pairs, ask students to review their notes on the reading and write two questions about each president. At least one question should be a *why* question. Now have students work in groups of four or five and take turns asking others in the group their questions.

4. Have each group share its most difficult questions. Discuss the answers and why those questions were the most difficult. Ask students to write the difficult questions and their answers in their notebooks.

Expansion

1. **Interpreting Political Cartoons.** Assign one of the cartoons on p. 140 to each group of three or four students. Have groups study their cartoon and answer the questions about it. Then ask them to take turns sharing their answers and titles with the class.
2. Symbols are the most difficult thing for students to assess. You may want to discuss some of the objects and/or symbols in the cartoons to help students understand their significance. For example, you may begin by explaining why the truck is delivering the world to Clinton.

HISTORICAL THINKING AND APPLICATION ACTIVITIES

1. Ask students to bring in a cartoon from their local newspaper. Remember to ask them to identify the source and the date. Have them use the same set of questions to discuss the cartoon. If students receive newspapers from other countries, the analysis can be expanded and related to the media section on p. 134. Ask students, *What does the cartoon tell you about the country's view of the issue?*
2. There have been many occasions when the vice president becomes president. Ask, *Who were the vice presidents of each of the four presidents studied?* Ask students to use an encyclopedia or the Internet to find out information about the vice presidents who served under each of the four presidents.
3. Have students study some of the economic vocabulary in this section, e.g., *deficit* and *surplus.* Ask students to illustrate the relationship between government income (taxes) and government expenditures (programs/spending).
4. Look on the Internet for the short version of the *Bush v. Gore* decision. Discuss the process by which that decision reached the Supreme Court.

THE UNITED STATES AND GLOBAL ISSUES — PAGES 140–141

Globalization

History Objectives: Evaluate the U.S. role in political struggles in the Middle East, Africa, Asia, and Latin America; assess the effects of international trade, transnational business, and overseas competition on the economy.

Language Objectives: Develop academic oral language; read for comprehension; use resources to find additional information; write what has been learned.

Historical Thinking Objectives: Analyze cause and effect relationships; use data to draw conclusions; gather needed knowledge of time and place to construct an explanation.

Learning Strategy Objectives: Explicit: Identify the learning strategies used to write notes about maps. **Implicit:** Use the previously introduced learning strategies *summarizing* to write the main ideas in the reading text, and *using resources* to investigate current information about countries where the United States has been involved in recent years.

PROCEDURES

Preparation

1. **Before You Read: Finding Out about Imported Products.** Have students work in pairs to examine the items they find in the classroom, at home, and around the school.
2. Assign students one of the categories listed in the exercise on p. 140 to explore. Students may benefit from being able to examine food products and music that are brought into the classroom. Items such as school supplies, clothing, electronics, and sports equipment will be available within the classroom, school, and at home.
3. Have students record their findings in their notebooks.
4. Work with students to make a class chart that shows each item and its country of manufacture. Identify its location on a world map.
5. Discuss with the class: *What does the information on the chart tell you about where things are manufactured? Is the whole item made outside the United States? What does it mean if the item is manufactured in one place, but materials for the product come from somewhere else?* Ask students if they have any questions about their data.
6. Have students write two or three sentences that summarize the class discussion about trade in their notebooks.

Presentation

1. See "How to Teach Reading Lessons," p. xi.
2. Have students work in small groups to discuss what they already know about globalization. Ask each

group to discuss how the information they found in the products activity could help them understand the next reading. Ask, *What information do you think you already know? What new information do you expect to find?* Have students write their ideas in their notebooks.

3. Have students first skim the reading selection to get the main ideas.

4. Have students work in pairs to reread the selection. At the end of each paragraph, have them decide on a sentence that summarizes the main idea (*summarizing*).

Practice

1. Have students work in small groups to compare and contrast their summaries. Have them consider these questions: *Are there vocabulary words that are new? How did you decide on the meanings of the words?*

2. Have each group share their summaries. Students should make any necessary additions or changes to their summaries in their notebooks. Ask, *Did your understanding of globalization change? If so, why? What is the new understanding?*

Self-Evaluation

1. **Understanding What You Read: Extending Information.** Have students look at a world map. Assign each pair of students one of the countries from the list on p. 141. Have students locate the area on the map and make a list of any information they already know about the assigned country.

2. Have students use an up-to-date encyclopedia or the Internet to find out about what happened in this country in the past year (*using resources*). Ask, *Why is this location important to the United States? What are the connections, if any, between this area and the United States (e.g., does this country trade with the United States)? Were there any connections between the United States and this location in the past? What were those connections and when did they exist?* Have students write the answers to these questions in their notebooks.

3. Have students share with the class the location of the country and the information they gathered about it. Ask students, *What conclusions can you draw about U.S. involvement in the world? Are any of the countries trading partners with the United States? How else is the United States involved outside its borders? Is U.S. involvement outside its borders today greater or less than it was fifty years ago?*

HISTORICAL THINKING AND APPLICATION ACTIVITIES

1. Use these questions for class discussion: *Is there a relationship between trade and foreign relations? What is it? How might a nation use its trade relations to build a connection with another country? Would the country have to have the same kind of government to trade with the United States?*

2. Ask students to locate information in the library or on the Internet about some alliances, e.g., the North Atlantic Treaty Organization (NATO), the United Nations (UN), the European Union (EU), the Warsaw Pact, the Southeast Asia Treaty Organization (SEATO), and the Organization of American States (OAS). Ask, *What countries are involved in each alliance? What are the goals of the alliance? Are the goals economic? Military? Social?* Have students write a short report on an alliance.

A TERRORIST ATTACK SHOCKS THE WORLD	Pages 142–143

The Events of September 11, 2001

History Objectives: Examine recent developments in domestic and foreign policy through a historical event; analyze images to review the history of the United States, its values, principles, and practices.

Language Objectives: Develop academic oral language; write ideas about terrorism and report them to the class; react to and discuss illustrations and write reactions.

Historical Thinking Objectives: Formulate historical questions; gather needed knowledge of time; identify problems and dilemmas; analyze the interests and values of various people; compare and contrast sets of ideas and values; build historical comprehension; analyze illustrations in historical stories.

Learning Strategy Objectives: Implicit: Practice the previously introduced learning strategies *tell what you know* to discuss terrorism, *predicting* to speculate about the information in each section of the reading text, *summarizing* to identify the main ideas, and *using imagery* to analyze and interpret a photo collage.

PROCEDURES

Preparation

1. See "How to Teach Reading Lessons", p. xi.

2. **Before You Read: Identifying What You Already Know.** Most students will have some recollection of the September 11 attacks and will probably have some opinions about what terrorism is (*tell what you know*). They may also be from other countries and have had different experiences from those born in the United States. Before students work in groups of three, ask each student to individually write down a definition of *terrorism* in his or her notebook. Then ask students to share their separate definitions with others in their group and develop one definition from the ideas of all three group members. They may combine ideas or use some words from each definition.

3. Next, ask each group to share their definitions with the class.

4. Write each group's definition on chart paper or on the board.

5. When all definitions are written, ask students to pick out the common ideas and together create a class definition of terrorism. The ever-changing definition of terrorism may make this a complex process; current events may allow students to seek definitions from newspapers or magazines.

6. In pairs, have students look over the headings on pp. 142–143 and the images on p. 142, and speculate about the type of information they will find in each section (*predicting*).

Presentation and Practice

1. Still in pairs, have students read pp. 142–143 a section at a time. At the end of each section, ask them to decide on the most important ideas and write them in their notebooks (*summarizing*).

2. Ask students to write a sentence about what they learned from the newspaper and from the cartoon illustration.

3. Discuss with the class any other information they have about the September 11, 2001 attacks or the *USA Patriot Act*.

4. Ask students to read the quote from Roger Spiller, which was written several months after the September 11, 2001 attacks. Ask them what they think it means. Have students work in pairs to decide on an answer and then share their answers with the class. Ask, *Are you, as students, writing history now? What can that mean for you?*

5. **Interpreting Images: Looking Back, Looking Forward** (p. 143). Begin by reviewing the threads that tie people and events of U.S. history together over time and across regions. Use these questions for class discussion: *What are the founding documents in the United States? What ideas do you remember from the Constitution, the Bill of Rights, and the Declaration of Independence that tell about what people in the United States believe about the country?* Help students identify "common threads," such as life, liberty, the pursuit of happiness, the rights of freedom of speech, freedom of press, etc. Have students list these beliefs in their notebooks.

6. Ask a student to read the quote at the bottom of p. 145.

7. In pairs, have students study the images on pp. 144–145 and answer the questions at the bottom of p. 143, writing the answers in their notebooks. Then have students share answers with the class.

Self-Evaluation

1. Provide students with more information about each family grouping. (See the Photo Collage section below.)

2. Ask students to look at the pictures again with the new information and decide what they think are the common threads. Have the class share their ideas.

Expansion

1. Brainstorm with students how they might construct an "American quilt" exhibit that tells their stories. Suggest that students bring in objects or images of their family's histories to use to develop a class exhibit.

2. After completing the exhibit, have students decide on a title for it or identify a quote that describes their picture of America. Display the exhibit in the classroom and invite other classes to come and see it.

Photo Collage, pages 144–145

The following information provides background on the images of the families in the photo collage on pp. 144–145. Family groupings are designated by the dotted lines.

Matsumoto Family—Northwestern United States
Reported by Amiko Matsumoto: My family immigrated to the United States from Japan in the early 1900s. My great grandfather worked in agriculture in Washington state, then in California. My grandfather, pictured with his family (standing in back) in the early twentieth century, had a store until World War II. My grandfather loved playing baseball. My father served in the Navy, then went

to college. My mother's ancestry is French/Swiss/British. I and my twin brothers (at college graduation) are fourth-generation Japanese Americans.

Lara Family—Southern California   Reported by Eduardo Lara: My family immigrated to the United States from Mexico in the 1970s. My great-grandmother and grandmother and uncle remained in Mexico. As one of four children, we tended a family garden at our home in Los Angeles county, following Mexican traditions. I graduated from college and have a masters degree, and I am currently teaching school in California.

Alvarado Family—Texas, New Mexico area   Reported by Diana Alvarado: My family is of Spanish descent. They immigrated to California via the Santa Fe route in the eighteenth century. They worked in occupations from ranching to store ownership (great-grandfather). My father served in World War II and recovered from wounds at V.A. hospital in California. My mother is from Thailand. I have B.A. and masters degrees, and I teach middle-school history in Virginia.

Seid Family—New York, New England area   Reported by Sylven Seid Beck: My father served in the U.S. Army in World War II. My paternal grandmother, father, and siblings came to the United States from Canton, China, in the 1920s. Wing On Wo was the name of my maternal grandfather's grocery store in Chinatown, New York, which has since been converted by my mother into an antique Chinese porcelain store. My sister, brother, and I celebrated our parents' fiftieth wedding anniversary in Chinatown in 1998. (Our brother, Stuart, a managing director in an investment firm, was lost in the World Trade Center attacks on September 11, 2001.)

Winters Family—Mid Atlantic, Florida area   Reported by Leonora Winters: My family is Native American (Cherokee, Seminole), African American, and Irish. My great-grandparents lived in South Carolina and Florida, later moving to New York City. My great-grandmother was head nurse at a Florida hospital. The photos show us celebrating Thanksgiving in Queens, New York, with my great aunt and uncle and family; also my parents celebrating July 4 in Queens, New York; Leonora, career army (Vietnam era veteran); member, first Combined Arms Services Staff School (CAS3), Ft. Leavenworth, Kansas.

Cheek Family—Oklahoma, Texas area   Reported by Elizabeth Cheek Jones: My great-grandfather was Cherokee and is pictured at Red Cloud Reservation in Oklahoma in the early twentieth century. His home there also housed the telephone exchange. My father served in the Navy in World War II. My brother served in the Air Force as a communications specialist and currently works in radio broadcasting.

Captain Family—Louisiana delta area   Reported by Yvonne Captain: We can trace our family as far back as the 1700s in Louisiana where they were brought as slaves. My great-grandparents are pictured at Hickory Flats, Louisiana, around 1904. The other photo, taken in Opelousas, Louisiana, in the early 1900s, is of my grandfather. My parents and siblings moved to California in the 1950s.

Uhl Chamot Family—Central United States area   Reported by Geoffroy Alain Chamot: My family immigrated to the United States from Germany in the 1700s, and later from England and Switzerland. They lived in Texas, Washington, DC, and overseas. My grandfather, who served in the Civilian Conservation Corps, is pictured holding his daughter, and his grandson in the photo below. My grandfather and father were international geologists. My grandmother (pictured with four generations—mother to great-grandmother) established a bilingual school in Bogotá, Colombia, where my mother had a birthday party with friends.

Anderson Family—Northern-Central United States area   Reported by Robert Anderson: My family immigrated from Europe to the United States in the seventeenth and eighteenth centuries. They lived in the Midwest. My maternal grandfather worked as a yard master for Chicago and Eastern Illinois Railroad in the early nineteenth century. My paternal grandfather, a business owner in Indiana, traveled with his children (my father and siblings) by Model-T Ford to Michigan in the 1920s. My mother and father married in 1939. My uncle served in World War II in the U.S. Army Air Corps, 8th Air Force, and flew B-24 bombers. Picnics were a summer activity during the 1950s.

HISTORICAL THINKING AND APPLICATION ACTIVITIES

1. Discuss these questions: *When is an event "history"? How can we be involved in making history?*
2. Have students think back over the events of the last fifty years—events that they read about in this book. Ask, *What is the event that you remember furthest in the past? What is the most recent event? Do you know more about one than the other? Why?* Explain to students that they may have more information about events that happened longer ago because they have had more time to find out information or to think about that event.
3. Ask students, *Do you think you are part of the history of the United States? In what ways?*
4. Ask students to think about the events that are represented by the images on the "quilt" on pp. 144–145. Have them make a time line of the events represented.

Four Presidents: 1980–2004

History Objectives: Identify events over four presidencies; examine relationships between these events.

Language Objectives: Comprehend information in a time line; develop academic oral language; research for additional information; make oral presentations to the class.

Historical Thinking Objectives: Use time lines; create time lines.

Learning Strategy Objectives: Implicit: Practice the learning strategies *classifying* and *using imagery* to understand a time line; *using resources, taking notes,* and *graphic organizers* to find additional information on one president and create a detailed time line; *classifying* to compare and contrast domestic and foreign policy issues and events; and *predicting* to speculate about upcoming historical events.

PROCEDURES

Presentation

1. Remind students that time lines are a visual way of describing the sequence of past events (*using imagery*). This time line covers a period of twenty-four years, in which there were four presidents of the United States. Show students how the events are grouped together next to each presidency, and remind them that grouping events and facts makes them easier to remember (*classifying*).

2. Ask students to keep an image of the time line in mind as they skim through the information on pp. 146–147 to get a general idea of the main facts (*using imagery*). Have students ask questions for clarification of any words they do not understand.

Practice

1. **Understanding What You Read: Using a Time Line.** Have students work in groups of three or four to review the time line and then select one of the presidents.

2. Have students read and follow the directions as they construct their presidential time lines. Have them use chart paper so that the time lines can be displayed when completed. Remind students that not all events in the time line were discussed in the unit, and not all events in the readings are in the time line. Ask students to look up new information on the presidential time line in reference books or on the Internet so they understand each event. Have them use these resources to find out about important events that happened after 2003.

3. Have students present their group's time line and also listen to the time line presentations of the other groups. Ask them to take notes about the other presidencies (*taking notes*).

4. Ask each group of students to refer to their time line as they list events in two categories—domestic and foreign—in their notebooks (*classifying*). Ask them to discuss how they would answer the question about the emphasis of each president, given the data available.

Expansion

1. **Write the Next Unit.** Encourage students to think about how history continues. This activity allows students to think about what they already know about a topic and make a guess (*predicting*) about what will happen next. In addition to the topics mentioned on p. 147, students may also have ideas about things they want to add, such as music, movies, or books to be written; what will happen to the Earth; their city, and so on.

2. Have students share their ideas with the class.

HISTORICAL THINKING AND APPLICATION ACTIVITIES

1. Have students look at all of the time lines together. Discuss what events, policies, and problems are the same in more than one presidency. Ask students why that might be the case. This provides an opportunity to talk about continuity and change in history.

2. Have students add graphics to their time lines. They can use magazines, newspapers, the Internet, or clip art. Be sure to have them properly credit sources with a caption.

3. Ask students what they think their roles will be in the future with regard to jobs they might have, places they might live, and the level of education they might receive. Encourage students to think about how knowing the past can help them think about the future.

Answer Key

BEGINNINGS TO 1877

Unit 1: The Earliest Americans

PAGE 4

1. herd
2. farmers
3. migrate
4. Asians
5. migration
6. hunters
7. continents
8. route
9. climate
10. settle

PAGE 5

A 1. Where Are Native Americans Today?
2. Why Did Asian Hunters Come to America?
3. What Happened to the Asian Hunters Who Migrated to the Americas?
4. Who Were the Earliest Americans?

B the first inhabitants of the continent.

PAGE 8

Answers will vary, but should at least contain the following information:

1. a bridge formed of land between Asia and North America
2. having to do with Asia; from Asia
3. large, wild animals; animals that the Asians followed over the land bridge
4. North, South (and Central) America
5. to grow plants for eating
6. a group of people with their own way of life
7. way of life
8. having to do with or related to a tribe or tribes
9. one of the first Americans
10. land used only by Native Americans

PAGE 9

1. F; They came when it was very cold.
2. T
3. T
4. NG
5. T
6. NG
7. NG
8. T
9. T
10. NG
11. F; They called them "Indians."
12. F; They speak the same language as the people around them.
13. T
14. NG
15. F; The Ice Age was many thousands of years ago.

PAGE 11

Map Skills

1. Alaska   2. Arctic Region

Understanding Bar Graphs

1. The Arctic Region
2. a. June, July, August, and September
   b. Because the days are longer. / There is daylight for 24 hours. / It's summer.
3. a. June, July, August, and September
   b. When it's summer in the northern hemisphere, it's winter in the southern hemisphere.
4. They are both very cold. They both have ice and snow.
5. June, July, August, and September are the warmest months in the Arctic and the coldest months in the Antarctic. / Some people live in the Arctic, but nobody lives in the Antarctic.

PAGE 12

A 1. hunters
2. bridge
3. migrate
4. Alaska; Canada

B 1. seals; whales
2. land

C 1. clothes; houses
2. fur and feathers
3. skins
4. whale
5. snow

PAGE 13

1. Mexico
2. Guatemala
3. Mexico
4. Peru
5. Iroquois
6. Anasazi
7. Inuit

PAGE 14

Paragraph 1: There were many different cultures in the Americas before Europeans arrived.

Paragraph 2: The three most important indigenous cultures in Central and South America were those of the Mayas, the Aztecs, and the Incas.

PAGE 15

Answers will vary but should contain this information:

1. He thought Cortés was the god Quetzalcoatl.
2. Because he wanted to claim the land and the riches of the Aztec Empire for Spain.
3. He became nervous because there were so many Aztecs and so few Spanish soldiers, and he didn't understand why Moctezuma was acting so friendly.
4. There were angry because he was friendly to the Spanish soldiers who had killed some Aztec chiefs; they no longer trusted Moctezuma as their leader.

PAGE 16

A 1. [in] New York State
2. hunting; fishing; farming
3. wars
4. tribes
5. council

B 1. Four Corners; Arizona; New Mexico; Colorado; Utah
2. corn; beans; hunted
3. into sides of cliffs
4. moved

C 1. Iroquois
2. Anasazi

PAGE 17

Which Foods Do You Eat?
Answers will vary.

Classifying
1. Answers will vary. Possible classifications:
Raw: avocados; peanuts; pepper; pineapple; squash; tomato
Cooked: corn; lima beans; manioc; peanuts; pepper; potatoes; pumpkin; squash; sweet potato; tomato

Unit 2: Explorers and Explorations

PAGE 20

People	*Things People Do*	*Places and Things*
bandits	convert	castle
crew	explore	colony
explorer	trade (*v.*)	furs
merchant		route
slaves		spices
		sugar cane
		trade (*n.*)

PAGE 21

A 1. trade
2. riches
3. religion
B 1. Asia
2. spices; ginger and cinnamon; spices made spoiled food taste better
3. [of] deserts, mountains, and bandits
C 1. astrolabe; compasses; maps; improvements in ships
D 1. money to fight wars, build, and buy luxuries
2. gold; silver; the Americas
3. the richest and most powerful country in Europe
4. sugar cane; cocoa; tobacco; furs
E 1. religion
2. Native Americans; African slaves; Christianity

PAGE 25

1. claimed
2. navigation
3. trade
4. voyage
5. vast
6. colony
7. persistent
8. stature

PAGE 26

1. North America, South America, Africa, Asia, Australia
2. Florida, Hawaii
3. No
4. Answers will vary.

PAGE 27

1. c
2. August
3. March
4. No, because it's too warm.

PAGE 28

1. c		6. h	
2. e		7. d	
3. a		8. g	
4. f		9. j	
5. b		10. i	

PAGE 29

1. T
2. F; Estevan was Noth African (former slave).
3. NG
4. T
5. T
6. NG
7. T
8. F; Estevan disappeared.
9. NG
10. F; Explorers never found the cities of gold.

PAGES 30–31

1. Florida
2. California
3. Florida
4. Florida, Texas
5. Colorado, New Mexico, Montana, Nevada
6. Texas, New Mexico, California
7. Montana
8. Nevada
9. Colorado
10. Answers will vary.

PAGE 38

See chart at the top of page 149.

PAGE 39

1. f		5. g	
2. c		6. b	
3. d		7. h	
4. a		8. e	

PAGE 40

1. a. July   b. 66°
2. a. July   b. 58°
3. a. January   b. −20°
4. a. January   b. 12°
5. a and b
6. Winters are warmer in Anchorage. Anchorage is near the Pacific coast. During the winter, the ocean breezes warm the land near the coast.

Unit 3: From Colonies to Nation

PAGE 44

1. Colonies and Missions in North America
2. Spanish Territories in the New World
3. U.S. Cities with Spanish History
4. Slaves Are Brought to the Colonies

PAGE 45

Comprehension Check
1. F; Parts of South America were called New Spain.
2. NG

CHART FOR PAGE 38

NAME	NATIONALITY	SPONSORING COUNTRY	DATES OF EXPLORATION	AREAS EXPLORED	IMPORTANCE OF EXPLORATION
Ponce de Leon	Spanish	Spain	1493–1521	Puerto Rico; eastern coast of U.S. and southern tip of Florida	Found gold; claimed Puerto Rico and Florida for Spain
De Soto	Spanish	Spain	1533–1541	Peru; Cuba; Florida; southeastern North America; states that are now Arkansas and Louisiana	Helped conquer Moctezuma; governor of Cuba; claimed SE U.S. for Spain
Champlain	French	France	1608	Coast of New France	Established first French colony in North America (Quebec)
Hudson	English	Netherlands; England	1609, 1610–1611	Coast of N. America and Hudson River; Hudson Bay, Canada	Claimed land along Hudson River for Netherlands; claimed land for England
Cabot	Italian	England	1497	Newfoundland, Canada	Claimed Nova Scotia, Newfoundland, and Grand Banks fisheries for England
Cartier	French	France	1533–1541	Coasts of Newfoundland, Quebec, and Nova Scotia	Established French presence in North America (Canada)
Cabeza de Vaca	Spanish	Spain	1528-1536	Parts of what are now Florida and Texas	Claimed areas for Spain

3. NG
4. T
5. T
6. T
7. F; San Juan, Puerto Rico was the first city founded, in 1521.
8. F; The mission in El Paso was founded in 1659 and the mission in San Antonio was founded in 1718.
9. F; The Spanish set up colonies in California last.

Scanning
Florida, New Mexico, Texas, California

PAGE 50
See chart below.

PAGE 51
A 1. Chief; tribe   2. colonists; 1621
B 1. Wampanoag   2. Massasoit and the Wampanoag; a feast of thanks to celebrate their first good harvest
C 1. very sick   2. warned; an attack
D 1. King; English colonists   2. two years   3. killed
E 1. Pilgrams   2. peace

PAGE 53
1. North America, South America, Europe, Asia, Africa, Australia
2. (Two of the following): North America, South America, Africa, Australia, Asia
3. Northern hemisphere (for students living in the U.S.)
4. Northern hemisphere
5. Answers will vary.

PAGE 54
1. December, January
2. June, July, August
3. June, July, August
4. January, February
5. Both Atlanta and Sydney have a warmer season and a colder season. In Atlanta, December, January, and February are the coldest months, but in Sydney they are the warmest months. In Atlanta, June, July, and August are the warmest months, but in Sydney they are the coldest months.
6. northern hemisphere
7. southern hemisphere

CHART FOR PAGE 50

	SPANISH COLONIES	JAMESTOWN	PLYMOUTH
1. Why established	To live Spanish way of life	Better life	Religious freedom
2. Problems of colonies	Labor	Land not good for farming	50% of Pilgrims died the first winter
3. How people made a living	Farms and sugar cane fields	Grew and sold tobacco	Grew corn, squash, and beans.
4. Relationship between Native Americans and the colonists	Bad	Poor at first	Good. Native Americans taught them to plant crops.
5. Type of government		Council	Mayflower Compact; agreed to live under one government and obey laws
6. Religion	Christian		Separatists
7. Importance of colonies	Settled and established missions	First permanent English colony	First colony for religious freedom

8. when it's warm in the northern hemisphere; when its warm in the southern hemisphere
9. Answers will vary.

PAGE 56
1. Quebec
2. Jacques Marquette and Louis Joliet
3. the Mississippi River to its mouth; the lands along the Mississippi River
4. to trap animals for their fur
5. the Native Americans
6. the Dutch
7. Manhattan
8. New Amsterdam
9. England and the Netherlands fought a war and the English won
10. Spain, France, and England

PAGE 58 (MAP ON PAGE 57)
1. Massachusetts, Rhode Island, Connecticut, New Hampshire, New York, New Jersey, Pennsylvania, Delaware, Virginia, Maryland, North Carolina, South Carolina, Georgia; England
2. 1. Portsmouth, New Hampshire
   2. Boston, Massachusetts
   3. Plymouth, Massachusetts
   4. New York City, New York
   5. Philadelphia, Pennsylvania
   6. Jamestown, Virginia
   7. Charleston, South Carolina
   8. Savannah, Georgia
3. They were all ports.

PAGE 59
1. France
2. Spain, England, France
3. France, England
4. Spain, Russia
5. They are the parts that are not shaded. Northern California, Oregon, and Washington.

PAGE 60
1. *Five of the following:* Mississippi, Alabama, Tennessee, Kentucky, West Virginia, Illinois, Indiana, Ohio, Michigan, Wisconsin. Other answers may also be acceptable.
2. Florida
3. Haiti, Martinique, Guadeloupe
4. Answers will vary, but should include the following information:
   - Montreal and Quebec were controlled by France before the French and Indian War and by England after the War.
   - Louisiana, New Mexico, and northern Texas were controlled by France before the War and by Spain after the War.
   - France claimed land to the east of the Mississippi River before the War but had to give the land to England after the War.
   - Spain had claimed Florida before the War but had to give it to England after the War.

- Before the War the French claimed the port of New Orleans; after the War they had to give it to Spain.

PAGE 61
1. Contributions to Life in the English Colonies
2. Early Life
3. Representing American Ideas
4. Importance in U.S. History

PAGE 63
1. cargo
2. import
3. intolerable
4. protest
5. right
6. ruler
7. British
8. fire a gun
9. Parliament
10. pass a law
11. representative
12. rule
13. taxes
14. repeal a law
15. provide
16. massacre
17. independent
18. allow

PAGE 66
1. F; It said that colonists could not settle there.
2. T
3. T
4. T
5. NG
6. T
7. F; Angry colonists threw snowballs at a group of soldiers and the soldiers fired their guns and killed five colonists.
8. NG
9. F; The Boston Tea Party was the protest against the tea tax.
10. F; Colonists dressed up as Native Americans did it.
11. T
12. F; Under the Acts, ships could not use Boston harbor until the colonists paid for the tea.
13. T
14. F; Many American colonists began to think this.

PAGE 68
Answers will vary, but the words should be defined in a similar way:
1. *Congress:* a meeting of representatives who will decide something
2. *Continental:* belonging to a continent
3. *delegate:* a person who is sent to a meeting to represent a larger group of people
4. *demands:* wants; things you say you must have
5. *loyal:* faithful; obedient to
6. *rebellion:* going against; fighting; disobeying

PAGE 72
Lexington, MA	April 19, 1775
Concord, MA	April 19, 1775
Boston, MA	June 1775
Trenton, NJ	December 1776
Saratoga, NY	October 1777
Valley Forge, PA	1777–1778
Charleston, SC	May 1780
Yorktown, VA	October 1781

PAGE 77

1. the U.S. Constitution
2. 11
3. the Bill of Rights
4. 194
5. religion; speak; meet; fair; printing things that the government doesn't like; many other rights
   a. It has provided a plan of government for the U.S. for more than 200 years.
   b. It is a model for constitutions of other new nations.

PAGE 79

Comprehension Check

1. Executive
2. Judicial
3. Legislative
4. Legislative
5. Legislative
6. Judicial
7. Legislative; Executive; Judicial
8. Executive
9. Legislative
10. Judicial

Find Out about Your Government

1. 18
2. 6
3. 2
4. Answers will vary.
5. Answers will vary.
6. Answers will vary.
7. 4
8. Answers will vary.
9. Answers will vary.

PAGE 81

1. Boston
2. Boston
3. Philadelphia
4. New York and Philadelphia

Unit 4: The Nation Grows

PAGE 84

1. canal
2. log cabin
3. plow
4. road

1. guide
2. frontier
3. path
4. log
5. pioneer

PAGE 85

1. Color the two territories
2. Choose three from the following: Ohio, Indiana, Illinois, Wisconsin, Michigan
3. Choose three from the following: Kentucky, Tennessee, Mississippi, Alabama, parts of Georgia

PAGE 86

1. T
2. NG
3. NG
4. F; It went from Virginia to Kentucky.
5. NG
6. T
7. T
8. NG

PAGE 87

1. 1803
2. Gadsden Purchase
3. Mexico
4. 1845
5. Florida
6. Answers will vary.

PAGE 88

1. Oregon country
2. Florida
3. Oregon country
4. Louisiana Purchase
5. Louisiana Purchase and Florida
6. Louisiana Purchase and Oregon country
7. Oregon country
8. Louisiana Purchase

PAGE 89

1. D
2. D
3. M
4. D
5. D

PAGE 90

1. Jefferson's Gift to His Country
2. Third President of the United States
3. Representative of the American People
4. Interests, Inventions, and Hobbies
5. Early Years

PAGE 93

See chart at the bottom of this page.

PAGE 94

1. The Rocky Mountains
2. In 1803, the Louisiana Purchase doubled the size of the U.S. The Rocky Mountains became the western border of the country. The Rocky Mountains were very difficult to cross and so they served as a natural boundary.
3. Answers will vary.

PAGE 95

See chart at the top of page 152.

PAGE 96

A
1. navy; ships; work on British ships
2. Americans in Northwest wanted more land
3. U.S. wanted British to stop telling Native Americans to attack U.S. settlers

B
1. British; White House in Washington D.C.
2. British attacked Fort Henry in Baltimore
3. Francis Scott Key saw battle, wrote song

C
1. trade freely; nations
2. Victory made U.S. proud; forgot about settling Canada
3. People moved west

CHART FOR PAGE 93

	WHAT HAPPENED	PLACE	DATE
The first winter camp. Lewis and Clark meet Sacajawea.	Fort Mandan	Winter 1804	
The most beautiful waterfall of the trip.	Great Falls	April 1805	
"The most difficult part of our voyage."	Rocky Mountains	August 1805	
"Ocean in view! O! The joy!"	Pacific Ocean	November 1805	
They return to tell the news.	St. Louis	September 1806	

Answers will vary but may include the following:

CONTINENT	A MAJOR MOUNTAIN RANGE	HIGHEST MOUNTAIN
North America	Rocky Mountains	Mt. McKinley, Alaska; Height: 20,320 feet
South America	Andes Mountains	Aconcagua, Argentina; Height: 22,834 feet
Europe	Alps	El'brus, Russia; Height: 18,510 feet
Africa	Atlas Mountains	Mt. Kilimanjaro, Tanzania; Height: 19,340 feet
Asia	Himalaya Mountains	Mt. Everest, Nepal / Tibet; Height: 29,028
Australia	Great Dividing Range	Mt. Kosciuszko; Height: 7,310 feet
Antarctica	Ellsworth Mountains	Vinson Massif; Height: 16,066 feet

PAGE 97

3. The United States wanted European countries to stay out of the Americas.

PAGE 99

1. T
2. NG
3. T
4. T
5. T
6. F; Many forty-niners traveled to California on the California Trail or by boat.
7. T
8. NG
9. F; A ghost town is a town with no people.
10. NG

PAGE 100

1. Europe, Africa, Asia
2. Antarctica, Asia
3. no
4. Answers will vary.

PAGE 101

1. northern
2. between 30° and 50°

PAGE 103

Answers will vary but should contain similar information.

1. *troops:* soldiers, men in the Army
2. *defeated:* beaten
3. *vetoed:* stopped, said no to, did not allow
4. *fired (someone):* dismissed from a job
5. *foreign:* not domestic, from another place
6. *obeyed:* did what someone said, did what one was told

PAGE 104

1. e
2. c
3. h
4. a
5. g
6. b
7. f
8. d

PAGE 108

1. 1836
2. 1853
3. 1821
4. 1836
5. 1846
6. 1848

PAGE 109

See chart at the bottom of this page.

PAGE 111

1. Thomas Jefferson, James Madison, James Monroe, Andrew Jackson
2. William Henry Harrison, John Tyler
3. William Henry Harrison
4. December 24, 1814
5. between the Hudson River and Lake Erie
6. 1833
7. Martin Van Buren
8. James K. Polk
9. James K. Polk
10. James K. Polk

Unit 5: The Civil War and Reconstruction

PAGE 115

Thinking about Differences

Answers may vary, but should contain at least four of the following differences:

TOPIC	NORTH	SOUTH
Land	suited to small farms	suited to large plantations
Factories	had more	had fewer
Income	mostly from manufacturing	mostly from agriculture
Taxes	wanted to tax imported goods	didn't want a tax on imported goods
Population (voters)	more people who could vote	fewer people who could vote
Representation in Congress	More members in House of Representatives	Fewer representatives in House of Representatives

CHART FOR PAGE 109

DATE	NAME OF TERRITORY	HOW ACQUIRED	FROM WHOM	STATES IN TERRITORY
1819	Florida	ceded	Spain	FL
1845	Texas	annexed	Texas	TX; part of NM, CO, KS, WY
1846	Oregon country	treaty	Great Britain	WA, OR, ID, part of WY
1848	Mexico Cession	by fighting war	Mexico	CA, NV, UT, part of WY, CO, NM, AZ
1853	Gadsden Purchase	purchased	Mexico	part of AZ, NM

Understanding Pie Graphs

1. 65% of pie graph darkened (North); 35% of pie graph white (South)
2. half; northern states; half; southern states; northern states; two-thirds; northern states; one-third; southern states

PAGE 117

Using Context
(Possible answers)

rare: not common; unusual; out of the ordinary
harvest: to cut down crops such as cotton and tobacco
captured: held somebody against their will; to be held against one's will
abolish: to do away with; to put an end to
conflict: a fight; a difference of opinion

PAGE 122

1. Arkansas, Tennessee, Virginia
2. Kansas, Missouri, Kentucky, Maryland
3. Union capital: Washington, D.C.
   Confederate capital: Richmond, Virginia
4. [Students will need to research this information.]
5. People were still settling this land. At the time of the Civil War, they had not yet asked to become states.
6. a. approximately 100 miles
   b. approximately 1,700 miles

PAGE 124

1. Bull Run, Petersburg, Chancellorsville
2. a. Bull Run
   b. 59,000; 62,500
   c. 3; 2
3. a. Memphis
   b. Texas, Louisiana, Arkansas
   c. South
4. a. Savannah, GA
   b. Charleston, SC; Columbia, SC; Raleigh, NC
   c. Atlanta

PAGE 125

A
1. 1809; log cabin in Kentucky
2. education; poor
3. lawyer

B
1. politics
2. Congress
3. "Honest Abe"
4. united
5. slavery

C
1. liked what he said
2. did not like Lincoln
3. 1860 elected President
4. southern states secede from Union

D
1. keep country together
2. Civil War started 1861
3. Lincoln made Emancipation Proclamation freeing slaves in southern states

E
1. 1864
2. Civil War ends; South surrenders
3. Lincoln shot to death five days later

PAGE 126

Answers will vary, but should contain some of the following information:

1. a. 1776; the thirteen colonies declared independence from Great Britain and became the United States of America
   b. to remember how and why the nation began
2. a. ordinary
   b. that he thought of himself as an ordinary person
3. a. that the North and South must work together, without anger and with forgiveness, to make the nation whole again

PAGE 129

1. a. Harriet Beecher Stowe
   b. She wrote *Uncle Tom's Cabin,* a book against slavery that influenced many people in the North to dislike slavery and want to fight to abolish it.
2. a. Robert E. Lee
   b. He was probably very sad. He had loyalty to the Union but did not want to fight against his native state, which was in the South.
3. a. Frederick Douglass
   b. yes
   c. They would be fighting a double battle: against slavery in the South and against prejudice in the North.
4. a. Clara Barton
   b. She founded the American Red Cross to distribute needed medical supplies for wounded soldiers.
   c. Yes, because she cared for wounded soldiers from both sides of the battlefield: North and South.

PAGE 133

Across
1. poor
2. rights
4. harvest
10. hero
11. survive
12. slave
13. tariff
14. ratify
16. candidates
17. unequal
18. unite
19. population
21. Amendment
22. free
23. Reconstruction

Down
1. plantation
3. injustice
5. segregation
6. slavery
7. sharecropper
8. Confederacy
9. repeal
11. secede
15. your
17. Union
20. rent

PAGE 135

Comprehension Check

1. F; Before the Civil War, Sojourner Truth began to do something that no black woman had ever done. She made speeches against slavery in cities all over the North.
2. T
3. NG
4. F; Women and blacks did not have voting rights in 1860; therefore Sojourner Truth could not have voted for Lincoln.

5. T
6. T
7. F; W.E.B. DuBois was born in Massachusetts.
8. F; He died in 1963.
9. T
10. F; Sojourner Truth died in 1883 when DuBois was 15 years old. He had not yet founded the NAACP.

Comparing and Contrasting
Answers will vary but should contain the following information.
Alike: Both Washington and Du Bois wanted blacks to have equal rights. Both were strong, important leaders.
Different: 1. Washington believed that blacks should first prove they could work hard and earn money. Then white Americans would give them equal rights. Du Bois did not believe that black Americans should depend on whites' acting fairly. He said that blacks must demand and fight for equal rights.

2. Washington was born a slave. He lived mostly in the South. Du Bois was born after the Civil War. He lived mostly in the North.

PAGE 137
Using Maps for Comprehension
1. Answers will vary.
2. Wyoming, Colorado, Utah, and Idaho
3. The West
4. The Southwest

What Do You Think?
1. The Declaration of Independence; the Declaration of Sentiments added the phrase "and women."
2. Answers will vary.
3. Answers will vary.

SINCE 1865

Unit 1: Industrialization and Change: 1865–1900

PAGE 4
double: to become twice as large
poverty: the opposite of wealth
fortune: a large amount of money
wealthy: rich
industry: a business that produces things
world power: a strong country
manufactured products: things made in factories
yacht: large, expensive boat

PAGE 5
Summarizing
Answers will vary, but should contain similar information:
1. *Four of the following:* acquired new land; grew in population; grew in power; grew in wealth; grew in art and literature
2. *Three of the following:* weak presidents; corrupt government; poverty; unemployment; poor working and living conditions for many Americans
3. John D. Rockefeller: oil
   Andrew Carnegie: steel
   William Vanderbilt: railroads
   J. Pierpont Morgan: banking
4. This period was called "The Gilded Age" because, on the surface, things looked golden. However, beneath the surface, many things were bad. Many people got very wealthy, but there was a lot of corruption, greed, and poverty.

Using Maps
Philippine Islands; 1898; acquired after the Spanish-American War
Guam; 1898; acquired after the Spanish-American War
Puerto Rico; 1898; acquired after the Spanish-American War
Hawaii; 1898; annexed
Alaska; 1867; purchased from Russia

PAGE 7
1. 1850: 9,000; 1900: 195,000
2. about 20,000 miles
3. 1880–1890; about 70,000 miles
4. about 2,400 miles

PAGE 9
Completing a Study Chart
See chart at the bottom of this page.

Cause and Effect
1. Many things became cheaper and more people could buy them; the United States sold more products to other countries; inventions made life easier
2. People worked very long hours and they did not earn much money; children worked in factories; bad working conditions; small businesses were forced out by large, powerful ones

CHART FOR PAGE 9

DATE	WHAT HAPPENED AND WHERE	WHY IMPORTANT
1790	First textile factory opens	More factories built; towns grew up around factories; people, especially women, moved from country to city
1830	First railroad companies started in SC and MD	Made transportation faster and easier
mid-1800s	Cheap way of making iron into steel invented	Steel used to build railroads and bridges
1859	Oil first found in Pennsylvania	Used to light homes and power machinery
1869	Railroad completed across the country	Made it easy for people from East to settle in West; also carried products to market

1. North America, South America, Europe, Africa, Asia, Australia
2. South America, Africa
3. *Ten of the following:* North Dakota, South Dakota, Nebraska, Kansas, Montana, Wyoming, Colorado, Texas, Oklahoma, New Mexico, Missouri, Iowa, Minnesota

PAGE 12

Answers will vary, but should contain similar information:

beef: meat that comes from cattle

corral: an area with a fence around it where the cattle were put

glamorous: exciting, full of glamour

herd: group of cattle

sunrise: the beginning of the day, when the sun comes up

wander: to walk away from the herd or the place where you belong

PAGE 15

Answers will vary, but should contain similar information:

A Important leader of the Sioux tribe

Medicine man

B Led sun dance for Sioux

Told people about plan for defeating white man: fight to kill

Fought General Custer at Little Bighorn and won

C U.S. sent forces to fight Sioux

Sitting Bull and Sioux fled to Canada

Many died of cold and starvation

In 1881, Sitting Bull and Sioux returned to SD and moved to reservation

D In 1890, Sioux start new religion: promised buffalo would return and Sioux could return to old way of life

Danced Ghost Dance

Army afraid, thought beginning of new war, killed Sitting Bull

E Wise and brave leader

Fought to save his people, land and way of life

PAGE 16

1. Africa   2. Europe
3. The Southwest

PAGE 17

1. Answers may include: water, food, proper clothing, shelter, transportation, tools, blankets, protection from sun, plants, animals, etc.
2. Answers will vary based on answers to number 1.
3. Answers will vary based on answers to number 1.

PAGE 19

1. Answers will vary, but may include: When was the camera invented? What is the Bessemer process? Who invented the sewing machine? Why was barbed wire important?
2. Answers will vary, but may include identification of *why* questions as difficult.

PAGE 22

Writing a Summary

Answers will vary, but should contain similar information:

Francis Cabot Lowell was a reformer who believed factory life did not have to be unpleasant. He hired women from nearby farms, gave them a place to live, paid them well, and encouraged them to attend church on Sundays. Jane Addams was another reformer who wanted to help the poor. She started Hull House, a settlement house, which provided classes, encouraged exercise, and prepared immigrants to become citizens. Jacob Riis also wanted to help the poor. He took photographs of where poor people lived and used these photographs to get conditions improved. Many states passed laws to make factories safer and cleaner.

Using Headings

1. *Early Immigrants;* from Spain, from England, and from other northern and western European countries
2. *Immigrants and Public Schools;* 1904
3. *A Nation of Immigrants;* yes
4. *How Immigrants Survived;* became farmers and business people, worked in factories, helped build railroads and bridges

PAGE 24

In the past

1. religious freedom, to live in a democracy, for better life
2. jobs included farming, business, factory work, and building bridges and railroads
3. gave children free education, taught children English (bilingual education and ESL), adult classes

Now

Answers will vary.

PAGE 25

Working with Study Questions

1. Answers will vary, but may include:
   1. What are immigrants?
   2. Where did early immigrants to the U.S. come from?
   3. Why did people come to the U.S. in the late 1800s?
   4. What jobs did immigrants have in the 1800s?
   5. What service did school provide for immigrants?
   6. Where did the immigrants in the 1900s come from?
2. Answers will be based on questions in number 1:
   1. People who come to a new country to settle and live.
   2. Spain, England, northern and western European countries.
   3. Came to U.S. for religious freedom; to live in democracy; for a better life.
   4. Farming; working in factories; building railroads and bridges.
   5. Taught English.
   6. Asia, North America, and South America.

PAGE 29

1. Andrew Johnson (1865), Chester A. Arthur (1881)
2. James Garfield
3. Wyoming gave the vote to women
4. telephone
5. Grover Cleveland
6. Chester A. Arthur
7. Andrew Johnson
8. Russia
9. Andrew Johnson
10. William McKinley

Unit 2: Starting a New Century: 1900–1940

Page 32

1. c 2. g 3. f 4. h 5. d 6. a 7. b 8. e

Page 34

1. Roosevelt wanted the U.S. to be more involved in international affairs; he made reforms at home including regulating big corporations, increasing the regulation of interstate commerce by the federal government, and setting standards for food and drugs. (Answers will vary based on students' opinions.)
2. Answers will vary, but may include: cars, washing machines, sewing machines, vacuum cleaners, radios, televisions, and microwaves
3. Answers will vary, may include: Appliances made life at home easier. Cars and transportation meant people did not have to live very close to their factory or office jobs.
4. Women had more options for jobs. Many worked in factories, but others did the cleaning, cooking, and caring for the children of their employers. Some women also did piece work or worked for the telephone company.

Page 35

join: become a member of
condition: the state of someone or something
threaten: claim you will hurt or cause harm to others in some way
unsafe: something that could cause harm

Page 37

1. The boll weevil began to thin the cotton crops, and poor farmers could not make enough money to live.
2. People who had already gone to the North wrote to friends and family in the South to tell them that there were jobs and better schools in the North.
3. Answers will vary, but may include: Poor conditions at home: lack of jobs, poor farming (due to natural or political factors), poor education.
4. Answers will vary, but may include: Good conditions in new country: more job opportunities, better treatment, better education, more political freedom.

Graphic organizers could include Venn diagrams and T-lists. Have students rewrite answers from questions 1 and 2 on one side, and questions 3 and 4 on the other side. Then compare.

Page 38

1. making mechanical drawings: drafting
2. hurt or wounded: injured
3. a contract that pays for medical help for workers: insurance
4. reporters or writers for a newspaper: journalists
5. people who make laws: legislators
6. people or groups that work to improve the lives of others: progressives
7. the farms, not the cities: rural areas
8. the cities, not the farms: urban areas
9. related to an occupation such as secretary or mechanic: vocational

Page 39

Answers will vary.

Page 40

1. f 2. k 3. j 4. h 5. i 6. e 7. n 8. g
9. l 10. m 11. o 12. a 13. c 14. d 15. b

Page 42

Prior to 1914: Secret agreements made
1914: Archduke of Austria assassinated in Bosnia; Germany declared war on Serbia; more countries joined the fight
1915: German U-boat sank *Lusitania,* 1200 people (including 100 Americans) died
1917: German submarines targeted American ships; Communists led by Lenin overthrew the czar in the Russian Revolution; Russia withdrew from the war; U.S. declared war on Germany in April; things started going better for the Allies after the arrival of U.S. troops
1918: War ended.

More information can be found in the library, on the Internet, by talking to people who remember the events, and by reading old newspapers.

Page 43

Similarities: airplanes used, tanks used, people in uniform, people injured, land destroyed.
Differences: In World War I: airplanes were simple, soldiers used hand-to-hand combat; Today: soldiers receive better medical attention, better transportation of troops.

Page 44

1. Germany
2. Russia
3. Russia and France
4. Answers will vary, but may include: Women take over jobs men had held; there is a decrease in birthrate.

Page 45

Studying Maps
Changes: Germany became smaller; Poland was created; Austria-Hungary was broken up; Czechoslovakia was created; Bosnia-Serbia became Yugoslavia; Latvia, Estonia, and Lithuania were created
Countries that became larger: Romania
Countries that became smaller: Germany

Summarizing
Answers will vary, but should include some of the following:

Fourteen Points was Woodrow Wilson's idea. It included things like control of land after war, trade, and other agreements between countries. The Treaty of Versailles included some of the ideas from the Fourteen Points, plus ideas from Britain and France. Germany was punished in many ways for starting the war. The treaty said that Germany would lose a great deal of land and weapons, and would have to pay for damage caused by the war. The Fourteenth Point was the creation of a League of Nations that could settle disputes before they became world wars. The U.S. Senate did not approve the treaty because they wanted the U.S. to stay out of international affairs.

1. *Restrictive Immigration Laws:* 170,000
2. *Intolerance toward African Americans:* race riots, lynch mobs, KKK
3. *Changes for the Better:* People in cities made more money than they had on the farm, there was better education in cities, women could vote
4. *The Red Scare:* Communists had encouraged workers in other countries to overthrow their own governments

PAGE 47

1. Answers will vary, but may include: What happened to people in the U.S. suspected of being Communists? Who worked against the discrimination of African Americans? What is a quota? How did all women in the U.S. gain the right to vote?
2. Answers will be based on questions in item 1: They were arrested and many had their rights denied. NAACP, the Urban League, and Ida B. Wells. A specific number. The Nineteenth Amendment.

PAGE 48

Analyzing Images
Answers will vary, but may include: watched baseball, went dancing, voted, listened to music

Reading and Taking Notes
Answers should include some of the following:
Good things in the 1920s: The war was over; people bought cars and traveled; they went to fairs and watched airplane stunt pilots; there were dance marathons; the creative outpouring of the Harlem Renaissance; jazz; people went to movies and listened to the radio; some people went to baseball games; real wages rose and life seemed much better
Bad things in the 1920s: Prohibition, smuggling and bootlegging; gangsters controlled crime in big cities

PAGE 50

share: a piece of ownership in a company
stock market: where owners sell shares
broker: person selling the shares
loan: the lending of money to be paid off in the future
goods: products
lay off: let workers go
investor: person who buys into a company
unemployed: without a job
salary: money earned for work
speculation: gambling that investment will increase over time
drought: serious lack of water
bonus: something extra
shack: building made of cardboard and metal

PAGE 53

Examples include:

CAUSES	EFFECTS
People speculated on investments	They lost their money and went further into debt
Drought ruined crops and farmland	Farmers from OK, TX, and KS moved west to CA

PAGE 54

Answers will vary, but should include some of the following:

Theodore Roosevelt, factories, Henry Ford, unions, immigration, Great Migration, Progressive Movement, World War I, Treaty of Versailles, Red Scare, Roaring Twenties, Prohibition, Al Capone, Dutch Shultz, Harlem Renaissance, Jelly Roll Morton, Duke Ellington, Langston Hughes, Zora Neale Hurston, Paul Robeson, drought, Black Tuesday, Bonus Army, Herbert Hoover

PAGE 55

Graphic organizers help to organize or order information. Organizers will vary but should contain similar information. See chart at the top of page 158.

PAGE 56

A Born 1884 in NYC; Theodore Roosevelt was her uncle; mother died when she was 8; father died when she was 10; lived with grandmother; went to boarding school in England; was a social worker; married Franklin Roosevelt; had six children

B Became active in Democratic Party, League of Women Voters, and Women's Trade Union League; assisted FDR after his illness, became his "eyes and ears"; campaigned for FDR; while in White House gave speeches, held press conferences, gave lectures and radio broadcasts; wrote newspaper column

C Resigned from DAR because they refused to allow Marion Anderson to sing at Constitution Hall; arranged for Anderson to sing at Lincoln Memorial; investigated working conditions; supported anti-lynching campaigns; sought fair housing for minorities; encouraged FDR to appoint first woman to cabinet; convinced Army Nurse Corps to admit black women; chosen by Truman to lead United Nations Human Rights Commission; helped draft Declaration of Human Rights.

D Active, caring, smiling presence in difficult times

PAGE 61

Answers will vary.

Unit 3: The United States Becomes a World Leader: 1940–1960

PAGE 66

Answers will vary, but should include some of the following information:

1. Germany was very poor; Germany had lost over 60% of its 11 million soldiers; Germany's factories and farms were terribly damaged; German people were starving; countries made it difficult for Germany to rebuild.
2. Everything in a country (natural resources, factories, farms, and businesses) is owned by the state instead of by individual owners.
3. A person must be totally loyal to the state.
4. Mussolini was the leader of Italy; Mussolini started fascism in Italy; he ruled with absolute power.
5. Francisco Franco was a Spanish military general; Franco led a revolt against the Spanish Republic starting the Spanish Civil War; he took power in Spain in 1939.

AGENCY/ACT	INITIALS	WHAT IT DID	WHO IT HELPED
Agricultural Adjustment Act	AAA	Tried to raise price of crops	Farmers
Rural Electrification Administration	REA	Brought electricity to rural areas	People in rural areas
Farm Security Administration	FSA	Provided loans so farmers could keep their farms	Farmers
National Labor Relations Act	NLRA	Allowed workers to bargain about wages and working conditions	Workers
Fair Labor Standards Act	FLSA	Set minimum wage at 25 cents/hour, set maximum hours of work week at 44, made it illegal to hire children under 16	Workers, children
Federal Emergency Relief Administration	FERA	Provided federal money to feed poor and pay for local projects like building roads	People in general
Civilian Conservation Corps	CCC	Gave unemployed young men jobs on conservation projects	Young men
Federal Housing Act	FHA	Provided low-interest loans for house building and repairs	People in general
Works Progress Administration	WPA	Gave jobs to millions of workers to build roads, bridges, and public buildings; It also hired artists, writers, and actors for public art projects.	Workers and artists
National Youth Administration	NYA	Provided part-time work to 16–25 year olds and allowed them to finish their education	16–25 year olds
National Housing Act	NHA	Gave money for low-income housing	Poor
Federal Deposit Insurance Corporation	FDIC	Insures people's money when they deposit it in a bank	General public
Securities Exchange Act	SEC	Created commission to regulate the stock market	Investors
Social Security Act	SSA	Provided monthly payments to people over 65	People over 65

6. Adolf Hitler was a German leader; Hitler threatened people who did not agree with him and he ignored the World War I treaty. He began to manufacture weapons and rebuild an army. He began to arrest Jews and others who he said were not "pure" Germans.

7. Japan was suffering from a depression. Japan moved into and took over a large area of northeastern China called Manchuria.

PAGE 67

conquer: defeat
invade: attack in order to conquer
alliance: an agreement between two or more countries or groups to work together
ally: a nation or group united with another in order to do something
overthrow: to cause to lose power
surrender: to yield

PAGE 68

Axis Powers	*Allies*
Germany	Great Britain
Italy	France
	Soviet Union

Poland: September 1939; France: June 1940; Belgium, Netherlands, Denmark, Norway: 1940; Soviet Union, Yugoslavia, Greece: 1941

Axis power not on the map: Japan.

PAGE 70

Answers will vary, but should contain similar information:

• The United States wanted to stay out of the war because it was thousands of miles away from Europe; the war didn't directly involved the United States; Americans would be divided about what side to support in the war.

• The United States finally entered the war because they were attacked or drawn into it.

PAGE 73

Answers will vary, but should include some of the following information:

1. Many men and women signed up to fight.
2. Women and African Americans starting working in factories to help the war effort.
3. Families contributed to the war effort by growing "victory gardens" and collecting rubber for use on military vehicles.
4. Many Japanese Americans were placed in U.S. internment camps. They lost their land, homes, and businesses.
5. Many people saw posters encouraging them to contribute to the war effort.

PAGE 74

1. Pearl Harbor is in the state of Hawaii.
2. United States lost at Pearl Harbor, Java Sea, and Wake Island. Beginning with the battles of Coral Sea and Midway, the United States won the battles listed on the map as they moved to retake islands.
3. The strategy was called "island hopping," as Allied troops moved from island battle to island battle to get closer to Japan.
4. Both in the Pacific—Midway near Hawaii, June 3–6, 1942; Guadalcanal in the Coral Sea, near Australia, August 1942–February 1943.

[page 149 answers]
1. September 1942
2. 11 months (May 1944 to April 1945)

CAUSES AND EFFECTS IN WORLD WAR II

CAUSE	EFFECT
Hitler invaded Poland.	Great Britain and France declared war on Germany.
Germany conquered most of Western Europe.	In May 1940, Britain stood alone without allies.
Franklin Roosevelt said that the U.S. must help democracies defend the "four freedoms"	The U.S. sent supplies and equipment to Britain.
Japan attacked Pearl Harbor	The U.S. entered World War II.
The U.S. needed to send secret messages in the war against Japan.	The U.S. used "Code Talkers" (Navajo Native Americans)
The U.S. led the Normandy invasion.	Many soldiers died because the Germans had weapons built into the beaches.
Hitler had a program to develop a master race.	12 million people were killed in concentration camps, 6 million of them were Jews
The Allies were losing many men fighting Japan and believed more would die.	The U.S. dropped the A-bomb on Japan.
Radioactivity from the A-bomb spread over large areas.	Survivors' skin was burned and made them ill with cancer. Large areas of land and water were contaminated.
People in Berlin were starving after the war	The Allies began the Berlin Airlift.
European countries had been damaged by the war.	The U.S. started the Marshall Plan to help them.
The United States helped European countries rebuild after World War II.	The U.S. was recognized as a world leader.

3. Battle of Stalingrad (1942); Battle of Anzio (May 1944); D-Day (June 1944); Battle of the Bulge (December 1944); Soviets capture Berlin (April 1945)
4. Answers will vary.

PAGE 75

A 1. Navajo from the southwestern part of the United States
2. Marines

B 1. soldiers fighting the war had to talk to each other
2. they did not want the enemy to hear what they were planning

C 1. Philip Johnston suggested the Navajo language could be used as a code
2. U.S. Marine Corps tested a pair of Navajo Marines
3. Navajo created code from their language
4. Navajo created new words and memorized all of them

D 1. Japanese not able to break code

PAGE 76

1. *The Effects of World War II;* Berlin was divided into four sectors
2. *Japan Surrenders;* The United States used the atom bomb to end the war
3. *Germany is Defeated;* May 8, 1945
4. *Japan Surrenders;* Hiroshima and Nagasaki
5. *Germany is Defeated;* Dwight David Eisenhower

PAGE 78

Identifying Cause and Effect
See chart at the top of this page.

Think about It!
Soviet Union, Russia, Soviets, Russians; The country changed names and governments over time; Russia, Russians; no longer controlled by communist government.

PAGE 80

Thinking about Effects
1. Many more elementary schools had to be built for the increase in children; many more high schools had to be built for the increase in teenagers.
2. There was increased competition for jobs.
3. Many more homes were built.
4. Many baby boomers are retiring now.

PAGE 80

Think about It!
Answers will vary, but may include: Israeli/Palestinian conflict; partitioning of India and Pakistan; Civil Rights movement; etc.

Prejudice could be reduced through education and the law.

PAGE 81

Answers will vary, but may include: The U.S. was allied with Great Britain, the Soviet Union, France, and China; the U.S. was a victor in World War II; the U.S. developed the atomic bomb.

The U.S. may have formed new alliances; the U.S. was more powerful than before World War II.

PAGE 84

Answers will vary, but should include some of the following information:

From General to President: Dwight Eisenhower and Richard Nixon were elected president and vice president. They took office in 1953.
Anti-Communism Affects People's Rights: People in the U.S. were uneasy about the Soviet Union and its leader, Joseph Stalin. Congress, led by Joseph McCarthy, passed many anti-Communist laws.
Fear of Atomic War: Many people in the United States were afraid of a nuclear attack from the Soviet Union. Many individuals and cities built bomb shelters.

POSITIVE RESULTS OF COLD WAR	NEGATIVE RESULTS OF COLD WAR	REASONS POSITIVE OR NEGATIVE
	Berlin Wall	Polarized world, divided families
	Boycott of Cuba still in effect	No trade, families have little contact
Space program advanced		Advanced technology, satellites forecast weather
Peace Corps		People helping others in need

PAGE 85

interstate: involving at least two states

segregation: the state of separating people by race or other characteristic

unconstitutional: a law or action that is not allowed by the United States Constitution

doctrine: a statement that tells what you believe in

civil rights: the rights guaranteed to a citizen

unmanned: containing no humans, or run by machines

PAGE 86

Answers will vary, but may contain information on changing interaction between racial groups in the United States and advances in transportation and other technologies.

Unit 4: Eras of Protest: 1960–1980

PAGE 94

integrate: to mix different things, ideas, or persons together

migrant worker: a person who travels from place to place to find jobs (often in agriculture)

integration: the mixing of different things, ideas, or persons together

internment: confinement

exile (n.): a person who has fled his or her homeland for various reasons

crisis: a difficult situation

confrontation: a face-to-face challenge

civil rights: the basic rights guaranteed to a citizen

sit-in: sitting in one place to bring attention to your cause

segregation: the separation of things, ideas, or people

voting bloc: a group that votes in the same manner

advocate (v.): to speak out in favor of

protest (n.): words or actions that show someone is against something

protest (v.): to speak out against something

intern (v.): to confine

confront: to challenge someone face to face

PAGE 98

See chart at the top of this page.

PAGE 101

Answers may vary, but should include the following information:

See chart at the bottom of this page.

PAGE 102

Answers will vary, but should include some of the following:

A Born 1929 in Atlanta, GA. Father and grandfather were ministers. Wanted to be a doctor. Changed his mind and became Baptist minister. Attended segregated schools. Attended Boston College for doctoral degree. Became

CHART FOR PAGE 101

AFRICAN AMERICANS AND CIVIL RIGHTS

DATE	GOALS	PEOPLE	METHODS USED	RESULTS
1954	Provide equal education for African American children	Thurgood Marshall	Legislation: decision by Supreme Court	*Brown v. Board of Education,* schools desegregated
1955	Integrate public transportation	Rosa Parks and other African Americans	Bus boycotts	African Americans were allowed to sit anywhere on the bus.
1960	Force restaurants to serve African American customers	Students and others	Sit-ins and peaceful non-violent protest	Restaurants had to follow the law and serve all customers.
1950s and 1960s	Defeat segregation and racism	Martin Luther King, Jr.	Peaceful protests including marches and protests, jailed . . . but continued to preach peace	People admired his ideas and followed his leadership. Civil Rights legislation passed.
1960s	Increase public awareness of discrimination against blacks	Freedom riders, civil rights marchers	Freedom rides, marching	Violence against freedom riders and marchers was televised on news. People were shocked and began to support protesters and their goals.
1960s	Self help, establish businesses run by blacks, elect black officials	Malcolm X, Stokely Carmichael, H. Rap Brown	Did not embrace non-violence. Challenged government if it did not enforce civil rights laws. Encouraged blacks to take pride in heritage and culture. Advocated for inclusion of African American history and culture in schools.	Increased awareness

known for speaking ability. Married Coretta. Had 4 children.

B Led bus boycott. Encouraged blacks to carpool or walk to work rather than ride bus. Violence against peaceful protesters brought media attention.

C Helped begin Southern Christian Leadership Conference to lead non-violent protests, marches, sit-ins, boycotts. Peaceful marchers attacked by police, police dogs, and others. Arrested. Wrote Letter from a Birmingham Jail encouraging people to disobey unjust laws. More joined struggle. March on Washington in August 1963. King gave "I Have a Dream" speech.

D Continued to organize marches. Received Nobel Peace Prize in 1964. Became involved in protests against involvement in Vietnam. Began working on gaining economic equality for blacks. In Memphis to help workers striking for better wages. Assassinated. Murder sparked riots.

E Great leader, inspired people, affected change. Civil rights laws giving African Americans voting rights and laws integrating schools, stores, transportation resulted from his leadership.

PAGE 103

1. *Women Seek Equality:* 1966
2. *Native Americans:* Organization formed to protect protesters and bring notice to their cause
3. *Hispanic Americans:* World War II veteran who led movement to help farm workers; formed National Farm Workers Association, a union seeking better working conditions for farmers
4. *Asian Americans:* Japanese Americans worked through courts to reclaim their property or to be paid for it. In 1982, the U.S. government apologized for injustice and in 1988 Congress agreed to pay $20,000 to each interned Japanese American still alive.
5. *Asian Americans:* Fleeing wars in their countries.
6. *Native Americans:* 800,000
7. *Women Seek Equality:* Non-violent methods, marches, spoke out for equality and a good education.
8. *Hispanic Americans:* Formed a large and vocal bloc to elect leaders who supported their issues

PAGE 109

Summaries will vary, but students should include information that answers the questions.

1. He was assassinated
2. Poverty, civil rights, war in Southeast Asia
3. Declared war on poverty, passed dozen major laws providing money and programs to fight poverty
4. By 1968, money that could have been spent on his programs was being spent on war in Southeast Asia

PAGE 110

1. China: they are next to each other and both countries are communist
2. By boat and airplane
3. By boat and airplane
4. Vietnam is in Southeast Asia, a wet tropical region; thick tropical vegetation to fight through

5. Answers will vary.
6. Answers will vary.

PAGE 112

Answers will vary, but may include the following:

1. Why did the U.S. become involved in the Vietnam War? How did President Johnson get more money for the war? How did students protest the war? What happened at Kent State University and Jackson Sate College? When was a cease fire reached? What happened in 1975? Should the U.S. interfere in the business of other countries?

PAGE 113

environment: air, water, soil, and all the other things that surround us
pest: something that is a bother, often insects
emissions: vapors released into air by machines
pesticide: chemical used to kill bugs
nuclear waste: the "trash" created when making nuclear power
nuclear plant: place that produces nuclear power
fragile: breakable
endangered: in danger of disappearing permanently
pollution: smog that is released into the air by cars, buses, planes, machines, and factories
conservation: the attempt to save or protect something

PAGE 118

1. détente 2. accord 3. unemployment
4. tap telephones 5. hostage 6. budget deficit
7. interest rate 8. strategic arms 9. inflation
10. recession

PAGE 119

See chart at the top of page 162.

Unit 5: The American Identity: 1980 to the Present

PAGE 124

Answers will vary, but may be similar to the following:

1. Economic opportunity, family, disaster, crime, educational opportunities
2. People in U.S. history moved for economic opportunity (westward expansion, Great Migration, Okies, etc.), to avoid violence (Great Migration), through forced movement (Trail of Tears, Japanese internment).

PAGE 125

Using Context
low-skilled job: work not requiring a great deal of education or expertise
high-skilled job: work that requires education and training
wages: money paid for work
high-tech industry: business dealing with technology such as computers and telecommunications
custodial work: jobs involving cleaning and upkeep of buildings
fast-food restaurant: places that pre-make food so that it is ready when ordered and can be delivered quickly to the customer

PRESIDENT	DOMESTIC EVENTS/PROBLEMS	FOREIGN EVENTS/PROBLEMS
Richard Nixon	High unemployment, budget deficit, inflation. Used government organizations to check up on protesters. Created a secret group when FBI refused to help. Group caught breaking into Democratic party office. Forced to resign.	Détente with communist countries. Traveled to China and initiated trade for first time since 1949. Visited Soviet Union and arranged SALT I, which limited number of nuclear weapons. Agreed to work with Soviet Union on space and health programs. Worked with Israel and Arab countries to build better relationships.
Gerald Ford	Recession, high unemployment, high price of gas.	Met with Soviet Union and began work on SALT II. No decisions made.
Jimmy Carter	Recession, high unemployment, high price of gas. Tried to revive economy. High inflation, high interest rates.	Worked with other nations to build peace in Middle East. Camp David Accords with Sadat and Begin were start of peace. In 1979, fifty Americans were taken hostage in Iran and held for over a year.

Finding Out More Information

1. Difference in education: low-skilled jobs are done by people with little education, while high-skilled jobs are done by people with a great deal of education
2. Difference in wages: low-skilled jobs pay low wages, while high-skilled jobs pay high wages

PAGE 127
Answers will vary.

PAGE 128
A 1. Loretta second and Linda sixth of seven children
2. Family of immigrants from Mexico
3. All seven children attended college.

B 1. Loretta earned bachelor's in economics in 1982 and MBA in 1984
2. Worked in business and economic
3. Linda earned B.A. in Spanish Literature and law degree
4. Worked as civil rights lawyer and labor activist

C 1. Loretta elected in 1994. In 4th term.
2. Interested in laws to do with education, crime reduction, economic development, and security.
3. Linda first term began in January 2003
4. Interested in laws on education, health care, public safety, and economy.

D 1. Loretta is member of House Armed Services Committee, Select Committee for Security, Committee on Education and the Workforce.
2. Both interested in helping people, especially those like their parents.

E 1. To work hard for change

PAGE 130
1. Important environmental issues may include: Increasing pollution from pesticides, increased waste from nuclear arms and power plants, fumes from factories, litter and trash, and global warming.
2. Answers will vary.
3. Answers may include some of the following: recycle, pick up trash, walk rather than drive, take public transit, set heat lower in winter and air lower in summer, conserve water, etc.

PAGE 131
See chart at the top of page 163.

PAGE 135
Using Graphs
1. a. Answers will vary, but may include sentences such as: The number of households in the United States with televisions increased between 1945 and 2000; The graphs tells how the number of televisions in the United States increased until almost all people (98.2%) have televisions.
   b. Answers may vary, but may be similar to: In 1984 few people had computers, but in 2000, 51% of households have a computer; In 16 years, the number of computers in the United States increased more than 40%.
   These graphs should encourage students to talk in mathematical terms, as well as describing the material on the graphs.
2. Answers may vary, but allow for discussion of how technology changes lives when so many people have access to television and the Internet. Discussion may also address the fact that many people do not have computers or Internet access. Students may discuss the relationship of televisions to computers and the information that each provides.

PAGE 136
1. i 2. h 3. a 4. g 5. d 6. e 7. j 8. b
9. k 10. f 11. c

PAGE 139
Study Questions
Questions and answers will vary, but may include some of the following:

Reagan: Why was Reagan called a great communicator? He was able to explain complicated issues in a simple way.

George H.W. Bush: Why did Bush have to raise taxes? Federal deficit kept growing.

Clinton: What was Clinton's platform during the campaign? Improve the economy.

George W. Bush: Why did unemployment increase during Bush's presidency? Business became bankrupt and laid off employees, some large corporations were caught telling lies about their earnings and many people lost jobs when the businesses were found out.

INVENTIONS

	MEDICINE	COMPUTERS	TRAVEL	COMMUNICATION
	1. MRI, CAT SCAN 2. MEDICAL ROBOTS AND LASERS 3. HUMAN GENOME	1. PCs 2. MICROPROCESSORS 3. CDs	1. HIGH SPEED TRAIN 2. ALTERNATIVE FUELS 3. SUBMERSIBLES	1. CELL PHONES 2. GLOBAL POSITIONING SYSTEM 3. LASER 4. RADAR
1. Who uses this invention? How do they use it?	1. Doctors use these to see inside people to diagnose illnesses 2. Repair damage in small or delicate body parts 3. Scientists may be able to treat genetic diseases	1. Just about everyone for work and entertainment 2. Most people benefit from these chips in cars, appliances and more 3. Stores large amounts of information, including music	1. Many people for travel 2. Makers and users of automobiles 3. Scientists	1. Many for more immediate communication 2. To find location on earth 3. Many for printers, scanners, X-rays 4. Meteorologist predict weather
2. What is another invention that is similar to this one?	X-ray	Calculators Floppy disks	Trains, submarines	Telephone
3. How did this invention change people's lives in the United States?	1. Less need for surgery 2. Less damage to patient 3. Cures for genetic diseases	1. Ease in computing 2. Decrease size of computer and use in small devices 3. Allows people to store large amounts of information	1. Faster travel 2. Decreased reliance on oil, improved air quality 3. Acquire knowledge about ocean	1. More immediate communication 2. Available in some cars, allowing for instant directions 4. Better forecast of weather allows for better preparation

PAGE 140

Interpreting Political Cartoons
See chart bottom of this page.

PAGE 142

Answers will vary.

PAGE 143

1. The people of the United States are young and old; they come from different ethnic backgrounds, different races, and different socio-economic levels; and they have different interests.
2. Answers will vary.
3. Each "picture" illustrates a belief in democracy, individual rights, and freedom.
4. By depicting just what he said: this is a country made up of different people, with different backgrounds, and different experiences who all believe that the United States is a good place (if not the best place) to live.

CHART FOR PAGE 140

	REAGAN/"STAR WARS"	BUSH FEEDING DOG	CLINTON WORLD
1. Who are people in cartoon? How do you know?	Reagan (caricature)	Bush (caricature)	Clinton
2. Describe what is happening in the cartoon.	Reagan is watching the Strategic Defense Initiative ("Star Wars") blow up various other government programs	Bush is overfeeding "dogs" with tax cuts; jobs are skinny, but the deficit is growing	The world is being delivered to Clinton
3. What does this cartoon tell you about this president?	The enormous expense of the Star Wars program took money away from other programs that needed funding	Bush attempted to solve economic problems through tax cuts, but this only succeeded in increasing the deficit	Countries around the world turned to the U.S. for help; U.S. concerned about issues all over the world
4. Decide on a good title for the cartoon.	Answers will vary.		

Land, People, Nation: Beginnings to 1877

CHECKLIST OF CONTENT, LANGUAGE, AND LEARNING STRATEGY OBJECTIVES

Student name _____ Date _____

Key: Level of Mastery   Yes = ☒   With help = ☑   Not yet = ☐

HISTORY AND GEOGRAPHY CONTENT OBJECTIVES
Can identify and explain or describe main ideas related to these topics:

Unit 1. The Earliest Americans
- ☐ Origins and migrations of first Americans
- ☐ Geographical characteristics of Polar Regions
- ☐ The Inuit
- ☐ The Aztec and Mayas and the Cortes conquest
- ☐ The Iroquois and the Anasazi
- ☐ Map and graph skills introduced in the unit

Unit 2. Explorers and Explorations
- ☐ Why people explore
- ☐ Early explorers of America: Columbus, Estevan
- ☐ Major European explorers in North America
- ☐ Geographical characteristics of Wet Tropical Regions and Northern Forest Regions
- ☐ Map and graph skills introduced in the unit

Unit 3. From Colonies to Nation
- ☐ Early Spanish, French, Dutch colonies in the New World
- ☐ Life in the colonies
- ☐ Geographical characteristics of Mid-Latitude Forest Regions
- ☐ Importance of Massasoit, Anne Hutchinson, Puritans
- ☐ Characteristics of thirteen English colonies
- ☐ French and Indian War
- ☐ Beginnings of democratic governments
- ☐ Issues of religious freedom and slavery
- ☐ Causes of War for Independence
- ☐ Declaration of Independence and major events of the American Revolution
- ☐ Importance of George Washington, Benjamin Franklin, and other heroes of War for Independence
- ☐ Major ideas of Constitution (especially Bill of Rights) and operation of the three branches of government
- ☐ Map and graph skills introduced in the unit

Unit 4. The Nation Grows
- ☐ Importance of pioneers (e.g., Daniel Boone); reasons why Americans moved west
- ☐ Acquisition of new territories, 1783–1853
- ☐ Accomplishments of Thomas Jefferson and of Lewis and Clark expedition
- ☐ Geographical characteristics of Highland Regions and of Mediterranean Regions
- ☐ War of 1812; Meaning of Monroe Doctrine
- ☐ Evaluation of policies during presidency of Andrew Jackson
- ☐ Importance of Native American leaders (Sequoyah, Osceola, Black Hawk, Tecumseh)
- ☐ Causes and results of Mexican-American War
- ☐ Presidents: 1801–1850
- ☐ Map and graph skills introduced in the unit

Unit 5. The Civil War and Reconstruction

- [ ] Reasons for dissension between North and South
- [ ] Reasons for secession of Southern states
- [ ] Major events in the Civil War
- [ ] Importance of Abraham Lincoln and other Americans of the Civil War period
- [ ] Major events and problems of the Reconstruction Period (e.g., women and African Americans)
- [ ] Presidents: 1850–1875
- [ ] Map and graph skills introduced in the unit

ACADEMIC LANGUAGE OBJECTIVES

Can use the following academic language skills:

- [ ] Defines and uses academic vocabulary related to history concepts
- [ ] Discusses and writes about prior knowledge on a topic
- [ ] Demonstrates comprehension of reading texts by identifying and recalling main ideas and details, comparing and contrasting, writing study questions, and summarizing
- [ ] Demonstrates comprehension of mini-lectures presented by teacher and peers
- [ ] Prepares and presents brief oral reports (Units 2–5)
- [ ] Discusses ideas and supports opinions
- [ ] Describes what has been learned orally and in writing
- [ ] Develops and writes research reports (Units 2–5)

LEARNING STRATEGY OBJECTIVES

Can identify the following learning strategies and use them independently:

- [ ] *Predicting:* Uses text headings to predict content; makes logical guesses about what will happen
- [ ] *Making Inferences:* Uses context to make logical guesses about new words; recognizes implied meaning
- [ ] *Taking Notes:* Writes down important words and ideas while listening or reading
- [ ] *Selective Attention:* Scans a reading text and/or listens for specific information
- [ ] *Cooperation:* Works collaboratively with peers to complete tasks
- [ ] *Classifying:* Groups or classifies words or ideas according to attributes
- [ ] *Tell/Use What You Know:* Recalls and uses prior knowledge to assist in completing a task (Units 2–5)
- [ ] *Using Imagery:* Uses and images to understand and/or represent information (Units 2–5)
- [ ] *Graphic Organizers:* Uses time lines, Venn diagrams, charts, etc. to show relationships between ideas and events (Units 2–5)
- [ ] *Summarizing:* Makes oral and written summaries of information read (Units 3–5)
- [ ] *Using Resources:* Finds and uses information from reference materials and the Internet (Units 3–5)
- [ ] *Planning:* Makes a plan or outline for research reports (Units 4–5)
- [ ] *Evaluating:* Evaluates own learning and learning strategies (Units 4–5)

Teacher's Comments:

_____

_____

_____

_____

_____

_____

_____

_____

_____

_____

_____

Land, People, Nation: Since 1865

CHECKLIST OF CONTENT, LANGUAGE, AND LEARNING STRATEGY OBJECTIVES

Student name _____ Date _____

Key: Level of Mastery   Yes = ☒   With help = ☑   Not yet = ☐

HISTORY AND GEOGRAPHY CONTENT OBJECTIVES
Can identify and explain or describe main ideas related to these topics:

Unit 1. Industrialization and Change: 1865–1900
- ☐ Changes in American life caused by the Industrial Revolution
- ☐ Geographical characteristics of Grassland Regions and Desert Regions of the world
- ☐ Role of cowboys in the West
- ☐ Policies affecting Native Americans
- ☐ Sitting Bull, Sioux leader
- ☐ American inventions: 1792–1903
- ☐ Reform laws and reformers in the late nineteenth and early twentieth centuries
- ☐ Immigrants to the United States in the late nineteenth and early twentieth centuries
- ☐ Map, graph, and photo analysis skills introduced in the unit

Unit 2. Starting a New Century: 1900–1940
- ☐ Changes made by industrialization at the turn of twentieth century
- ☐ Labor unions
- ☐ Immigration and migration
- ☐ The Progressive Movement
- ☐ Causes and effects of World War I
- ☐ Treaty of Versailles
- ☐ The 1920s
- ☐ The Great Depression and the New Deal
- ☐ Eleanor Roosevelt
- ☐ Franklin D. Roosevelt and other presidents: 1900–1940
- ☐ Important leaders
- ☐ Map, graph, and image analysis skills introduced in the unit

Unit 3. The United States Becomes a World Leader: 1940–1960
- ☐ Economic depression and the world
- ☐ Nazism, communism, fascism
- ☐ Causes and conduct of World War II
- ☐ The Code Talkers
- ☐ Life in United States after World War II
- ☐ The Cold War
- ☐ Inventions and scientists: mid-twentieth century
- ☐ Three presidents
- ☐ Map, graph, and photo analysis skills introduced in the unit

Unit 4. Eras of Protest: 1960–1980
- ☐ The New Frontier and the Cold War
- ☐ Civil rights movements (African American, Hispanic, Asian American, Native American, women)
- ☐ Martin Luther King, Jr.
- ☐ John F. Kennedy and Lyndon Johnson
- ☐ Causes and results of Vietnam War

- [ ] The environment
- [ ] Important leaders
- [ ] Presidents Nixon, Ford, Carter
- [ ] Map, graph, and photo analysis skills introduced in the unit

Unit 5. The American Identify: 1980 to the Present

- [ ] Changes in work
- [ ] Organization and roles of schools
- [ ] Congresswomen Loretta Sánchez and Linda Sánchez
- [ ] Changing environment and technology
- [ ] Effects of changes in media
- [ ] Causes and effects of globalization
- [ ] Presidents Reagan, Bush, Clinton, Bush
- [ ] Impact of terrorism
- [ ] Map, graph, and photo analysis skills introduced in the unit

ACADEMIC LANGUAGE OBJECTIVES

Can use the following academic language skills:

- [ ] Defines and uses academic vocabulary related to history concepts
- [ ] Discusses and writes about prior knowledge on a topic
- [ ] Demonstrates comprehension of reading texts by identifying and recalling main ideas and details, summarizing, completing a study chart, writing study questions, and identifying cause and effect
- [ ] Demonstrates comprehension of mini-lectures presented by teacher and peers
- [ ] Prepares and presents brief oral reports
- [ ] Discusses ideas and supports opinions
- [ ] Describes what has been learned orally and in writing
- [ ] Develops and writes research reports

LEARNING STRATEGY OBJECTIVES

Can identify the following learning strategies and use them independently:

- [ ] *Using Imagery:* Uses images to understand and/or represent information
- [ ] *Summarizing:* Makes oral and written summaries of information read
- [ ] *Graphic Organizers:* Uses and creates time lines, Venn diagrams, charts, etc. to show relationships between ideas and events
- [ ] *Predicting:* Uses text headings to predict content; makes logical guesses about what will happen
- [ ] *Tell/Use What You Know:* Recalls and uses prior knowledge to assist in completing a task
- [ ] *Making Inferences:* Uses context to make logical guesses about new words; recognizes implied meaning
- [ ] *Selective Attention:* Scans a reading text and/or listens for specific information
- [ ] *Taking Notes:* Writes down important words and ideas while listening or reading
- [ ] *Cooperation:* Works collaboratively with peers to complete tasks
- [ ] *Using Resources:* Finds and uses information from reference materials and the Internet
- [ ] *Classifying:* Groups or classifies words or ideas according to attributes (Units 2–5)

Teacher's Comments:

_____

_____

_____

_____

_____

_____

_____

_____

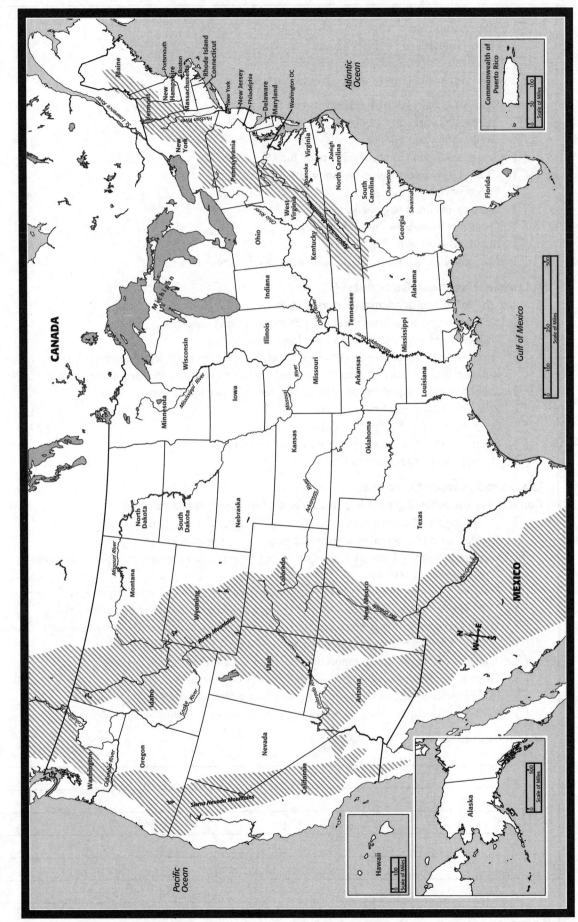

UNITED STATES

Beginnings to 1877

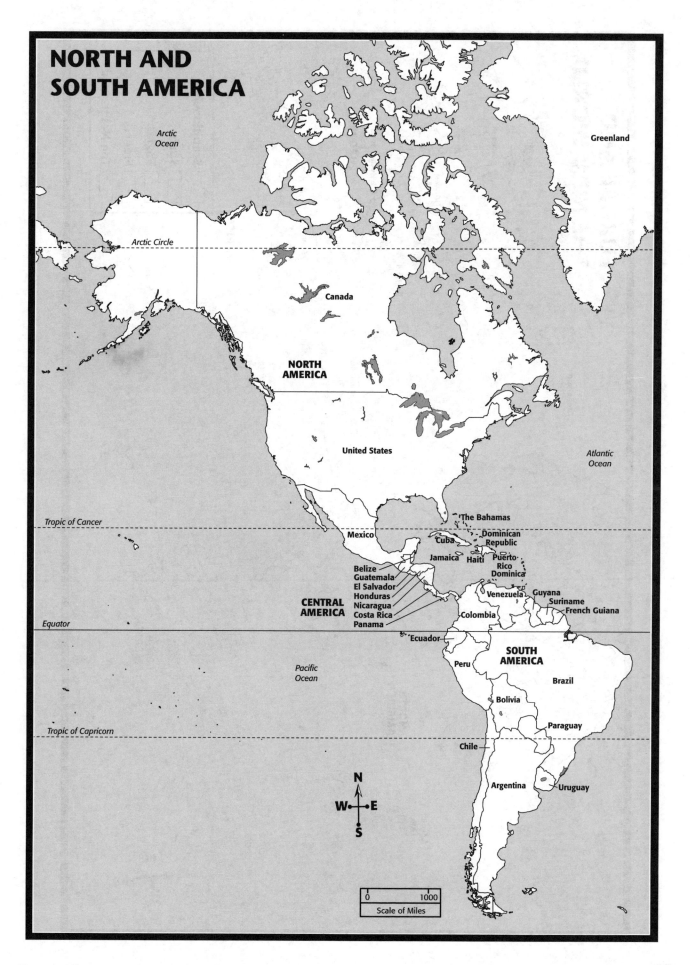

NORTH AND SOUTH AMERICA

Arctic Ocean

Greenland

Arctic Circle

Canada

NORTH AMERICA

United States

Atlantic Ocean

Tropic of Cancer

The Bahamas

Mexico

Cuba

Dominican Republic

Jamaica   **Haiti**   **Puerto Rico**

Dominica

Belize
Guatemala
El Salvador
Honduras
Nicaragua
Costa Rica
Panama

CENTRAL AMERICA

Venezuela   **Guyana**
Suriname
French Guiana

Colombia

Equator

Ecuador

SOUTH AMERICA

Peru

Pacific Ocean

Brazil

Bolivia

Paraguay

Tropic of Capricorn

Chile

N
W · E
S

Argentina

Uruguay

0   1000
Scale of Miles

169

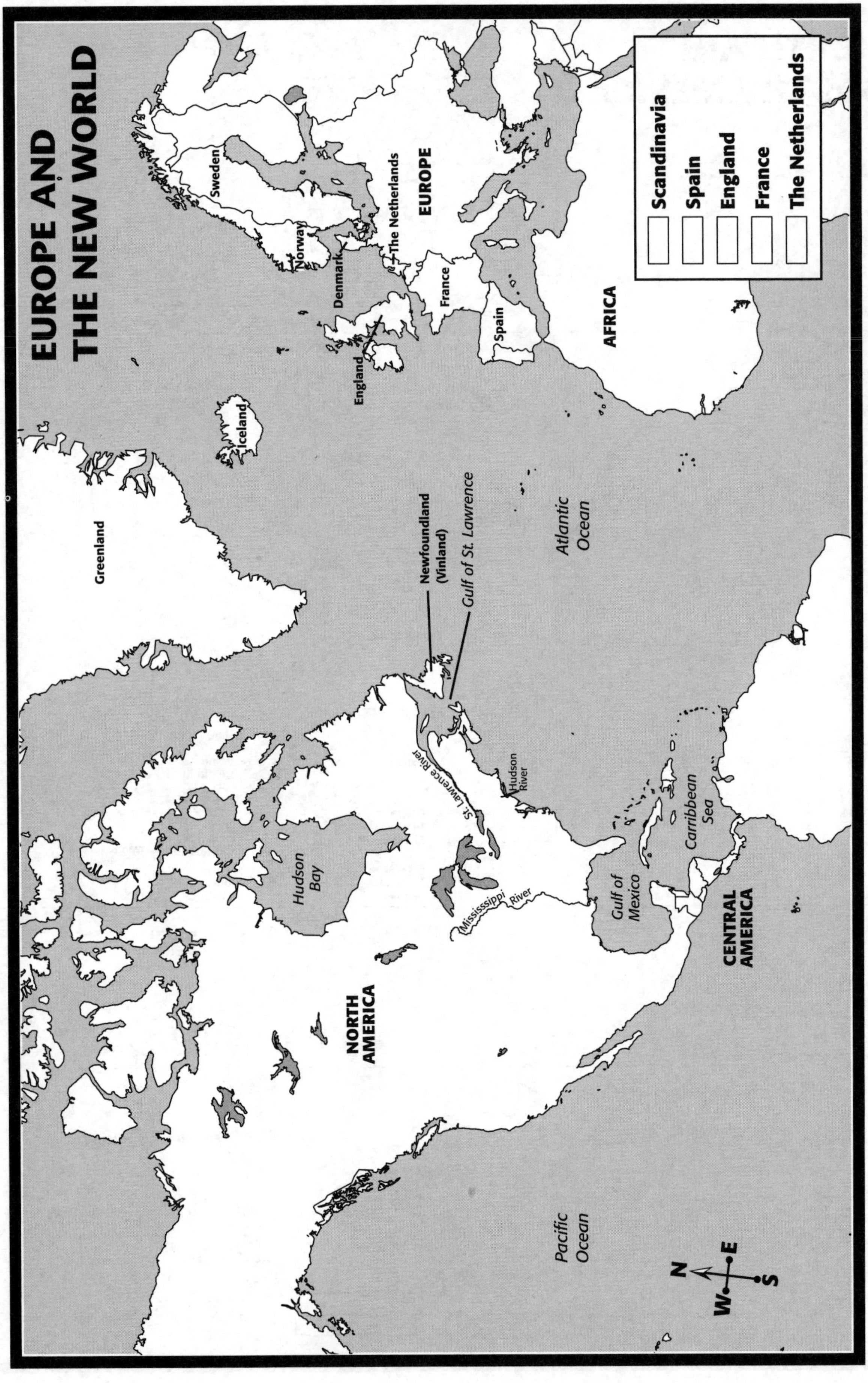
EUROPE AND THE NEW WORLD
Scandinavia
Spain
England
France
The Netherlands
Sweden
Norway
Denmark
The Netherlands
EUROPE
France
Spain
England
AFRICA
Iceland
Greenland
Newfoundland (Vinland)
Gulf of St. Lawrence
Atlantic Ocean
St. Lawrence River
Hudson River
Hudson Bay
Mississippi River
Gulf of Mexico
Carribbean Sea
CENTRAL AMERICA
NORTH AMERICA
Pacific Ocean
N
E
S
W

SOME SPANISH CLAIMS IN NORTH AMERICA

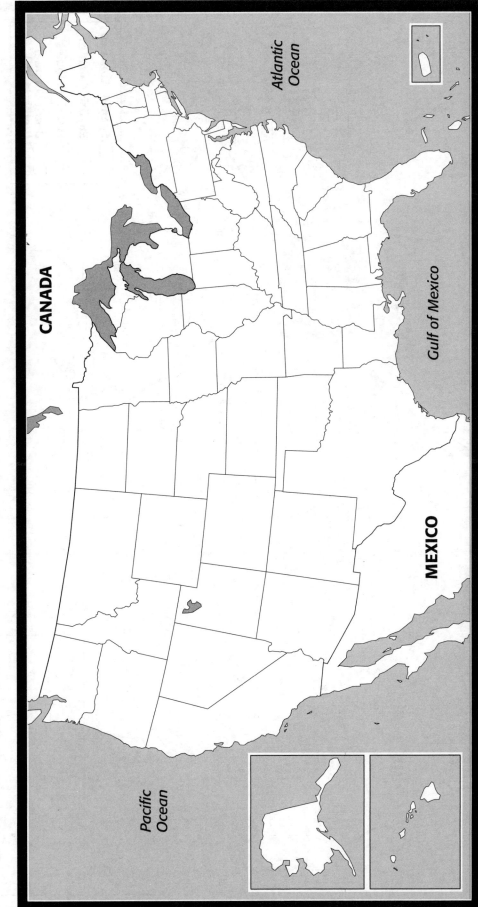

CANADA

Atlantic
Ocean

Gulf of Mexico

MEXICO

Pacific
Ocean

THE UNITED STATES AND SOUTHERN CANADA

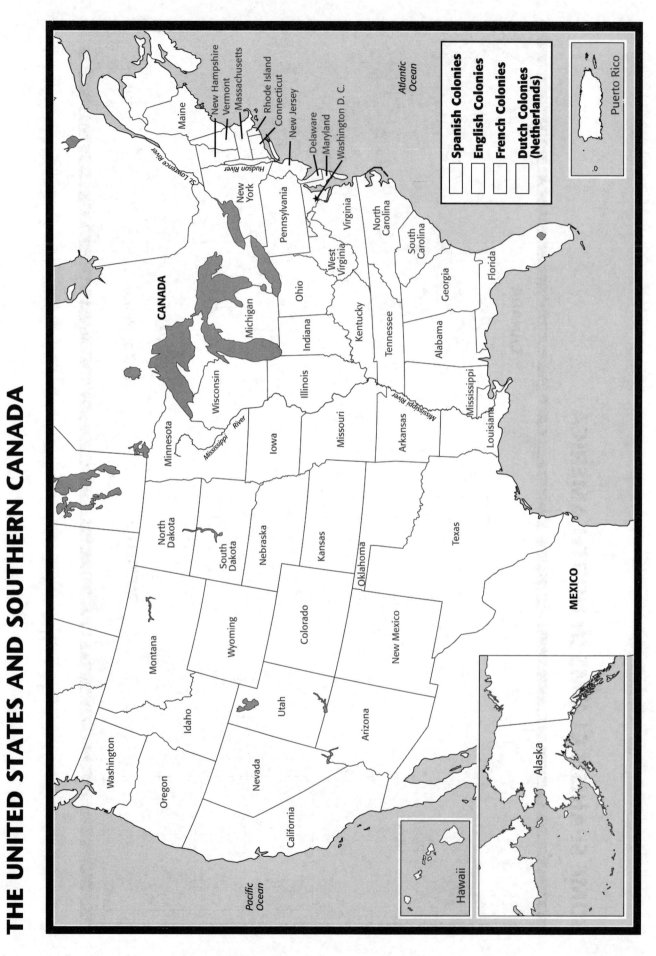

Maine

New Hampshire
Vermont
Massachusetts
Rhode Island
Connecticut
New Jersey
Delaware
Maryland
Washington D. C.

St. Lawrence River

Hudson River

New York

Pennsylvania

Virginia

West Virginia

North Carolina

South Carolina

Georgia

Florida

Spanish Colonies
English Colonies
French Colonies
Dutch Colonies (Netherlands)

Puerto Rico

Atlantic Ocean

CANADA

Michigan

Ohio

Indiana

Kentucky

Tennessee

Alabama

Mississippi

Louisiana

Wisconsin

Illinois

Missouri

Arkansas

Mississippi River

Minnesota

Mississippi River

Iowa

North Dakota

South Dakota

Nebraska

Kansas

Oklahoma

Texas

MEXICO

Montana

Wyoming

Colorado

New Mexico

Idaho

Utah

Arizona

Washington

Oregon

Nevada

California

Pacific Ocean

Alaska

Hawaii

Beginnings to 1877

THE UNITED STATES IN 1783

THE UNITED STATES IN 1853

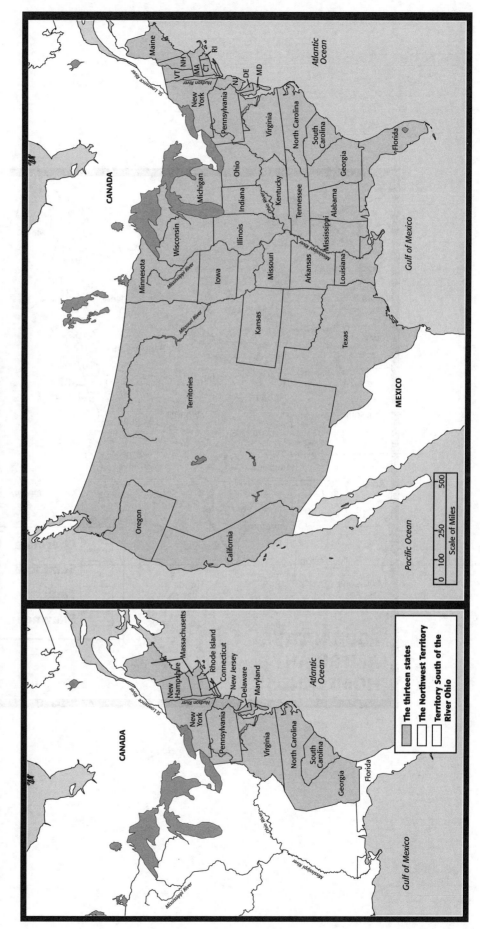

Map: The United States in 1853

- CANADA
- Maine
- VT, NH, MA, CT, RI
- New York
- Pennsylvania
- NJ, DE, MD
- Virginia
- North Carolina
- South Carolina
- Georgia
- Florida
- Atlantic Ocean
- Ohio
- Michigan
- Indiana
- Kentucky
- Tennessee
- Mississippi
- Alabama
- Ohio River
- Wisconsin
- Illinois
- Iowa
- Missouri
- Arkansas
- Louisiana
- Mississippi River
- Gulf of Mexico
- Minnesota
- Missouri River
- Kansas
- Texas
- Territories
- MEXICO
- Oregon
- California
- Pacific Ocean
- St. Lawrence River
- Hudson River

Scale of Miles
0 100 250 500

Map: The United States in 1783

- CANADA
- Massachusetts
- New Hampshire
- Rhode Island
- Connecticut
- New Jersey
- Delaware
- Maryland
- New York
- Pennsylvania
- Virginia
- North Carolina
- South Carolina
- Georgia
- Florida
- Atlantic Ocean
- Ohio River
- Mississippi River
- Gulf of Mexico
- St. Lawrence River
- Hudson River

Legend:
- The thirteen states
- The Northwest Territory
- Territory South of the River Ohio

CANADA

L. Superior

L. Huron

L. Michigan

L. Ontario

L. Erie

St. Lawrence River

Hudson River

Mississippi River

Wisconsin

Minnesota

Iowa

Illinois

Michigan

Missouri

Indiana

Ohio

West Virginia

Kentucky

New York

Pennsylvania

Virginia

Maine

VT

NH

MA

CT

RI

NJ

DE

MD

Arkansas

Tennessee

North Carolina

South Carolina

Alabama

Georgia

Mississippi

Louisiana

Florida

Pacific Ocean

	Cherokee
	Seminole
	Sauk
	Shawnee

FOUR NATIVE AMERICAN HOMELANDS

 Beginnings to 1877

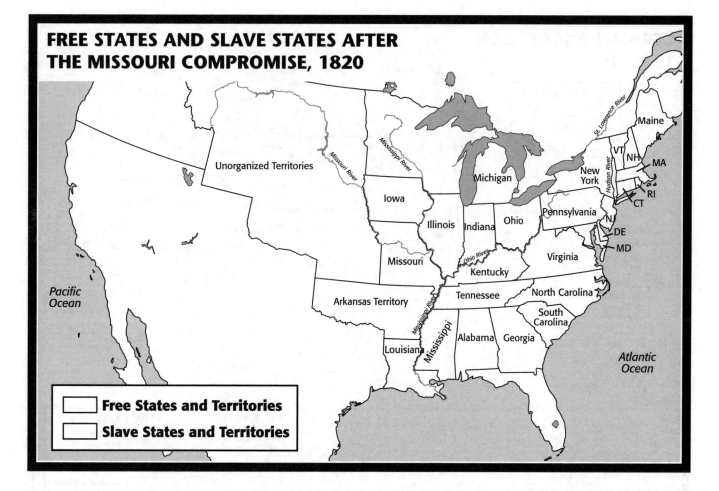

FREE STATES AND SLAVE STATES AFTER THE MISSOURI COMPROMISE, 1820

Unorganized Territories

Iowa

Illinois

Missouri

Arkansas Territory

Louisiana

Mississippi

Alabama

Georgia

Tennessee

Kentucky

Indiana

Ohio

Michigan

Virginia

North Carolina

South Carolina

Pennsylvania

New York

Maine

VT

NH

MA

RI

CT

NJ

DE

MD

Pacific Ocean

Atlantic Ocean

Missouri River

Mississippi River

Mississippi River

Ohio River

St. Lawrence River

Hudson River

☐ **Free States and Territories**

☐ **Slave States and Territories**

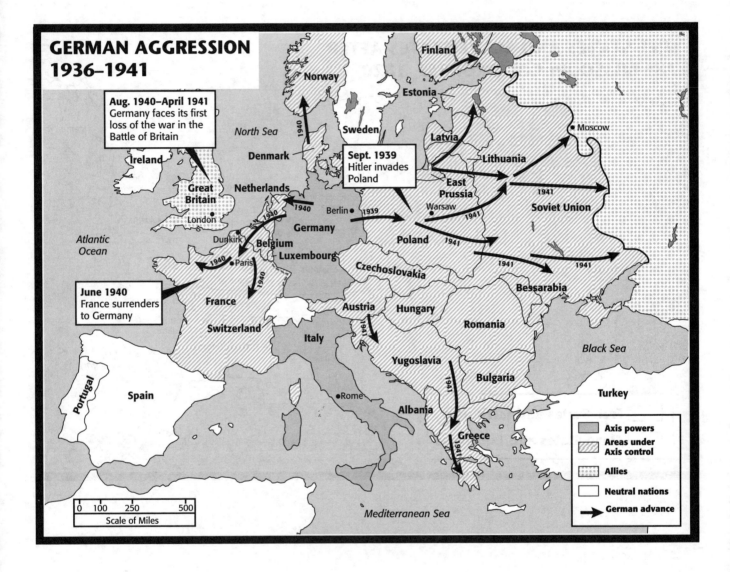

GERMAN AGGRESSION 1936–1941

Aug. 1940–April 1941
Germany faces its first loss of the war in the Battle of Britain

Sept. 1939
Hitler invades Poland

June 1940
France surrenders to Germany

Norway

North Sea

Sweden

Finland

Estonia

Denmark

Ireland

Great Britain

London

Netherlands

Berlin

Germany

Dunkirk

Belgium

Luxembourg

Paris

Atlantic Ocean

France

Switzerland

Portugal

Spain

Italy

Rome

Latvia

Lithuania

• Moscow

East Prussia

Warsaw

Soviet Union

1941

Poland

Czechoslovakia

Austria

Hungary

Bessarabia

Romania

1941

Yugoslavia

Bulgaria

Black Sea

Albania

Greece

Turkey

Mediterranean Sea

1939

1940

1941

	Axis powers
	Areas under Axis control
	Allies
	Neutral nations
→	German advance

0 100 250 500
Scale of Miles

   Since 1865

CROSSWORD PUZZLE

Use words from the box to complete the crossword puzzle.

| Amendment |
| candidates |
| Confederacy |
| free |
| harvest |
| hero |
| injustice |
| plantation |
| poor |
| population |
| ratify |
| Reconstruction |
| rent |
| repeal |
| rights |
| secede |
| segregation |
| sharecropper |
| slave |
| slavery |
| survive |
| tariff |
| unequal |
| Union |
| unite |
| your |

ACROSS

1. Having little or no money.
2. The 14th Amendment said that all Americans, black or white, had the same _____.
4. To pick or gather crops.
10. A person who does brave things and is admired by other people.
11. To go through hard times and come out alive.
12. A person who is owned by another person.
13. A tax on goods made in other countries and then sold in the United States.
14. To approve a law by voting for it.
16. There were four _____ in the presidential election of 1860.
17. Not the same (in size or treatment, for example).
18. To join together.
19. The number of people in a place such as a city, state, or country.
21. The 13th _____ ended slavery in the United States.
22. After the Civil War, the slaves were _____.
23. The rebuilding of the South after the Civil War.

DOWN

1. A very large farm where only one crop is grown.
3. Unfairness.
5. Under _____, black children had to go to different schools from the ones that white children went to.
6. A system in which one person can own another person.
7. A _____ rented land from a plantation owner and gave some of the crops to the owner as rent.
8. During the Civil War, the southern states were called the _____.
9. To abolish, or do away with, a law.
11. When Lincoln was elected president, eleven southern states decided to _____.
15. Belonging to you.
17. During the Civil War, the northern states were called the _____.
20. To pay money in order to live in a house or use land or property owned by someone else.